offbeat
spanish

by Glenn Flear

Published by Everyman Publishers plc, London

First published in 2000 by Everyman Publishers plc, formerly Cadogan Books plc, Gloucester Mansions, 140A Shaftesbury Avenue, London WC2H 8HD

Copyright © 2000 Glenn Flear

The right of Glenn Flear to be identified as the author of this work has been asserted in accordance with the Copyrights, Designs and Patents Act 1988.

All rights reserved. No part of this publication may be reproduced, stored in a retrieval system or transmitted in any form or by any means, electronic, electrostatic, magnetic tape, photocopying, recording or otherwise, without prior permission of the publisher.

British Library Cataloguing-in-Publication Data
A catalogue record for this book is available from the British Library.

ISBN 1 85744 242 3

Distributed in North America by The Globe Pequot Press, P.O Box 480, 246 Goose Lane, Guilford, CT 06437-0480.

All other sales enquiries should be directed to Everyman Chess, Gloucester Mansions, 140A Shaftesbury Avenue, London WC2H 8HD
tel: 020 7539 7600 fax: 020 7379 4060
email: dan@everyman.uk.com
website: www.everyman.uk.com

The Everyman Chess Opening Guides were designed and developed by First Rank Publishing.

EVERYMAN CHESS SERIES (formerly Cadogan Chess)
Chief Advisor: Garry Kasparov
Advisory Panel: Andrew Kinsman and Byron Jacobs

Typeset and edited by First Rank Publishing, Brighton.
Production by Book Production Services.
Printed and bound in Great Britain by The Cromwell Press Ltd., Trowbridge, Wiltshire.

Contents

BIBLIOGRAPHY

Books

Encyclopaedia of Chess Openings Volume C (third edition), Alexander Matanovic (Sahovski Informator 1997)

Capablanca's 100 Best Games of Chess, Harry Golombek (Bell 1972)

Schliemann - Jänisch Gambit, Hagen Tiemann (Schachverlag 1990)

Spanish: Schliemann (Jaenisch), Leonid Shamkovich & Eric Schiller (Batsford 1983)

Ruy Lopez Bird's Defence, Colin Leach (Caissa 1985)

4...d5 in the Cordel Defense Spanish Game, Andrzej Filipowicz & Jerzy Konokowski (Chess Enterprises 1981)

Spanish without ...a6, Mikhail Yudovich (Batsford 1986)

Periodicals

Informators 1-78

New in Chess yearbooks 1-56

Chessbase Magazine

Websites

The Week in Chess

Infoxadrej

PREFACE

The purpose of this book is to give the reader a thorough grounding in each of the defences covered here, whether the reader is intending to play the Spanish with White or Black. In each variation, strong pointers to best play by both sides should help the reader to construct his repertoire.

The Spanish, or Ruy Lopez, is one of the most solid and respectable of Black's defences to 1 e4. After 1...e5 2 ♘f3 ♘c6 3 ♗b5 many games then continue with 3...a6, whereupon both players have at their disposal a myriad of systems, which in many cases have been deeply analysed. One of these systems 4 ♗xc6, the Exchange variation, has the reputation of giving White long-term winning chances (due to a superior pawn structure) whilst limiting Black's potential for counterplay. The variations analysed in this book avoid this annoying possibility.

We shall be examining possibilities for both sides when Black chooses to vary as early as the third move. His reasons can be varied, avoiding masses of main-line theory, a surprise weapon, or avoiding the Exchange variation. By choosing the variation so early, Black has a major influence on the type of game that follows.

The popular Berlin Defence (as successfully chosen four times by Kramnik in his London match against Kasparov), some variations of the Classical, the old-fashioned Steinitz and Smyslov's 3...g6, could be all be described as 'solid'. The gambit-style Schliemann and 4...f5 in the Classical are risky attempts to wrest the initiative. The Bird's with 3...♘d4 and Cozio's 3...♘ge7 are 'complex' strategic variations often leading to unusual pawn structures. Other third moves are experimental and probably not correct against best play by White.

In fact, in each chapter there are a number of options enabling players of every style a chance to find their own types of position and their own ways of interpreting the opening.

In the layout of material take note of the following points:

Chapters 7 and 8 should be studied together as there are some transpositional possibilities and Chapters 2 and 4 are both allied to Chapter 3. Apart from these links the book can be considered as nine mini-books in one.

White players should be able to find a testing line in each chapter. Players of the black pieces will find sufficient material in each chapter to be able to play their chosen variation to a high standard.

In order to play any of the lines detailed in

this book, Black doesn't have to learn that much theory (a practical consideration in the real world) but beware(!), this also holds true for your opponent, so study well the system of your choice and be ready to change, just in case your opponents have also read this book!

In most of the chapters Black can equalise (or at least get very close), as well as often having the benefit of surprise and a major influence on what type of game will result. All this for very little learning time required, what more can you ask?

Glenn Flear
Baillargues, France, November 2000

INTRODUCTION

After the moves **1 e4 e5 2 ♘f3 ♘c6 3 ♗b5** we arrive at the position which defines the Spanish (or Ruy Lopez) Opening.

One can already gain an idea into the likely strategy of both sides by studying the implications of these, ever so automatic, opening moves.

1 e4 – claims some central squares and space, as well as preparing the development of the king's bishop.

1...e5 – idem.

2 ♘f3 – develops a piece with gain of time, as Black's e-pawn is en prise.

2...♘c6 – develops a piece and defends the e5-pawn.

3 ♗b5 – develops a piece with threats against the defender of the e5-pawn and along the a4-e8 diagonal, pointing at the black king.

Early days, but what can we already conclude? Having the advantage of the opening move allows White to create threats, whereas Black is so far on the defensive.

In fact many of White's opening plans revolve around an attempt to eliminate or undermine the e5-pawn. The reasoning being if this fortified defensive outpost is breached then White controls the centre. So look out

for repeated efforts by White to play ♘xe5, d2-d4, or c2-c3, followed by d2-d4.

The various chapters involve different ways of trying to resolve the White pressure on e5. The two extremes are the Schliemann (3...f5), which immediately counter-attacks the e4-pawn, (hoping for quick development and general confusion, at the risk of losing the precious e5-pawn), and the Steinitz (3...d6) which reinforces the e5-point even at the risk of denying the king's bishop an active posting.

The Bird's (3...♘d4) releases the pressure on the e5-point but loses time and allows the White e- and f-pawns a chance to advance.

In both the Berlin and the Classical Defences Black develops pieces in natural fashion, and is not committing himself yet to any particular strategy, but 'is ready for anything'. Typically Black will switch readily between the defence of the e5-point and the counter-attack on e4.

The Cozio and Smyslov (where ...g6 and ...♗g7 are typically played early) prepare either, the defence of the e5-pawn by the bishop, or (in the case that the e5-pawn is exchanged) to obtain play along the long a1-h8 diagonal.

CHAPTER ONE

The Schliemann Defence

1 e4 e5 2 ♘f3 ♘c6 3 ♗b5 f5

The Schliemann Defence (sometimes referred to as the Jaenisch Gambit) is a sharp and risky attempt to wrest the initiative from White's hands. Tactical and correspondence players have long been associated with the intricacies of the line and several books have been written on the subject.

For the unprepared white player there are many dangers and the line can be fun but a word of caution...there are a number of quieter positional tries that stop Black getting too excited and keep a modest edge. For the White player, learning some theory and going down one of the main lines can be rewarding, as I'm not convinced that the Schliemann is 100% sound.

> ## Game 1
> ### Tiviakov-Inkiov
> *Macedonia 1998*

1 e4 e5 2 ♘f3 ♘c6 3 ♗b5 f5 4 ♘c3

see following diagram

This is White's principal choice. Alternative fourth moves are discussed in Games 9-11.

4...fxe4 5 ♘xe4 d5 6 ♘xe5 dxe4 7 ♘xc6 ♕g5

Other moves for Black are studied in game 5.

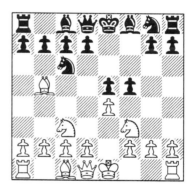

8 ♕e2 ♘f6 9 f4 ♕xf4

This capture has almost totally replaced 9...♕h4+ (see Game 4) in recent years.

10 ♘e5+

This is generally considered to be the main line of the Schliemann. The other important moves here are 10 ♘xa7+, as in game 3, and 10 d4, as in game 2.

10...c6 11 d4 ♕h4+ 12 g3 ♕h3 13 ♗c4 ♗e6

The continuation 13...♗d6 14 ♗f7+! ♔e7 15 ♗b3 is given by Keres as offering White a clear advantage.

14 ♗g5

Not the only way to maintain an opening

advantage. There is also a good case for 14 ♗f4 ♖d8 15 0-0-0 ♗d6 16 ♗g5 ♕f5 (after 16...0-0 Bologan's 17 ♕f1! is difficult to meet), Bologan-Chandler, Germany 1994, when after 17 h4 ♗xe5 18 ♖hf1 ♕g4 19 dxe5 ♖xd1+ 20 ♖xd1 ♕xe2 21 ♗xe2 ♘d7 22 ♖d4 White's bishop pair promises him the better ending. If Black were to try 14...0-0-0 (instead of 14...♖d8), then following 15 0-0-0 ♗d6 16 ♔b1 ♖he8 17 ♖hf1, Popovic-Inkiov, Palma de Mallorca 1989, White keeps some pressure as his pieces are well placed and as in the main game, the isolated e-pawn requires attention.

14...0-0-0

Inkiov's move-order avoids 14...♗d6 15 ♖f1!? 0-0 16 ♗xf6 gxf6 17 ♘d7!, leading after 17...♖f7 18 ♘xf6+ ♔h8 19 ♗xe6 ♕xe6 20 ♘g4 c5 21 ♖xf7 ♕xf7 22 ♖d1 to an edge to White (analysis by Dvoirys).

15 0-0-0 ♗d6

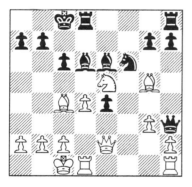

A well-known position. White has tried several moves, all three below yielding a small edge:

a) 16 g4 ♖he8 (or 16...♗xc4 17 ♘xc4 ♖he8 18 ♘e3, An.Bykhovsky) 17 ♗xe6+ ♖xe6 18 ♘f7 ♖de8 19 ♘xd6+ ♖xd6 20 ♗f4 ♖d7 21 g5, Antoniewski-Ilczuk, Poland 1999.

b) 16 ♘f7 ♗xf7 17 ♗xf7 ♖hf8 18 ♗c4 ♖de8 19 ♖hf1 h6 20 ♗f4, Yudovic-Boey, correspondence 1975.

c) 16 ♗xe6+ ♕xe6 17 ♕c4 ♖he8 18 ♕xe6 ♖xe6 19 ♘c4 ♗e7 20 c3 ♘d5 21

♗xe7 ♖xe7 22 ♔d2 b5 23 ♘e5 ♔c7 24 ♖he1 ♘f6 25 ♔e3, Van Riemsdijk-Martins, Brazil 1998.

16 ♕f1 ♖he8 17 ♗xf6 gxf6?!

More precise was 17...♕h6+ 18 ♔b1 ♕xf6 19 ♕xf6 gxf6 20 ♗xe6+ ♖xe6 21 ♘f7 ♖f8 (after 21...♖d7, Tiviakov intended 22 ♘h6, aiming for the f5-square) 22 ♘xd6+ ♖xd6 23 c3

when White, who has the better structure, will blockade and pressurise the e- and f-pawns.

18 ♘f7 ♕xf1 19 ♗xe6+!

An improvement on 19 ♘xd6+ ♖xd6 20 ♗xe6+ ♖exe6 21 ♖hxf1 ♖d5, when Black was more active than in the analogous position in the previous note (Kholmov-Ageichenko, Moscow 1996), but even here White may count on a slight pull.

19...♖xe6 20 ♖hxf1 ♖d7 21 ♘h6

Playing for more than in the slightly favourable double rook ending.

21...e3 22 ♖de1 ♗f8 23 ♘f5 c5 24 c3 cxd4 25 ♘xd4 ♖e4 26 ♔c2!?

26 ♖xf6 was also good; 26...♗g7 27 ♖f3 ♗xd4 28 cxd4 e2 29 ♖f2 ♖de7 30 ♔c2 and White will exchange the two central pawns and have a clear extra pawn.

26...♗c5 27 ♔d3 ♖g4 28 ♖f4 ♖xf4 29 gxf4 ♗xd4 30 cxd4 ♖g7 31 ♖xe3 ♔d7

The attempt to activate with 31...♖g2 is thwarted by 32 ♖e2, aiming to come to e4 and f5 with the king.

32 ⁣Rg3! ⁣Re7 33 ⁣Rh3 ⁣Kd6 34 ⁣Rh6 ⁣Ke6 35 ⁣Ke4 ⁣Rf7 36 b3! b6 37 h4 ⁣Re7 38 d5+ ⁣Kd6+ 39 ⁣Kf5 ⁣Kxd5 40 h5 ⁣Kd4 41 ⁣Rxf6 ⁣Kc3 42 ⁣Rd6 ⁣Re2 43 ⁣Rc6+ ⁣Kb2 44 ⁣Rc7 a5 45 ⁣Rb7 ⁣Rh2 46 ⁣Kg5 ⁣Rg2+ 47 ⁣Kh6 ⁣Rf2 48 ⁣Rxb6 ⁣Rxf4 49 ⁣Kxh7 1-0

The main line of the Schliemann offers a small edge to White.

Game 2
Kamsky-Piket
Groningen 1995

---

1 e4 e5 2 ⁣Nf3 ⁣Nc6 3 ⁣Bb5 f5 4 ⁣Nc3 fxe4 5 ⁣Nxe4 d5

The less popular 5...⁣Nf6 is the subject of game 7.

6 ⁣Nxe5 dxe4 7 ⁣Nxc6 ⁣Wg5 8 ⁣We2 ⁣Nf6 9 f4 ⁣Wxf4

10 d4

Here White is more concerned with completing development rather than pawn snatching with 10 ⁣Nxa7+ (see the next game).
10...⁣Wd6

10...⁣Wh4+ 11 g3 ⁣Wh3 12 ⁣Ne5+ c6 13 ⁣Bc4, transposes to the main line (see Game 1).
11 ⁣Ne5+

11 ⁣Nxa7+? c6 12 ⁣Nxc8 ⁣Wb4+ 13 c3 ⁣Wxb5, Kir.Georgiev-Inkiov, Bulgaria Championship 1988, is simply good for Black, as the knight is trapped.
11...c6 12 ⁣Bc4 ⁣Be6

13 c3

13 ⁣Bf4, has been known and analysed for 30 years. Then 13...⁣Bxc4 14 ⁣Wxc4 ⁣Wd5 15 ⁣Wb3 ⁣Wxb3 (15...⁣Rd6!? – Tiemann) 16 axb3 ⁣Bd6 (16...⁣Nd5!? – Tatai and Zinser) was unclear in Keres-A.Zaitsev, USSR 1971.
13...⁣Bxc4 14 ⁣Nxc4

14 ⁣Wxc4 is solidly countered with 14...⁣Wd5.
14...⁣We6 15 0-0 ⁣Be7

This represents an improvement on previous theory (Palkovi-Szell, Hungary 1991) which continued 15...⁣Bd6?! 16 ⁣Nxd6+ ⁣Wxd6 17 ⁣Bg5 (winning a pawn) 17...⁣Wd5 18 ⁣Bxf6 gxf6 19 ⁣Rxf6 0-0-0 20 ⁣Wg4+ ⁣Rd7 21 ⁣Re6 and Black had no compensation.
16 ⁣Bg5 0-0 17 ⁣Rae1 ⁣Rae8 18 ⁣Nd2

Piket suggests 18 a4!?, just keeping the tension.
18...⁣Wxa2?

Kamsky points out 18...⁣Wd5!, as 19 ⁣Wc4!?

(and certainly not 19 ♗xf6? ♗xf6 20 ♘xe4, which is refuted by 20...♗xd4+! 21 cxd4 ♕xd4+, as Black wins at least a pawn) 19...b5 looks fine for Black.

19 ♗xf6 ♗xf6 20 ♘xe4

20...♖e6!

The best defence, as both 20...♗e7? 21 ♘d6! ♗xd6 22 ♕xe8 and 20...♖d8 21 ♖xf8+ ♖xf8 22 ♘c5 ♕f7 23 ♕e6! are very bad.

21 ♕g4 h6! 22 ♖xf6!

Leading to the win of a pawn, but the fight is far from over.

22...♖fxf6 23 ♘xf6+ ♖xf6 24 ♕c8+ ♔h7 25 ♕xb7 a5 26 h3 ♖g6?

26...a4! 27 ♕b4 ♖g6 was more robust.

27 ♕b8! a4 28 ♖e8

Forcing the black monarch out into the open.

28...♖e6 29 ♖h8+ ♔g6 30 ♕g3+ ♔f7 31 ♖b8 ♕b1+ 32 ♔h2 ♖e1 33 ♖b7+ ♔e6

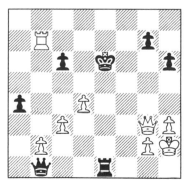

34 d5+! ♔xd5 35 ♖d7+ ♔c4 36 ♖d4+ ♔b3 37 c4+ 1-0

Black resigned as 37...♔xb2 38 ♖d2+♔a1 39 ♕a3+ or 37...♔b4 38 ♕a3+♔a5 39 ♕c5+ are hopeless.

Game 3
Palac-Zelic
Pula 1996

1 e4 e5 2 ♘f3 ♘c6 3 ♗b5 f5 4 ♘c3 fxe4 5 ♘xe4 d5 6 ♘xe5 dxe4 7 ♘xc6 ♕g5 8 ♕e2 ♘f6 9 f4 ♕xf4 10 ♘xa7+

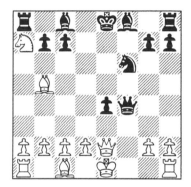

10...♗d7

The only good move. Others (10...c6 11 ♘xc8 ♖xc8 12 ♗c4, Winslow-Carrion, New York 1994, and 10...♔d8 11 d4 ♕h4+ 12 g3 ♕h3 13 ♘xc8 ♔xc8 14 ♗f4, Gufeld-Miasnikov, Riga 1960) both leave White well on top.

11 ♗xd7+ ♔xd7

Capturing the other way is inadequate; 11...♘xd7 12 ♘b5 0-0-0 13 d4 ♕f6 14 ♗e3 (14 ♕c4 c6 15 ♖f1, as suggested by Tseitlin, may be even better) 14...c6 15 ♘c3 ♗b4 16 ♕c4 and Black had nothing for his sacrificed pawn, Ruderfer-Agzamov, USSR 1966.

12 ♕b5+

Despite the exchange of queens after 12 d4 ♕f5 13 ♕b5+ ♕xb5 14 ♘xb5, Black is sufficiently active; 14...c6 15 ♘c3 ♗b4 16 ♔e2 (or 16 ♗d2, which is met by the shot 16...e3! 17 ♗xe3 ♖he8 18 ♔d2 ♘e4+ with equality as in Todorovic-N.Ostojic, Novi Sad 1992) 16...♗xc3 17 bxc3 ♖a4 and Black drew comfortably in Adams-Lautier, Terrassa 1991.

12...♔e6 13 ♕b3+ ♔d7 14 ♕b5+

White has a perpetual check, if he wants it, but can he play for more?

14...♔e6 15 ♕b3+ ♔d7

16 ♕xb7

Courageous! Instead, 16 ♕b5+ and a draw was agreed in Zso.Polgar-Timmerman, Dutch League 1998.

The other winning try is not so dangerous for Black. After 16 ♘b5 ♗c5 17 ♕h3+ (Ulibin considers that neither 17 ♕f7+ ♗e7 18 ♘d4 ♕e5 19 c3 nor 17 d4 e3 18 ♖f1 ♕h4+ 19 ♔d1 ♕g4+ give any advantage) 17...♕g4 18 ♕xg4+ ♘xg4 19 ♘c3 ♖hf8 20 ♘xe4 ♖fe8 21 d3 ♘f2 22 ♖f1 ♘xe4 23 dxe4 ♖xe4+, Black's initiative is worth at least a pawn, Ulibin-Timmerman, Cappelle la Grande 1998.

16...♗d6 17 ♕b5+ ♔e6 18 ♕b3+ ♔e7!

18...♔d7 is inferior as it allows 19 ♕f7+ ♔d8 (19...♗e7 20 ♘c6 ♔xc6 21 ♕xe7 ♖he8, is no improvement) 20 ♘c6+ ♔c8 21 ♘e7+ ♗xe7 22 ♕xe7 ♖e8 23 ♕c5 e3 24 dxe3 ♖a4 25 g3 ♕f3 26 ♖f1 and White converted his advantage into the full point, Gentinetta-Pezzi, correspondence 1998.

19 ♘c6+ ♔d7 20 ♘d4 ♕h4+ 21 g3 ♕h3 22 ♕b5+

I get the impression that White is doing

well about here but Palac never quite consolidates.

22...♔d8 23 ♘f5 ♖f8

24 d4?!

White should have taken the opportunity to lop off the bishop with 24 ♘xd6 cxd6 25 b3.

24...♕g2

Now this move has the added punch of hitting c2.

25 ♖f1 ♕xh2 26 ♗f4 ♗xf4 27 ♖xf4 ♕xc2 28 ♖f2 ♕d3 29 ♕xd3 exd3 30 ♘xg7 ♔d7

31 0-0-0

It's never too late to castle! White retains an extra pawn but his structure is very broken and he is not able to get close to winning.

31...♖xa2 32 ♖xd3 ♖g8 33 ♖xf6 ♖xg7 34 ♔b1 ♖a5 35 ♖df3 ♖ag5 36 ♖f7+

♔d6 37 ♖xg7 ♖xg7 38 ♔c2 ♔d5 39 ♔d3 ♖g5 40 b4 h5 41 ♖e3 c6 42 ♔c3 ♖f5 43 ♔d3 ♖g5 44 ♖e5+ ♖xe5 45 dxe5 ♔xe5 46 ♔c4 ♔d6 47 ♔d4 ♔c7 48 ♔c5 ♔b7 49 b5 cxb5 50 ♔xb5 ♔c7 51 ♔c5 ♔d7 52 ♔d5 ♔e7 53 ♔e5 h4 ½-½

10 ♘xa7 has not previously been considered by theory as a way to obtain an advantage. Here, however, Palac bravely took the second pawn and was probably well on the way to winning. So another reason for Schliemannites to worry!

> ### Game 4
> ## Timman-Böhm
> *Wijk aan Zee 1980*

1 e4 e5 2 ♘f3 ♘c6 3 ♗b5 f5 4 ♘c3 fxe4 5 ♘xe4 d5 6 ♘xe5 dxe4 7 ♘xc6 ♕g5 8 ♕e2 ♘f6

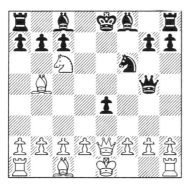

9 f4

White defends his g2-pawn and gains time. Instead 9 ♘xa7+!? ♗d7 10 ♗xd7+ ♘xd7 11 f4! was a recent improvement on 11 ♕xe4+? ♔d8 12 ♕xb7 ♖xa7 13 ♕xa7 ♕xg2 14 ♖f1 ♗c5 15 ♕a6 ♖e8+ and Black was winning in D.Thomas-Boskovic, USA 1975.

After 11 f4, the game Kaminski Henris, Pardubice 1996 continued 11...♕c5 12 ♘b5 ♕xc2 13 ♘c3. Now Black should have played 13...♘c5, whereupon Kaminski analyses 14 ♕h5+ ♔d8 15 0-0 ♕d3 16 ♕g5+ ♔c8

17 ♕f5+ ♔b8 18 ♕f7, which he concludes as unclear.

9...♕h4+

The text move has been largely abandoned as inferior to 9...♕xf4. The present game is one of the foremost reasons.

10 g3 ♕h3

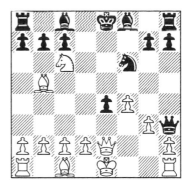

11 ♘e5+

The sequence 11 ♘xa7+ ♗d7 12 ♗xd7+ ♕xd7 13 ♘b5 0-0-0 gives Black unnecessary counterplay, as in the game Estrin-Neishtadt, correspondence 1963, which continued 14 b3 c6 15 ♘a3 (or 15 ♘c3 ♗c5) 15...♕d4 16 c3 ♕a7 and White is a long way from getting organised.

11...c6 12 ♗c4

12 ♘xc6? fails to 12...a6 13 ♗a4 ♗d7.

12...♗c5

Alternatives have been found wanting, for instance 12...h5 13 d3 h4 14 ♗e3 hxg3 15 0-0-0 gxh2 16 dxe4, Liberzon-Wockenfuss, Bad Lauterberg 1977, and 12...♗e6 13 b3 ♗c5 14 ♗b2 0-0-0 15 0-0-0, Adorjan-Rigo, Hungarian Championship 1976.

13 d3

Otherwise 13 d4 ♗xd4 14 ♗f7+ ♔d8!? is unclear according to Tiemann, but if the text continuation is (as I suspect) over-rated, then White players may like to investigate the game Zapata-Gi.Garcia, Medellin 1992, which continued 13 c3 ♗f5 14 d4 exd3 15 ♘xd3+ ♗e7 16 ♗d2! ♗g4 17 ♕f1 0-0-0 18 ♘e5 and White simplifies favourably.

13...♘g4

The critical move. Instead 13...exd3 14 ♘xd3+ ♗e7 15 ♘e5 ♗f5, as suggested by Zvetkovic, looks bad after 16 ♗e3 0-0-0 17 ♘f7.

14 ♘f7

14 d4?!, led nowhere after 14...♘xe5 15 ♕xe4 ♗xd4 16 fxe5 ♕g4 17 ♕xg4 ♗xg4, Karpov-Parma, Portoroz/Ljubjana 1975.

Instead of the text, 14 ♕xe4 is another good move. Then the continuation 14...♘f2 15 ♗f7+ ♔e7! is not really that clear, but Tiemann continues with 16 ♕c4 ♗b6 17 ♖f1 ♕xh2 18 ♕b4+ c5 19 ♕d2 ♘g4 20 ♕xh2 ♘xh2 21 ♖h1, and White keeps an edge.

14...♗f2+ 15 ♔d1

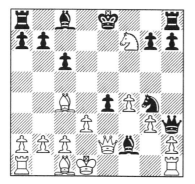

15...e3

15...♘e3+ fails to obtain a playable game, for example 16 ♗xe3 ♗g4 17 ♗xf2 ♗xe2+ 18 ♔xe2 exd3+ 19 ♔f3! and White was winning, Tiemann-Lehmann, correspondence 1980.

16 ♕f3 ♘h6!

White wins comfortably after both 16...♘xh2 17 ♕e4+ ♔f8 18 ♗xe3, Kavalek-Ljubojevic, Amsterdam 1975, and 16...♘f6 17 f5 ♖f8, Nunn-Rumens, London 1977, and now simply 18 ♗xe3, (Keres and Parma) seems to be sufficient, for example 18...♕g4 19 ♘d6+ ♔d7 20 ♕xg4 ♘xg4 21 ♗f4 etc.

17 ♕e4+ ♔f8 18 ♗xe3

All sources just quote the remainder of the game as if Black is already lost. But is he?

18...♗g4+?

Now Black is definitely lost, but after the natural 18...♗xe3! things don't seem that clear to me. 19 ♘xh8?? ♗g4+ 20 ♔e1 ♖e8 and 19 ♘xh6?? ♗g4+ 20 ♘xg4 ♕xg4+ 21 ♔e1 ♖e8 both lose for White while 19 ♘g5 doesn't seem right after 19...♕h5+ 20 ♔e1 ♕e8, defending neatly.

I consider 19 ♕xe3 ♘xf7 (but not 19...♗g4+? 20 ♔d2 ♘xf7 21 ♖ae1) 20 ♖e1 as leading nowhere after 20...♕d7! 21 ♕c5+? (21 ♔d2 ♘d6 22 ♗b3 is well met by 22...b6, with ...♗b7 and ...♖e8 to come) 21...♕d6 22 ♖e8+?? ♔xe8 23 ♗xf7+ ♔e7 and Black wins. Instead of 20 ♖e1 White should settle for 20 ♕c5+! ♔g8 21 ♕e7 (after 21 ♖e1 Black can defend with 21...♗g4+ or 21...h6) 21...♗g4+ 22 ♔d2 ♖f8 23 ♕xb7 (23 ♖ae1?! ♗d7),

when White has certainly obtained sufficient compensation for the piece, but can hardly be described as winning.

19 ♔d2 ♖e8 20 ♘e5 1-0

White has two pawns and a safe king, whereas Black's is open to the wind.

In conclusion, against 9...♕h4, White can obtain the better of it. However, if my improvement on move 18 is correct, not by as much as previously thought.

Game 5
Timman-Piket
Wijk aan Zee (2nd matchgame) 1995

---

1 e4 e5 2 ♘f3 ♘c6 3 ♗b5 f5 4 ♘c3 fxe4 5 ♘xe4 d5 6 ♘xe5 dxe4 7 ♘xc6

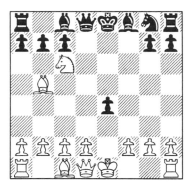

7...♕d5

The capture, 7...bxc6, has almost never been played, but is it so bad? Following 8 ♗xc6+ ♗d7 9 ♕h5+ ♔e7 10 ♕e5+ ♗e6 11 f4 (after 11 ♗xa8 {11 d4 ♔f7} 11...♕xa8 12 ♕xc7+ ♔e8 13 0-0 ♗e7 14 d3 ♔f7 White may have the material advantage of rook and three pawns for a couple of minor pieces, but the risk is that Black's pieces will come into play with great effect) 11...exf3 (if 11...♘h6? 12 f5! ♘xf5 13 ♖f1 White's initiative is too strong) 12 0-0 ♖b8 13 d4 ♖b6! (rather than 13...♘f6?! 14 d5 ♕d6 15 ♕xe6+ ♕xe6 16 dxe6 ♔xe6 17 ♗xf3, and White emerged with a clear extra pawn, Gipslis-Tringov, Varna 1962) 14 ♖xf3 ♘f6 15 d5 ♖xc6 16

dxc6 ♕d1+ 17 ♖f1 ♕d6 the ending looks playable for Black. Another area of research for Schliemann addicts!

8 c4 ♕d6

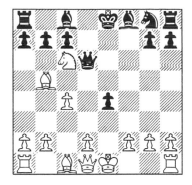

9 ♕h5+

Popular, but not necessarily the strongest. With 9 ♘xa7+ White grabs a second pawn but Black then obtains a lead in development. However, I suspect that there is insufficient compensation. After the logical sequence 9...♗d7 10 ♗xd7+ ♕xd7 White has two tempting tries:

a) 11 ♘b5 ♘f6 12 0-0 ♗c5 13 b4!? (13 d4 exd3 14 ♖e1+ ♔f7 15 ♗e3 ♗xe3 16 ♖xe3 ♖ad8 yields a position that has been tried on several occasions, the conclusion being that Black's big passed pawn yields sufficient compensation) 13...♗xb4 14 ♕b3 ♗c5 15 ♗a3 ♗xa3 16 ♘xa3 0-0 17 ♘c2 is recommended by Tiemann as giving a small edge to White.

b) 11 ♕h5+! (the most testing) 11...g6 12 ♕e5+ ♔f7 13 ♘b5 (13 ♕xh8!? isn't bad, but 13...♘f6 14 ♘b5 ♖d8 15 0-0 ♗c5 16 ♕xd8 ♕xd8 is considered to yield about equal practical chances) 13...c6 14 ♕d4! ♖d8 (the complications after 14...♕e7 15 ♕xh8 ♘f6 16 b3 ♖d8 17 ♗b2 ♗g7 18 ♗a3!, as in Lawton-Finlayson, England 1985, seem better for White) 15 ♕xd7+ ♖xd7 16 ♘c3 ♘f6 17 b3!.

---

see following diagram

So, pausing for breath, we see that White has two extra pawns in the ending, but Black has some practical compensation as the d2-pawn in particular is open to attack. Some references prefer White while some feel that Black has enough pressure. The game Vogt-Möhring, Leipzig 1975 continued with 17...♗c5 18 ♘a4 ♗a7 (18...♗d4 19 ♗b2 b5 20 ♗xd4 ♖xd4 21 cxb5 cxb5 22 ♘c3 b4 23 ♘e2 ♖d7 24 ♖c1, Jansa-Becx, Copenhagen 1987, when White was close to winning, was no improvement either) 19 ♗b2 ♖hd8 20 ♗xf6 and White had a clear advantage.

The other alternative 9 c5?! is no longer played as after 9...♕xc5 10 ♕a4 ♘f6 11 d4 ♕b6 12 ♘e5+ c6 13 ♗c4 ♗b4+, Rantanen-Sollid, Gausdal 1981, Black is doing well. Here 14 ♔e2 is recommended, but both 14...♖f8, or even 14...♕xd4!, look promising.

9...g6 10 ♕e5+ ♕xe5 11 ♘xe5+ c6 12 ♗a4

12 ♘xc6? loses a piece to the pin 12...a6 13 ♗a4 ♗d7.

12...♗e6!?

12...♗g7 is not bad. After 13 d4 exd3 14 ♗f4 (or 14 0-0!? then 14...♗e6!, intending to castle long) 14...g5 15 ♗g3 ♗f5 16 0-0-0 ♖d8 17 ♖he1 ♘e7 18 ♖e3 ♖d4 19 ♘xd3 ♖xc4+ 20 ♗c2 ♔f7 21 ♔d2! ♖d4 22 ♔e2 White was restricted to a very small pull, Am.Rodriguez-Barreras, Cienfuegos 1979.

13 d4

Velimirovic-Vasiukov, Yugoslavia vs.

USSR 1973, was fairly balanced after 13 b3 ♗g7 14 ♗b2 a6 15 b4 ♘h6 16 0-0 0-0.

13...exd3 14 ♗g5!

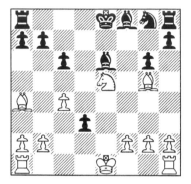

14...♗g7

Kuijf points out that 14...♗b4+? 15 ♗d2 ♗d6 only helps White after 16 ♗c3.

In an earlier game 14...♗e7 was tried but after 15 ♗xe7 ♘xe7 16 ♖d1 0-0-0 17 ♗b3 ♘f5 18 ♖xd3 Black didn't have much compensation for the lost pawn, Wolff-D.Gurevich, Worcester 1986.

15 0-0-0 ♗xe5

If instead 15...h6!? 16 ♗f4 g5 17 ♗g3 0-0-0 18 ♖he1 ♗xe5 19 ♗xe5 ♖h7, White has the bishop pair but Black seems to be doing okay.

16 ♖he1 h6

Kuijf suggests 16...♔f7 17 ♖xe5 ♗xc4, as a better defence.

17 ♖xe5 hxg5?

Black should have tried 17...♔f7 18 ♗e3 ♗xc4, although Timman prefers White slightly after 19 ♗b3, as he has a lead in development and will recuperate the pawn.

18 ♖xe6+ ♔f7 19 ♖d6! ♘f6 20 ♖1xd3 g4

After 20...♖h4 Timman intended 21 ♗b3! c5 22 ♖f3 ♖f4 23 ♖xf4 gxf4 24 ♗d1, when the bishop comes to f3 and White should be able to exploit his extra pawn.

21 f3

Opening up Black's king.

21...♖xh2 22 fxg4 ♘e4 23 ♖f3+ ♔g7 24

♖d7+ ♔h6 25 ♖e3! ♘c5?

Losing at once, but 25...♘g5 26 ♖xb7 ♖xg2 27 ♗xc6 ♖xg4 28 ♗d5 is probably lost in the long run.

26 g5+ 1-0

26...♔h5 loses a piece to 27 ♗d1+ etc.

So 9 ♕h5+ leads to an ending where White keeps a small edge, but the real problem for 7...♕d5 is that 9 ♘xa7+ wins two pawns for insubstantial compensation.

Game 6
Nisipeanu-Mi.Tseitlin
Budapest 1996

---

1 e4 e5 2 ♘f3 ♘c6 3 ♗b5 f5 4 ♘c3 fxe4 5 ♘xe4 d5 6 ♘g3

A safe way of 'copping out' from the sharp 6 ♘xe5.

6...♗g4

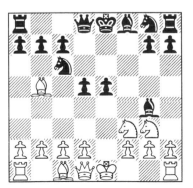

6...♗d6? loses a pawn to a well-known trick; 7 ♗xc6+ bxc6 8 ♘xe5 ♗xe5 9 ♕h5+, while 6...e4?!, was made to look dubious in a 1986 game Moiseev-Ivanov, after 7 ♘d4 ♕f6! 8 ♕h5+ ♔e7! 9 ♘df5+! (preferable to 9 ♘xc6+ bxc6 10 ♗a4 g6 11 ♕e2 h5, with a double-edged struggle ahead) and now 9...♔d8 (Tiemann) is met by 10 ♘e3, (Flear) and I prefer White.

7 h3

7 0-0 is not dangerous after 7...♕f6!, when 8 ♖e1 0-0-0 9 ♗xc6 bxc6 10 d3 ♘e7 11 ♗g5 ♗xf3 12 ♗xf6 ♗xd1 13 ♗xe7 ♗xe7 14 ♖axd1 ♗d6 was equal in Geller-Tseitlin, Moscow 1982.

7...♗xf3 8 ♕xf3

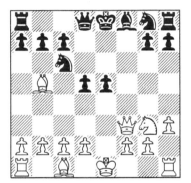

8...♘f6

This seems to be a better choice than 8...♕d6 9 ♕h5+ g6 10 ♗xc6+ bxc6 11 ♕e2 ♘e7 12 b3 ♗g7 13 a4!? (13 ♗b2, followed by 0-0, ♖ae1 and ♕a6 gives a small, risk free edge) 13...e4 14 ♗a3 ♕e6 15 ♖d1 ♘f5 16 0-0 ♘d4 17 ♕a6 ♘xc2 18 ♗c5 with complications that turned out in White's favour in Kupreichik-Yagupov, Groningen 1995.

9 ♘h5

9 0-0 ♗d6 10 ♘h5 doesn't create that many problems, for example 10...e4 11 ♘xf6+ ♕xf6 12 ♕xf6 gxf6 13 d3 0-0-0 14 dxe4 dxe4 15 ♖e1 f5 16 ♔f1 ♖de8 17 ♗h6 ♖e6 and Black had equalised, Karpov-Lautier, Ubeda 1994.

9...♕d6 10 ♘xf6+ gxf6 11 ♕h5+

The point of White's move-order becomes clear. Black has to move his king.

11...♔d7

11...♔e7 12 c3 ♗g7 13 0-0 ♘d8 14 d4 ♘e6 is suggested as a reasonable alternative for Black by Mikhail Tseitlin. The game continuation also seems perfectly sound.

12 0-0

The ending after 12 c3 ♖d8 13 ♕g4+ ♕e6 was equal in Westerinen-Parma, Dortmund 1975.

12...a6!?

Black can also get a good game with 12...♖d8, as 13 d4 (or 13 c3 ♔c8 14 ♗e2 ♔b8 15 d3 ♘e7 16 ♗e3 f5, with unclear play in A.Ivanov-Inkiov, Gausdal 1991) 13...♔c8 14 dxe5 fxe5 15 ♗g5 ♗e7 16 ♗xc6 bxc6 17 ♗xe7 ♕xe7 18 ♖ae1 e4 19 f3 ♕c5+ 20 ♖f2 exf3 21 ♕xf3 gives him no real problems, Gdanski-Lautier, Polanica Zdroj 1991.

13 ♗e2 ♘d4!

More active than 13...♖e8 14 c3 ♔d8 15 ♗g4 e4 16 d4!, Kochiev-Kupreichik, USSR 1974, when Black's king is not ideally placed and capturing en passant will only open lines for White.

14 ♗g4+ ♔c6 15 c3 ♘e6 16 d4 ♘g7 17 ♕f7 h5!

Black's eccentrically placed king shouldn't be a problem.

18 dxe5 fxe5 19 ♗f3 e4?!

Safer is 19...♕e6 20 ♕xe6+ ♘xe6, when 21 c4 e4 22 cxd5+ ♔xd5 23 ♖d1+ ♘d4 24

♗e3 ♗g7 is only equal.

20 c4!

An interesting try as otherwise 20 ♗e2 ♕e6 gives nothing.

20...exf3 21 ♗f4 ♕e7 22 ♕xd5+ ♔b6 23 ♗e3+ c5 24 b4 ♖d8!

The best defence.

25 ♕xf3

White could have headed for a favourable double-rook ending with 25 ♗xc5+!? ♔c7 26 ♗xe7 ♖xd5 27 ♗xf8 ♖g5 28 ♗xg7 ♖xg2+ 29 ♔h1 ♖xg7 30 ♖ae1.

25...♘e6 26 ♖ae1 ♕d7?!

Here Black missed his chance with 26...♕g7! and following 27 bxc5+ ♘xc5! 28 ♕f5! ♕c7 29 ♗g5 the game would have been unclear.

27 ♕f6 ♗d6 28 ♖d1

28 ♕xe6! ♕xe6 29 ♗xc5+ was simpler.

28...♕c6 29 ♖xd6! ♕xd6 30 bxc5+ ♘xc5 31 ♖b1+ ♔c6 32 ♕f3+ ♔d7 33 ♖d1 ♘d3 34 ♗f4 ♕g6 35 ♖xd3+ ♔c8 36 ♖d5 ♕c6 37 ♕a3 ♖hg8! 38 ♗d6!

Certainly not 38 ♖c5?? ♖d1+ 39 ♔h2 ♖xg2 and it's mate!

38...b6?!

Better was 38...h4.

39 ♕xa6+ ♕b7 40 ♕xb7+ ♔xb7 41 ♗b4

With the time control safely navigated, White has the time to consolidate his material advantage of three pawns for the exchange, which seems to be enough to win the game.

41...h4 42 ♗e7 ♖de8 43 ♗xh4 ♖e4 44 ♗g5 ♖xc4 45 ♗e3 ♖a8 46 ♖b5 ♖a6 47 g4 ♔c6 48 ♖f5 ♖b4 49 ♖f6+ ♔d5 50 ♔g2 ♔e5 51 ♖g6 ♔e4 52 ♔g3 ♖a3 53 h4 ♖b1 54 h5 b5 55 h6 ♖xa2 56 ♖c6 ♔d5 57 h7 ♖a8 58 ♖h6 ♖h8 59 ♗g5 ♖g1+ 60 ♔f3 1-0

In conclusion it can be said that 6 ♘g3 doesn't lead to an advantage.

Game 7
Boto-M.Peric
Bosnia and Herzegovina 1998

---

1 e4 e5 2 ♘f3 ♘c6 3 ♗b5 f5 4 ♘c3 fxe4 5 ♘xe4 ♘f6

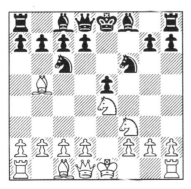

This move is less common than 5...d5.

6 ♘xf6+

6 ♕e2 leads to unclear play after 6...d5 7 ♘xf6+ gxf6 8 d4 ♗g7 9 dxe5 0-0 when

White has not been able to prove an advantage, for instance 10 e6 ♘e5 11 ♗f4 c6 12 ♗d3 ♘xd3+ 13 ♕xd3 ♗xe6 14 ♘d4 ♗g4 15 0-0 ♕d7 16 ♖fe1 ♖fe8, Klovans-Souleidis, Germany 1993.

6...♕xf6

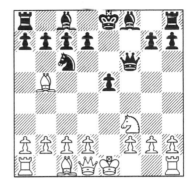

7 0-0

7 ♕e2 is a prelude to snatching a pawn; 7...♗e7 8 ♗xc6 dxc6 9 ♘xe5 (9 ♕xe5 ♗g4 10 ♕xf6 ♗xf6 gives Black enough practical compensation) 9...♗f5 10 d3 0-0 11 0-0, when it seems that White has a clear extra pawn. However, after 11...♖ae8 12 d4 ♗d6 13 f4 ♗xe5 14 dxc5 ♕g6 15 ♖f2 h5, Unzicker-Tseitlin, Moscow 1982, Black's total control of the light squares gives him a positional blockade sufficient to hold.

7...♘d4 8 ♘xd4 exd4 9 b3

The main line used to start with 9 ♖e1+, but it doesn't trouble the second player; 9...♗e7 10 ♕e2 c6 11 ♗d3 d5 12 b3 0-0 13 ♕xe7 ♕xf2+ 14 ♔h1 ♗h3 15 ♖g1? (correct is 15 gxh3, allowing a repetition as in Adorjan-Parma, Moscow 1977) 15...♖ae8 and Black was on top in Kalegin-Tseitlin, USSR 1986, as 16 ♕xf8+ is met by 16...♕xf8!.

9...c6 10 ♖e1+ ♗e7 11 ♗a3!

New. Previous theory continued with 11 ♗c4 b5 12 ♗d3 0-0 13 ♕e2 d5 14 ♕xe7 ♕xf2+ 15 ♔h1 ♗h3 16 ♖g1 ♖ae8 17 ♗a3 ♖xe7 18 ♗xe7, Friedrich-Schlesinger, West Germany 1988, and now 18...♖f7 is considered as unclear by Friedrich.

11...d6 12 ♕h5+! g6

12...♕f7 allows 13 ♖xe7! ♔xe7 14 ♗xd6+ ♔f6 15 ♕e5+ ♔g6 16 ♗d3+ ♗f5 (after 16...♔h6 17 ♗e7! leads to a quick win) 17 ♕g3+ ♔f6 18 ♗e5+ ♔e7 19 ♕g5+ and Black can resign.

13 ♕d5

Picturesque.

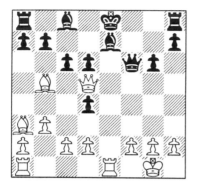

13...♔d8

13...♔d7 is met by 14 ♗b2, when 14...♖e8 15 ♗xd4 ♕f4 16 ♗a4 keeps up the pressure.

14 ♗xc6 bxc6 15 ♕xc6 ♖b8 16 ♖xe7!!

Correctly eliminating Black's best defensive piece.

16...♕xe7

Boto points out that after 16...♔xe7 17 ♕c7+ ♔d7 18 ♖e1+ ♔f7 19 ♕xd7+ ♔g8 20 ♕xa7 White also has a winning position.

17 ♗xd6 ♕b7 18 ♕c5 ♖a8

18...♖e8 was a more resistant continuation. However, 19 ♗xb8 ♕xb8 20 ♕xd4+ ♗d7 21 ♕h4+ gives White a fistful of pawns for the piece.

19 ♖e1 ♕b6 20 ♗c7+! ♕xc7 21 ♕g5+ 1-0

see following diagram

Black resigned in view of the continuation 21...♔d7 22 ♖e7+ ♔c6 23 ♖xc7+ ♔xc7 24 ♕e5+.

An impressive display that seriously puts into doubt the soundness of the adventurous 5...♘f6.

1 e4 e5 2 ♘f3 ♘c6 3 ♗b5 f5 4 ♘c3 ♘d4?!

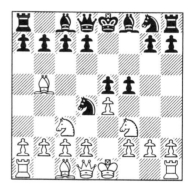

An extremely tricky variation, but objectively not that good. After this convincing correspondence game became known just about everyone gave up the line.

5 ♗a4

This retains the pin on the d-pawn.

The following four alternatives seem reasonable but tend to be double-edged:

a) 5 exf5 and now:

a1) 5...♘xb5?! 6 ♘xb5 d6 7 d4 e4 8 ♘g5 ♗xf5 9 ♕e2 ♕d7 10 g4 ♗g6 11 ♘e6, Pokojowczyk-Lipski, Krakow 1978, is terrible for Black.

a2) Another try 5...♘f6 has its points, as after 6 ♘xe5 ♗c5 7 0-0 0-0 8 ♘f3 c6 9 ♘xd4 ♗xd4 10 ♗e2 d5 11 ♗f3 ♗xf5 12 ♘d2 ♙h6 13 d4, Vasilchuk-Stein, USSR 1966, Black has some compensation for the pawn.

a3) 5...c6 ♘xe5 ♕e7 7 0-0 ♔d8 8 ♖e1 ♘xb5 9 ♘xb5 cxb5 10 d4, when Nunn prefers White slightly but of course the position remains very unclear.

b) 5 ♘xd4 exd4 6 ♘d5!? c6 7 exf5 ♕g5! is totally wild.

c) 5 ♘xe5 can be met by the extraordinary sequence 5...♕f6 6 ♘f3 ♘xb5 7 ♘xb5 fxe4 8 ♕e2 ♕e7!, after which White can take the rook but will eventually lose the stranded knight on a8. Instead White can play 9 ♘fd4 d6 10 0-0 ♘f6 11 d3 a6 (Tiemann), but Black is okay.

d) After 5 ♗c4 c6 a dichotomy for White:

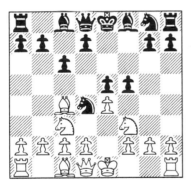

6 ♗xg8 and 6 0-0.

d1) 6 ♗xg8 ♖xg8 7 0-0 ♕f6 (or 7...d6!?) 8 exf5 d5! (instead 8...♘xf3+?! turned out badly in Sax-O.Rodriguez, Las Palmas 1978 after 9 ♕xf3 ♗e7 {9...d5?! allows 10 ♘xd5! cxd5 11 ♕xd5, with ♖e1 and d4 to follow} 10 d4 d5 11 dxe5 ♕xf5 12 ♕e2 ♗e6 13 ♗e3 ♕xe5 14 ♖ae1 ♔f7 15 f4 with a strong initiative for White) 9 ♘xe5 ♘xc2 is given by Larsen as unclear.

d2) 6 0-0 ♘f6!? 7 ♘xe5 fxe4 8 ♘f7 ♕c7! (not getting in the way of the bishop; instead 8...♕e7?! 9 ♘xh8 d5 10 ♗e2 ♗f5 11 d3

0-0-0 12 ♗e3 ♘xe2+ 13 ♘xe2 g6 14 dxe4 dxe4 15 ♕e1 ♗g7 16 ♕a5 was basically winning for White in Geller-O.Rodriguez, Las Palmas 1976) 9 ♘xh8 d5 10 ♗e2 ♗d6 11 h3

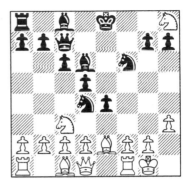

is murky, but somehow one feels that White's material advantage should count for something.

I think that Black can do better with 6...d6 7 ♘xd4 exd4 8 ♘e2 fxe4 9 ♗xg8 ♖xg8 10 d3 (Scholl-Brenndorf, correspondence 1969), when I now prefer 10...d5! with equal chances (rather than the game continuation 10...♗g4 11 dxe4 ♕b6 12 a4 a5 13 h3 ♗xe2 14 ♕xe2, when White had an edge).

5...♘f6

On 5...c6 6 ♘xe5 ♕f6 the move 7 ♘d3! seems to diffuse Black's activity. Then after 7...fxe4 8 ♘xe4 ♕g6 9 0-0 d5 10 ♘g3 ♗d6 11 ♖c1+ ♘e7 12 ♘e5 and White is well on top.

6 ♘xe5

There are a couple of less convincing alternatives:

a) 6 exf5 ♗c5 7 0-0 0-0 8 ♘xd4 ♗xd4! is unclear according to Keres. 8...exd4?! is inferior and in the game Chandler-Inkiov, Nis 1983 White was better after 9 ♘e2 d5 10 d3 ♗xf5 11 ♗f4 ♗d6 12 ♗xd6 ♕xd6 13 ♘xd4 ♘g4 14 g3 ♕h6 15 h4.

b) 6 0-0 ♗c5 7 ♘xe5 0-0 8 exf5 d5 gives Black excellent play for his gambit, for example 9 ♘f3 ♗xf5 10 ♘xd4 ♗xd4 11 ♘e2 ♗g4 12 c3 ♕e7 13 ♗b5 ♖ae8 14 cxd4 ♗xe2

15 ♗xe2 ♕xe2 16 d3 c6 and Black is not worse, Stoica-Ciocaltea, Bucharest 1980.

6...♗c5

6...♕e7!? is suggested as a possible improvement by Van der Tak. The following game suggests that the idea is playable; 7 f4 c6 8 d3 b5 9 ♗b3 d6 10 ♘f3 ♘xb3 11 axb3 b4 12 ♘e2 fxe4 13 dxe4 ♘xe4 14 0-0 d5 15 ♗e3 ♕b7 16 ♘g5 ♘f6 17 f5 ♗d6 18 ♘d4 0-0 19 ♘de6, Bondar-Smolensky, correspondence 1978.

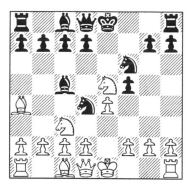

7 ♘d3!

Precisely played, as 7 0-0 0-0 8 ♘d3 is met by the positional piece sacrifice 8...fxe4! 9 ♘xc5 d5 and play becomes very sharp. Now 10 d3 ♘g4 11 ♘5xe4 dxe4 12 ♘xe4 ♕h4 13 h3 (Timman-Hermann, Bad Lauterberg 1977) can be met with 13...♘e5! 14 f4 ♗g4 15 ♕d2 ♗f3 (Mechkarov), when White can grab material but his king comes under a strong attack. After the further 16 fxe5 ♗xe4 17 ♖xf8+ ♖xf8 18 dxe4 ♘f3+ 19 gxf3 ♖xf3 20 ♗b3+ ♔h8 21 ♗e6 ♕g3+ 22 ♕g2 ♕e1+ 23 ♔h2 ♖f2 a draw is the most likely result.

7...♗b6

What else? 7...♕e7?! 8 e5 0-0 9 0-0 ♘g4 10 h3 is dubious for Black and 7...fxe4 is no better; 8 ♘xc5 c6 (or 8...0-0 9 d3! ♕e7 10 ♗e3 ♕xc5 11 dxe4 and wins) 9 d3 (9 ♘5xe4 is also good) 9...d5 10 ♗e3 etc., with a clear advantage to White.

8 e5 ♘e4

Following 8...♘g4 9 ♘d5! ♕h4 10 g3!

♕h3 11 ♘3f4 ♕h6 12 c3 Black's attacking pretensions are thwarted.

9 ♘d5 0-0

9...♕g5 10 0-0 c6 11 ♘xb6 axb6 12 ♗b3 ♘xb3 13 cxb3, intending f3, gives White the advantage according to Hamarat.

10 0-0 c6 11 ♘xb6 axb6

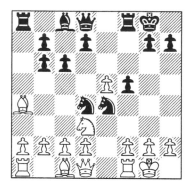

12 ♗b3+

12 c3 may be even stronger as Black has no compensation for the pawn.

12...♘xb3 13 cxb3 d6 14 b4! dxe5 15 ♕b3+ ♔h8 16 ♘xe5 ♕e7 17 f4 ♗e6 18 ♕h3 ♔g8 19 d3

White has managed to organise himself and is even threatening to complete his development! He has an extra pawn and the Black initiative has withered away.

19...♘f6 20 a3 ♘g4 21 ♖e1 ♘xe5 22 ♖xe5 ♖f6 23 ♗d2 ♕d7 24 ♗c3 b5 25 ♖ae1 ♖d8 26 ♕e3 ♔f7

27 g4!

A neat way of increasing the pressure.

27...♖g6

If 27...♖e8 28 g5 ♖g6 29 h4 h5 30 ♕e2 ♖h8 31 ♔h2 Black is virtually in zugzwang!

28 ♔f1! 1-0

Black resigned as after 28...♕c8 (or 28...fxg4 29 f5) 29 gxf5 ♗xf5 30 ♖xf5+♕xf5 31 ♕e7+ ♔g8 32 ♕xd8+ White wins easily.

Game 9
Apicella-Sharif
French League 1991

1 e4 e5 2 ♘f3 ♘c6 3 ♗b5 f5 4 d3

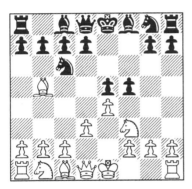

This move has been popular but doesn't really test Black that much.

4...fxe4

Keeping the tension with 4...♘f6!? is another idea. Then 5 0-0 (5 exf5 led to unclear play after 5...♘e7 6 0-0 c6 7 ♗c4 d6 8 ♖e1 ♗xf5 9 ♗g5 ♕d7 10 ♘c3 h6 11 ♗xf6 gxf6, Kindermann-Geenen, Thessaloniki Olympiad 1988) 5...♗c5 6 ♘xe5 is given as an advantage to White in some works, but after 6...♘xe5 7 d4 ♘xe4 8 dxc5 ♕e7 (Shamkovich and Schiller) the position is not at all clear.

5 dxe4 ♘f6 6 0-0

6 ♕d3 can be met with the cheeky 6...♗b4+!?, when after 7 c3 (7 ♘c3 d6 8 ♗d2 ♗xc3 9 ♗xc3 ♗d7 10 0-0-0 ♕e7, In-

cutto-Spassky, Mar del Plata 1960, proved to be better for Black who has useful assets in the shape of his solid central majority and use of the f-file) 7...♗c5 8 0-0 (Black gets enough play for the pawn after 8 ♗xc6 bxc6 9 ♘xe5 ♕e7 10 f4 ♗b7 11 ♘d2 d6 12 ♘ef3 0-0, according to Inkiov) 8...d6 9 a4 a6 10 ♗c4 ♕e7 11 ♘bd2 ♗e6 12 b4 ♗a7 13 ♗xe6 ♕xe6 14 ♘c4 h6 15 ♗e3 0-0 Black has a good game, Kindermann-Inkiov, Berlin 1986.

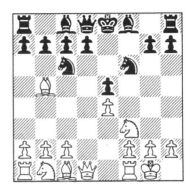

6...♗c5

The alternative 6...d6 (intending ...♗e7) is perhaps less ambitious as the bishop on c5 is more active than on e7 but this isn't necessarily an inferior option. After 7 ♘c3 ♗e7 8 ♕d3 (8 ♗c4 should be met by 8...♘a5!, fighting for the important a2-g8 diagonal) 8...♗g4 9 h3 ♗xf3 10 ♕xf3 0-0 11 ♕d1 ♔h8 12 ♗e3 ♘b8 13 ♗e2 c6 14 ♗f3 ♘bd7 (Gobet-Milligan, European Junior Championship 1981) 15 a4 offers a slight pull. White has his bishops and keeps ideas of ...b5 or ...d5 under observation, but Black remains solid.

If instead 7 ♕d3, then standard theory continues 7...♗g4 8 h3 ♗xf3 9 ♕xf3 ♗e7 (9...♕d7 is more accurate according to Schiller and Shamkovich, but this has yet to be tested at a high level) 10 ♕d3 (preventing Black from castling) 10...a6 11 ♗c4 b5 12 ♗b3 ♘d4 13 ♗g5, as in Ermenkov-Damjanovic, Alicante 1978, and concludes 'with an edge to White'. However, this seems too optimistic and should be revised, so read on! The game continued 13...♘d7 14 ♗e3

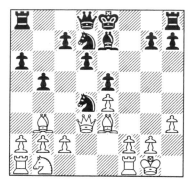

14...♘xb3?! (14...♘c5! is a clear improvement; 15 ♕d1 ♘dxb3 16 axb3 and now 16...♘xe4 17 ♕d5 ♘f6 18 ♕c6+ ♔f7 is not worse for Black) 15 axb3 c6 16 c4 0-0 17 ♘c3 ♕c8 and 18 ♖a2! duly gave Ermenkov his edge due to pressure on the queenside.

7 ♘c3

Critical is 7 ♕e2 d6 8 ♕c4 ♕e7 9 ♘c3 (9 b4?! looks dubious after 9...♗e6 10 ♕c3 ♘xe4 11 ♕d3 ♘xf2!) 9...♗d7 10 ♘d5 ♘xd5 11 exd5 ♘d4 12 ♗xd7+ ♕xd7 13 ♘xe5!? (13 ♘xd4 ♗xd4, as in A.Martin-Inkiov, Gausdal 1989, is equal) 13...♕f5 14 ♘d3 b5 15 ♖e1+ ♔f7 16 ♕c3 ♕xd5 17 ♗e3 (Kalegin-Vi.Ivanov, USSR 1991), and now 17...♕c4! (17...♖he8 has been played, but White can get an edge without risk by playing 18 ♘xc5 dxc5 19 ♗xd4) 18 ♕xc4+ bxc4 19 ♘xc5 ♘xc2 20 ♘a6 (20 ♘e4?! ♖hb8! looks promising for Black), with an edge to White according to Kalegin. However after Black's best 20...c5, he only has one pawn and rook for the two pieces but White's knight on a6 requires freeing. A possible continuation is 21 ♖ac1 ♘xe1 22 ♖xe1 ♖hc8 23 b4 cxb4 24 ♘xb4 ♖ab8 and with his active rooks and useful passed c-pawn I'm not sure that Black is worse.

7...d6 8 ♗g5

8 ♗c4 gets nowhere after 8...♘a5 9 ♗b5+ ♘c6.

8...0-0 9 ♘d5 ♔h8 10 ♘h4 ♘d4

The recent try 10...♗e6!?, was fairly successful; 11 ♗c4 (11 ♗xf6 gxf6 12 ♕h5 ♖g8) 11...♗xd5 12 ♗xd5 ♘e7 13 ♕d3 ♘exd5 14 exd5 ♕d7 15 ♗e3 ♗xe3 16 fxe3 ♕g4 and Black had equal chances in Markovic-Matulovic, Cacak 1998.

11 ♗c4!?

11 ♗d3 led to no advantage in Grinberg-Parma, Buenos Aires Olympiad 1978, after 11...c6 12 ♗xf6 (12 ♘xf6!?) 12...gxf6 13 ♘e3 ♘e6 14 ♘ef5 ♗g7.

The text provokes ...b5, which is space gaining, but may give something for White to nibble at on the queenside (see move 22).

11...b5 12 ♗d3 c6 13 ♘xf6 gxf6 14 ♗e3 ♖g8 15 ♔h1 ♖g4 16 g3 ♖g8

Hoping to bring the bishop into play on g4

or h3. Instead 16..♕g8? 17 c3 ♘e6 is inadequate after 18 ♘f5.

17 f3

Not 17 c3?, as 17...♗g4! 18 f3? ♘xf3! wins a pawn.

17...♗h3 18 ♖g1 ♘e6 19 ♕d2 ♗xe3 20 ♕xe3 ♘g5 21 f4 ♘f7 22 a4!

Now that White has consolidated the other wing, it's time to soften up the queenside.

22...a6 23 ♗e2 ♗e6 24 ♗h5 ♕e7 25 f5 ♗d7 26 ♗xf7 ♕xf7 27 g4!

With ideas of a timely g4-g5.

27...c5!

Hoping to activate the bishop.

28 ♖ad1 ♕f8 29 ♖g3

A key position.

29...♖g5!?

As Apicella points out, Black can go wrong with 29...♗c6?! 30 ♖h3 ♔g7 31 g5, but the most precise is perhaps 29...♖a7! 30 ♘f3 ♗c6 31 h4 ♖d7 32 g5 d5 with counterplay.

30 ♘g6+

Winning the exchange but Black has enough resources to hold.

30...hxg6 31 h4 gxf5 32 hxg5 f4 33 ♖h3+ ♔g7 34 gxf6+ ♕xf6 35 ♕d3 ♗c6! 36 ♕xd6 ♗xe4+ 37 ♔g1 ♕xd6 38 ♖xd6 ♖e8

38...♗xc2? is bad after 39 axb5 axb5 40 ♖c3.

39 c3 bxa4 40 ♖xa6

40...♗g6?!

More precise was 40...♖d8 41 ♖xa4 ♖d1+ 42 ♔f2 ♗d3 and the plan of pushing the e-pawn equalises, for example 43 ♖a5 e4 44 ♖xc5 e3+ 45 ♔f3 e2 46 ♖c7+ and White forces a perpetual as it's too risky for Black to come closer to the centre.

41 g5!

Black now has to defend, but he is equal to the task.

41...e4 42 ♖a7+ ♗f7 43 ♖h4 e3 44 ♔f1 ♔g6 45 ♖xf4 ♗b3 46 ♖g4 ♔f5! 47 ♖g1 ♗c4+ 48 ♔e1 ♖b8! 49 ♖xa4 ♖xb2 50 ♖xc4 ♖b1+ 51 ♔e2 ♖xg1 52 ♔xe3 ♖e1+ 53 ♔d3 ♖d1+ 54 ♔c2 ♖d5 55 ♖a4 ♔xg5 56 ♔b3 ♔f6 57 ♔c4 ♔e6 58 ♖a5 ♖d1 59 ♔xc5 ♔d7 60 c4 ♖h1 61 ♔b6 ♖c1 62 ♖c5 ♖b1+ 63 ♖b5 ♖c1 64 c5 ♔c8 65 ♖b2 ♔b8 66 ♔c6+ ♔c8 67 ♖h2 ♔b8 68 ♖h8+ ♔a7 69 ♖h7+ ♔b8 70 ♖b7+ ♔c8 71 ♖e7 ♔b8 72 ♖e8+ ♔a7 73 ♖d8 ♖c2 74 ♔d6 ♔b7 75 ♖d7+ ♔c8 76 ♖g7 ♖c1 77 ♔c6 ½-½

Game 10
J.Polgar-Ivanchuk
Dortmund 1997

---

1 e4 e5 2 ♘f3 ♘c6 3 ♗b5 f5 4 d4 fxe4 5 ♗xc6

Another modern approach to calm things down. Theoreticians used to get excited about a messy piece sacrifice, which comes about after the sequence 5 ♘xe5!? ♘xe5 6 dxe5 c6. Now if White moves his bishop Black has ...♕a5+ and ...♕xe5 with a solid extra pawn. White therefore offers a piece to get ahead in development with 7 ♘c3!?

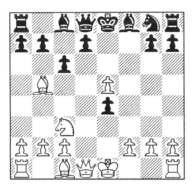

and now:

a) 7...♕e7 8 ♗f4 (again holding onto the e-pawn is the only way to create problems) 8...cxb5 9 0-0 ♕c5 10 ♘xe4 ♕c6 11 ♖e1 b6 12 ♕h5+ ♔d8 13 ♖ad1 g6 14 ♕h3 h6 15 e6 ♖h7. This analysis is given by Anjuhin, who sensibly concludes with 'unclear'.

b) Another reasonable way to refuse is 7...d5!?, when 8 exd6 ♘f6 9 ♗c4 ♗xd6 10 ♗g5 ♗f5 11 ♕e2 ♕e7 12 0-0-0 0-0-0 13 f3 b5 led to equal chances in Pettersson-Ballbe, correspondence 1974.

c) 7...cxb5 8 ♘xe4 d5 (to give some breathing space) 9 exd6 ♘f6 with a further split:

c1) 10 ♕d4 ♗e7! 11 ♗g5 (11 ♗f4 0-0 12 ♗e5 ♗f5 13 dxe7 ♕xe7 14 ♘d6 ♘g4 is again given as unclear by Hachian, although after 15 f4 I prefer White!) 11...h6 12 ♗h4 ♗f5 13 0-0-0, J.Diaz-Am.Rodriguez, Cuban Championship 1982, when Rodriguez suggests 13...g5 14 ♖he1 ♔f7 15 ♘xg5+ hxg5 16 ♖xe7+ ♔g6 17 ♗g3 as unclear.

c2) 10 ♗g5 ♕a5+ 11 ♘c3 b4 12 ♗xf6 gxf6 13 ♘d5 b3+! (13...♗e6 14 ♕h5+ ♔d8 15 0-0-0 gave White a powerful attack in Glek-Jandemirov, USSR 1983) 14 c3 ♗e6 15 ♘c7+ ♔d7 16 0-0 ♗xd6, with an unclear

game, Piskov-Jandemirov, USSR 1984.

It's true that there is still much unresolved here, but 5 ♘xe5 has lost its topicality.

5...dxc6

Best. The continuation 5...exf3?! 6 ♗xf3 c6 7 dxe5 ♕a5+ 8 ♘c3 ♕xe5+ 9 ♗e3 yields White a useful lead in development. Otherwise 5...bxc6 6 ♘xe5 ♘f6 7 0-0 (7 ♗g5 also looks promising) transposes to game 11, note to Black's 4th move, which is good for White.

6 ♘xe5

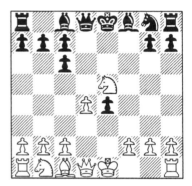

6...♗f5!?

A new idea when played immediately. Black has previously played 6...♘f6 7 ♗g5 and only now 7...♗f5, when White can try either 8 ♘c3 ♗b4 9 0-0, or 8 c3 ♗d6 9 ♕b3, in either case Black has an uphill struggle to equalise.

The aggressive queen sortie 6...♕h4, is tempting but Black gets into hot water after 7 ♕e2! ♘f6 8 h3 ♗e7 9 g3 ♕h5 10 g4 ♕h4 11 ♗f4 0-0 12 ♘d2 ♗e6 13 ♘ef3! (Tiemann).

7 0-0 ♗d6

With this move-order Black can put off the decision whether or not to go to h4 with his queen until later, depending on circumstances.

8 ♕h5+!?

Provoking Black's next move to create potential targets on the dark-squares.

8...g6 9 ♕e2 ♕h4!

A good choice. This way White's bishop is

denied f4, g5 and h6, while White cannot harass the queen in the same way as after 6...♕h4.

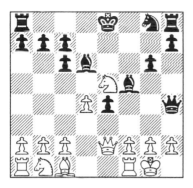

10 ♘c3 ♘f6 11 f3 ♗xe5!

11...0-0? fails to 12 fxe4 ♘xe4 13 ♖f4.

12 dxe5 exf3 13 ♖xf3 ♕d4+ 14 ♔h1 ♘e4!

Much better than 14...♘g4?! 15 h3 h5 16 ♗g5! (Matulovic) when Black has no useful moves.

15 ♘xe4 ♕xe4 16 ♖f2 ♕xe2 17 ♖xe2

White has the better pawn structure but with opposite bishops it's not that dangerous for Black.

17...♗g4 18 ♖e1 ♖f8 19 ♔g1 ♗e6 20 ♗g5 a5 21 a3 ♖f5 22 ♗f6 ♖f4 23 ♖ad1 b5 24 c3 b4 25 axb4 axb4 26 cxb4 ♖xb4 27 ♖d2 ♖a2 28 ♖d8+ ♔f7 29 ♖e2 ♖bxb2 30 ♖xb2 ♖xb2 31 ♖h8 h5 32 ♖h7+ ♔f8 33 ♖xc7 ♖c2 34 ♖e7 ♗d5 35

e6 ♖e2 36 ♖f7+ ♔e8 37 ♖e7+ ♔f8 ½-½

Ivanchuk's clever move order offers Black good chances of equalising.

Game 11
Am.Rodriguez-Sirvent
Terrassa 1995

1 e4 e5 2 ♘f3 ♘c6 3 ♗b5 f5 4 ♗xc6

This capture is often associated with taking the sting out of Black's position and just playing for the better structure. A simple and effective plan that is hard to counter.

4...dxc6

4...bxc6?! is probably not good; 5 d4! fxe4 6 ♘xe5 ♘f6 7 0-0 c5 (or 7...♗e7 8 ♘c3 0-0 9 ♖e1 with a big advantage for White – Petronic) 8 ♘c3 cxd4 9 ♘xe4! ♗b7 (9...♘xe4 10 ♕f3) 10 ♘g5 ♗d5 11 ♕xd4 and Black was struggling in S.Jovanovic-Bokan, Yugoslav Championship 1996.

5 ♘c3 ♘f6 6 ♕e2

6...fxe4

6...♗d6 has been fairly popular but doesn't equalise. After 7 d4 ♗b4 (or 7...exd4 8 e5 dxc3 9 exf6+ ♔f7 10 ♕c4+ ♔g6 11 0-0, Am.Rodriguez, with sharp play where Black's king is exposed) 8 0-0 ♗xc3 (8...exd4 9 e5!, Am.Rodriguez-Cruz Lopez, Olot 1995, 9...♘d5 10 ♗g5 ♗e7 11 ♘xd5 cxd5 12 ♗xe7 ♕xe7 13 ♘xd4 with a positional edge – Am.Rodriguez) 9 bxc3 fxe4 10 ♘xe5 0-0 11 ♗a3, Milos-O.Rodriguez, Spain 1992,

White has an edge as he has the more active pieces. Play could continue 11...♖e8 12 f3 exf3 13 ♕xf3 ♗e6 14 ♕d3 and White is better.

7 ♘xe4 ♗g4

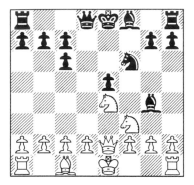

8 d3

8 h3 may be even stronger, for example 8...♗h5 (on 8...♗xf3 9 ♕xf3 ♘xe4 10 ♕xe4 ♕d5 11 d3 Black will sooner or later exchange into an inferior ending, for instance the game Tolnai-Morvay, Budapest 1991 continued 11...♗c5 12 f3 0-0 13 ♔e2 ♗b6 14 ♗e3 ♕xe4 15 dxe4 ♗xe3 16 ♔xe3 ♖ad8 17 ♖ad1 ♖d6 18 ♖d3 ♖fd8 19 ♖hd1 when White's 4 vs. 3 kingside majority gave him a clear advantage) 9 d3 ♕d5 10 g4! (a clearer way to an advantage than 10 0-0 as in Gusev-I.Zaitsev, Dubna 1979, when 10...♗xf3 11 ♕xf3 0-0-0 is then recommended by Zaitsev as equal; White retains the better structure and the better bishop so I believe that he retains a slight pull) 10...♗f7 11 c4 ♗b4+ 12 ♗d2 ♗xd2+ 13 ♘exd2 ♕e6 14 ♘xe5 0-0-0 15 f4 h5 16 ♘df3 ♗e8 17 ♘g5 and White soon won, Milos-Van Riemsdijk, Brasilia 1993.

8...♗b4+

Trying to provoke c3 in order to obtain a target on d3. The inferior 8...♗e7 9 h3 ♗xf3 10 ♘xf6+ ♗xf6 11 ♕xf3 0-0 12 0-0 ♗g5 13 ♗xg5 ♕xg5 14 ♕g4 ♕h6 15 ♖ae1 offered White all the chances in Hecht-Loffler, Bundesliga 1986.

9 c3

9 ♗d2 is worth consideration.

9...♗e7 10 h3 ♗xf3 11 ♕xf3 0-0!

An improvement on Velimirovic-Ristic, Novi Sad 1995, where White obtained good knight vs. bad bishop after 11...♕d5 12 ♗g5 0-0-0 13 ♗xf6 gxf6 14 ♔e2 ♔b8 15 ♖hd1.

12 ♔e2 ♘xe4 13 ♕xe4 ♗g5!

The exchange of the remaining minor pieces limits White's advantage to a minimum.

14 ♗e3 ♗xe3 15 ♕xe3 ♕d5 16 f3 c5 17 ♖hd1 ♖ad8

White can continue to improve his position whereas Black has to wait and see. Black's doubled c-pawns and isolani on e5 enable White to keep nibbling away to see if something gives.

18 ♖d2 ♖f6 19 ♖ad1 b6

19...♕xa2!? 20 ♕xc5 ♖c6 was an alternative.

20 b3 ♖g6 21 ♔f2 ♖gd6 22 ♖e1 ♕e6 23 ♕g5 h6 24 ♕h4 ♕f5

After 24...♖xd3? White would play the x-ray 25 ♕xd8+!.

25 ♖e4 g5 26 ♕h5 ♔g7

26...♖xd3 27 ♖xd3 ♖xd3 28 ♕e8+ ♕f8 29 ♕xe5 leaves Black's king too exposed.

27 ♖de2 ♖e6 28 ♖2e3 ♖de8 29 h4 ♖g6 30 ♖e1 ♕d7

Rodriguez suggests 30...♖ee6 as more resistant.

31 d4 cxd4 32 cxd4 ♖f8 33 dxe5 ♖f4 34 e6 ♕e7 35 ♖xf4 gxf4 36 ♕e5+ ♖f6 37 ♖e4 ♔h7 38 h5 a5 39 ♔f1 ♔g7 40 ♖xf4

♕xe6 41 ♕xc7+ 1-0

White exchanges off all the pieces.

Summary

The Schliemann can be fun but probably doesn't equalise against a well-booked up opponent. In games 10 and 11 White plays an early ♗xc6 keeping Black calm and generally keeps a small positional edge. If Black varies early from the main line then games 4, 5, 7 and 8 illustrate the dangers.

The main line is sounder (game 1) but with correct play White maintains his opening edge deep into the game.

1 e4 e5 2 ♘f3 ♘c6 3 ♗b5 f5 4 ♘c3 *(D)*

> 4 d3 – *Game 9*
> 4 d4 – *Game 10*
> 4 ♗xc6 – *Game 11*

4...fxe4

> 4...♘d4 5 ♗a4 ♘f6 6 ♘xe5 ♗c5 7 ♘d3 – *Game 8*

5 ♘xe4 d5

> 5...♘f6 – *Game 7*

6 ♘xe5

> 6 ♘g3 – *Game 6*

6...dxe4 7 ♘xc6 *(D)* **♕g5**

> 7...♕d5 8 c4 ♕d6 9 ♕h5+ – *Game 5*

8 ♕e2 ♘f6 9 f4 ♕xf4 *(D)*

> 9...♕h4+ – *Game 4*

10 ♘e5+

> 10 ♘xa7+ – *Game 3*
> 10 d4 – *Game 2*

10...c6 11 d4 ♕h4+ 12 g3 ♕h3 13 ♗c4 ♗e6 – *Game 1*

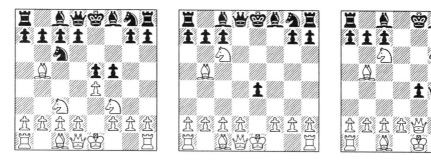

     4 ♘c3   *7 ♘xc6*   *9...♕xf4*

CHAPTER TWO

The Berlin Defence

1 e4 e5 2 ♘f3 ♘c6 3 ♗b5 ♘f6

At the time of writing, the most fashionable of all the variations covered in this book. This is almost certainly set to continue as some ideas were even tested in the recent Kasparov-Kramnik match. The plan of capturing on e4 and then retreating the knight can be compared to Petroff's Defence in that Black is primarily concerned with solidity, rather than counterplay, in the early stages.

The main line detailed in games 12-15, leads to an early exchange of queens followed by some intricate manoeuvring. Rapid development is secondary to finding quality squares for the pieces.

The chapter represents a useful exercise in the study of the strengths and weaknesses of doubled pawns, as ♗xc6 is a common theme.

Another plan, combining ...♘f6 with ...♗c5, a hybrid variation between the Berlin and Classical, is covered in Chapter Three.

Game 12
Adams-Z.Almasi
Las Vegas 1999

---

1 e4 e5 2 ♘f3 ♘c6 3 ♗b5 ♘f6 4 0-0

The main line. For fourth move alternatives see Game 21.

4...♘xe4 5 d4

5...♘d6

The main alternative 5...♗e7 is discussed in games 18-20.

6 ♗xc6 dxc6 7 dxe5 ♘f5

For the provocative 7...♘e4!? see Game 16.

8 ♕xd8+ ♔xd8 9 ♘c3

The early exchange of queens is typical of the Berlin. Black has the bishop pair to compensate the inferior pawn structure and, because of a misplaced king, is behind in development.

If we compare with the Spanish Exchange variation (1 e4 e5 2 ♘f3 ♘c6 3 ♗b5 a6 4 ♗xc6 dxc6) we note another difference; White's e-pawn is already on e5 rather than e4. This factor gives chances for Black to use the d5- and f5-squares for his pieces (White's options c2-c4 and g2-g4 are not without risk) and gives him greater chances of indefinitely blockading the kingside majority.

It will become clear that this queenless middlegame is far from drawish, offering rich ideas for both sides.

9...♔e8

For 9...♗d7 see Game 14.

Another plan is to put the bishop on e6 and decide on the king's destination later:

a) 9...♗e6 10 ♘g5 ♔e7 (aiming for a well-centralised king before concentrating on routine development) 11 ♖d1 h6 12 ♘xe6 ♔xe6 and if White goes to dislodge the king with 13 g4 ♘h4 14 f4 then 14...h5, Daniliuk-Aleksandrov, Krasnodar 1995, gives adequate counterplay.

b) 9...h6 10 h3 ♗e6 11 g4 (the less direct continuation 11 b3 b6 12 ♗b2 ♔c8 13 ♖ad1 ♔b7 14 ♘e2 ♗c5 15 ♘d2 ♖ad8 16 ♘e4 ♗e7, Ehlvest-Korchnoi, Reykjavik 1988, is again reminiscent of game 14) 11...♘e7 12 ♘d4 ♗d7 13 ♗f4 c5 14 ♘de2 ♔c8 15 ♖ad1 b6 (the loosening 15...g5?! 16 ♗g3 ♘g6 17 f4, Geller-Romanishin, USSR Championship 1977, turned out badly for Black who should avoid such line-opening whilst behind in development) 16 ♗g3 h5 17 f3 ♗c6 is given by Velickovic as a shade better for White, but it often comes down to a question of taste if there is nothing concrete.

In Kasparov-Kramnik, London (9th matchgame) 2000, after 9...h6, Kasparov first played 10 ♖d1+ ♔e8 and only now 11 h3 whereupon 11...a5 12 ♗f4 ♗e6 13 g4 ♘e7 14 ♘d4 ♘d5 15 ♘ce2 ♗c5 16 ♘xe6 fxe6, leads to a typical position where White has a theoretical edge, but Black is very solid.

Kasparov was unable to make significant progress in the game continuation; 17 c4 ♘b6 18 b3 a4 19 ♗d2 ♔f7 20 ♗c3 ♖hd8 21 ♖xd8 ♖xd8 22 ♔g2 ♖d3 23 ♖c1 g5 (here holding up the kingside is successful due to Black's activity reducing the effectiveness of any white play based on f4 or h4) 24 ♖c2 axb3 25 axb3 ♘d7 26 ♖a2 ♗e7 27 ♖a7 ♘c5 28 f3 ♘xb3 29 ♖xb7 ♘c1 30 ♘xc1 ♖xc3 and the players agreed a draw.

The bishop on d7 is less exposed to immediate attack, but the e6-square is more natural, especially if an eventual ♘xe6 proves to be nothing special for White.

10 h3 ♘e7

The plan of switching the knight to g6 and adopting a wait-and-see attitude has become fashionable of late.

Instead 10...h5 (weakening the g5-square) 11 ♖d1 ♗e6 12 ♘g5 ♗e7 13 ♘xe6 fxe6 14 ♘e4 is easier to play for White (Prasad-Prakash, Madras 1994) as the black pawn structure will require a careful defence.

11 ♘e4 ♘g6 12 ♖e1 c5

Typical is 12...h6 preventing a white piece from coming to the g5-square. After the sequence 13 ♘d4 c5 14 ♘b5 ♚d7 15 f4 ♚c6 16 a4 ♗e7 17 g4 (so far, so good, but...read on!) 17...h5 18 ♘f2 hxg4 19 hxg4 f5 20 exf6 ♗xf6, Kotronious-Van den Doel, Korinthos 2000, Black had counter-chances against the White pawns. We will see other examples of the king coming to the excellent c6-square.

More common after 12...h6 is 13 ♗d2 when the passive reply 13...♗d7 in Luther-Van den Doel, Venlo 2000 allowed 14 b4! ♖d8 15 a4 ♗e6 16 a5 ♗d5 17 ♘d4 when White had a significant space advantage.

If b2-b4 is a positional threat Black does best to play 13...c5, even if it doesn't hit anything. Now we look at two possibilities:

a) 14 a3!? is an interesting idea; White cedes space on the queenside, but with this structure he may be able to switch back there later. His immediate goal, however, is to advance on the other wing. Ulibin-Grabarczyk, Bydgoszcz 2000 continued 14...a5 15 ♖ad1 ♗e6 16 g4 ♗d5 17 ♚g2 a4 18 ♚g3 ♖d8 19 h4 and White was pressing.

b) 14 a4 a5 (14...♗e6?! 15 a5, Fressinet-Jonkman, Mondariz Zonal 2000, gave White strong pressure, as in the main game) 15 h4 b6 16 h5 ♘e7 17 ♘d6+ (here this combination is less effective than in Adams-Almasi; Black retains the two bishops and his queenside is rock-solid) 17...cxd6 18 exd6 ♗e6 19 dxe7 ♗xe7 with equal chance in Kulaots-Yemelin, Tallinn 2000.

13 a4!?

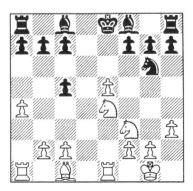

White gains space and can, if desired, develop his queen's rook via a3.

Instead 13 c4 was unsuccessful in Peng Xiaomin-Z.Almasi, Las Vegas 1999, as after 13...♗e6 14 b3 h6 15 ♗e3 b6 16 ♖ad1 ♗c7 17 ♘c3 ♗d8 (the start of a noteworthy manoeuvre) 18 ♗c1 c6 19 ♘e4 ♗c7 20 ♗b2 ♚e7 Black had a good game.

13...h6?!

Largely as a result of the lessons learnt from this game, competing for space on the wing with 13...a5 is now standard. Then Wedberg points out that 14 e6?! ♗xe6 15 ♘eg5 is dubious on account of 13...♗a6!. Instead White should play 14 ♘c3 h6 15 ♘b5 ♚d7, leading us to a position in which piece pressure alone is insufficient to dent Black's defences, for example:

a) 16 ♖a3 ♗e7 17 ♖c3 b6 18 ♘d2 ♚c6 19 ♘e4 ♚b7 20 f4 h5 21 ♖f3 h4 occurred in Boudre-Markowski, Cannes 2000, where White's initiative had just run out of steam.

b) White can try 16 e6+!?, a crazy idea that might just be good, for instance 16...fxe6 17 ♖xe6 ♚xe6 18 ♘xc7+ ♚d7 19 ♘xa8 ♚c6, Dominguez Perez-Miles, Varadero 2000, which at first sight looks odd with the knight stuck in the corner, but in the game White continued with the sharp 20 ♗f4!? ♘xf4 21 ♘e5+ and after 21...♚d5 22 ♖e1 ♗f5 23 ♘c7+ ♚d6 24 ♘b5+ ♚e6 25 ♘g6+ ♚f6 26 ♘xh8 g5 27 ♖e8 ♚g7 28 c3 ♗d7 29 ♖b8 ♗c6 30 f3 ♘e6 a draw was agreed, with a knight stuck in the other corner! This time the knight is lost, but White can obtain a second pawn with 31 ♖a8 so perhaps he could have played on.

14 a5!

Gaining space and preparing to pressurise the c5-pawn.

14...♗f5 15 h4!?

Aiming to dislodge the knight on g6.

15...♗e7

15...h5 gives away the g5-square.

16 ♘d6+!

A tactical shot leading to a good ending

where White maintains the initiative.

16...cxd6 17 exd6 &e6

Perhaps 17...&xc2! 18 dxe7 &xe7 19 &e3 &c6 20 &xc5+ &d7 21 &ac1 &b3 22 &c3 &e6 may restrict White to an edge.

18 dxe7 &xe7

Black's king, denied the right to castle, is his main problem. Apart from being a target for White's active pieces his rooks are slow to come to the centre.

19 &e5 &f5 20 &a4 &e7 21 &f4 &ac8 22 b4! b6 23 bxc5 bxc5 24 &a3 g5 25 &fe4 &xh4

26 &xf7!

The breakthrough!

26...&xf7 27 &xe6 &he8

This holds off the attack, but loses a number of pawns. Instead 27...&c7 is inadequate as 28 &b2 and &f6+ will be fatal.

28 &xe8 &xe8 29 &xe8 &xe8 30 a6! &d7 31 &xc5 &c6 32 &xa7 &b5 33 &c5! &xa6 34 &f8 g4 35 &xh6 &f5 36 &g5 &b5 37 &f6 &c4 38 &f1 &d5 39 &e2 &c4 40 f3 gxf3+ 41 &xf3 &d5 42 g4 &d6 43 &f4 &e6 44 &d4 1-0

Game 13
Acs-Pinter
Lillafured 1999

One of White's main weapons is the advance g2-g4 kicking the knight, gaining space and preparing a pawn roller with f2-f4-f5 and eventually e6 or f6.

1 e4 e5 2 &f3 &c6 3 &b5 &f6 4 0-0 &xe4 5 d4 &d6 6 &xc6 dxc6 7 dxe5 &f5 8 &xd8+ &xd8 9 &c3 &e8

9...h5 stops the kingside expansion at the cost of a weakening to the g5-square. As a result White kept a nagging edge in Ljubojevic-Salov, Linares 1990 after 10 &g5+ &e7 11 &ad1+ &e8 12 &e2 &h6 13 h3 &f5 14 &d2 &d8 15 &fd1 &xg5 16 &xg5 &e7 17 &d4 &c8 18 c4 f6 19 exf6+ &xf6 20 h4.

10 h3

Preparing g2-g4.

10...a5

The g2-g4 expansion plan has been used in analogous positions; 10...h6 11 &f4 &e6 12 g4 &e7 13 &g3 &d5 14 &e4 in Bologan-Keitlinghaus, Ostrava 1993, and 10...&e6 11 g4 &e7 12 &g5 &c4 13 &e1 &d5 14 &d1 h6 15 &e4 &b4 16 &e3 in de Firmian-Miles, Biel 1990. Essentially White has space and the potential for a pawn roller whereas Black aims to frustrate and counter when possible.

Miles has also experimented with 10...&b4?! 11 &e4 &e6 12 c3 &f8 13 g4 (yet again!) 13...&e7 14 &g3 &g6 15 &e1 &d5 16 &d4 &h4 17 &g5 &f3+ 18 &xf3 &xf3 19 c4 c5 20 &h5 and now Black had great difficulty in completing his development, Rowson-Miles, Southend 2000.

11 g4

In the position after 11 a4 &e6 12 &d1 h6

13 g4 ♘e7 14 ♘d4 g5!? 15 ♘e4 ♗g7, Ernst-Rausis, Stockholm 1997, Black has counterplay against the e-pawn, White chances against the loosened black kingside.

In Sebag-Rainfray, Naujac 2000, Black failed to stop White's central expansion; 11 ♖e1 a4 12 ♘e4!? (or simply 12 a3) 12...a3 13 b3 ♘e7 (a bit slow) 14 ♗d2 ♘g6 15 ♘d4 ♗d7 (15...c5! 16 ♘b5 ♔d7) 16 f4 ♘h4 and 17 e6! yielded White a useful initiative.

11...♘e7 12 ♔g2

White can also play for an immediate pawn-rush. Black has to stay on his toes and react actively, for instance 12 ♘h2!? h5! 13 f4 hxg4 14 hxg4 ♘d5 15 ♘e4 ♘b4 16 ♖f2 ♗e6 17 a3 ♗d5 18 axb4 ♗xe4 19 ♖e2 (not 19 ♖xa5? in view of 19...♖xa5 20 bxa5 ♗c5) 19...♗d5 20 bxa5 ♖h3 as in Wahls-Z.Almasi, Germany 1997. Black has dynamic counterplay due to White's exposed king.

12...h5 13 ♔g3 ♘g6

14 ♘e4

The manoeuvre 14 ♘e2 a4 15 ♘f4 (exchanging the knight on g6) was unclear after 15...♘xf4 16 ♗xf4 ♗e7 17 ♖fe1 c5 18 ♗g5 ♗e6, Van Riemsdijk-Marciano, F.lista 1998. Essentially exchanging a pair of knights helps Black (who has a space disadvantage) to complete his development, so this is not a particularly dangerous plan.

Instead, 14 ♗g5?! is not recommended as Black reacts with the blow 14...f6! as in the game Yurtaev-G.Giorgadze, Elista 1998.

White now abandoned a pawn for insufficient compensation with 15 ♗e3 (because he didn't fancy facing Black's initiative after 15 exf6 ♗d6+ 16 ♔g2 hxg4 17 hxg4 ♔f7!) 15...fxe5 16 ♖fe1 ♗d6.

14...♗e7

When playing the text move, Black has to keep aware of the ♘d6+ trick on the e-file, hence the next couple of moves. To avoid this tactical shot, Wedberg prefers ...♗e6 (now or after 15 ♖e1) continuing the development process. Equally possible is the space gaining 14...a4.

15 ♖e1 ♔f8

More natural is 15...♗e6, because if 16 ♘eg5?! (White should think about completing his development with say a4, ♗d2 and ♖ad1) then 16...♗d5 17 ♘d4 (the careless 17 e6? loses to 17...♗d6+) 17...hxg4 18 hxg4 ♔d7!? (Wedberg) and Black aims to double on the h-file if given half a chance.

16 ♗g5 ♗e6 17 ♖ad1 ♗d5 18 ♗xe7+ ♔xe7 19 ♘d4

19...♖ae8?!

Wedberg criticises this as passive, preferring 19...h4+! 20 ♔h2 ♖hd8, which stops the immediate advance of the f-pawn.

20 f4 ♔f8 21 ♘f5 ♗e6 22 ♘e3 ♗c8?!

Another passive move, after which Black is squeezed deep into the ending. The best chance could be the rather daring 22...♗xa2!?, as after 23 b3 a4 24 bxa4 Black can try the tricky 24...♗d5!?, whereupon 25

♘xd5 cxd5 26 ♖xd5 hxg4 27 hxg4 is countered by 27...♖h3+.

23 ♖d4 b6 24 ♖ed1 ♖h6 25 ♖d8 ♖h8 26 c4 hxg4 27 hxg4 ♔e7 28 ♖8d4 ♔f8 29 ♖d8 ♔e7 30 ♖xe8+ ♖xe8 31 ♘f5+ ♔f8 32 ♘h4 ♘xh4 33 ♔xh4 a4 34 ♘c3 ♗e6 35 b3 axb3 36 axb3 ♗c8 37 ♔g5 f6+

Perhaps 37...♔e7 38 f5 ♖h8 hoping for breathing space was a better try.

38 exf6 gxf6+ 39 ♔xf6 ♗xg4 40 ♖d3 b5

Exchanging as many pawns as possible.

41 cxb5 cxb5 42 ♘xb5 c6 43 ♘c7 ♖c8 44 ♖d6 c5 45 ♘d5 ♖b8 46 ♖b6 ♖d8 47 ♘e7 ♔e8 48 ♘g6 ♖d4 49 ♔g5 ♗h3 50 ♘e5 ♖d5 51 ♔f6 ♔d8 52 ♖c6 ♖d4 53 f5 ♖b4

Now Black should hold.

54 ♖d6+ ♔e8 55 ♖c6 1-0

After 55...♔d8 (or even 55...♗xf5 56 ♔xf5 ♖xb3 57 ♔e6 ♔f8 58 ♔f6 ♔g8) 56

♔e6 ♗xf5+ 57 ♔xf5 ♖xb3 58 ♔e6 ♖b8 the ending is drawn, but the result given in all sources is '1-0'. If this is not a mistake, then this either indicates a loss on time, or an incomplete score.

Game 14
Kasparov-Kramnik
London (3rd matchgame) 2000

---

1 e4 e5 2 ♘f3 ♘c6 3 ♗b5 ♘f6 4 0-0 ♘xe4 5 d4 ♘d6 6 ♗xc6 dxc6 7 dxe5 ♘f5 8 ♕xd8+ ♔xd8 9 ♘c3 ♗d7

This modest bishop development, allied with the aim of walking the king to the queenside, has recently become popular.

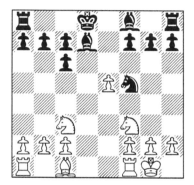

10 b3

10 h3 h6 11 ♗f4 didn't lead to a White win when Shirov was faced with this opening a couple of months before the K-K match. Two rounds later, in the same tournament, Shirov had a second crack at the white side of this variation. He decided that the bishop was better placed on b2 to facilitate the thematic advance f2-f4. Kasparov decides to follow Shirov's plan.

Shirov-Z.Almasi, Polanica Zdroj 2000 continued 11...b6 12 a4 a5 13 ♖ad1 ♔c8 14 b3 ♗b4 15 ♘e4 ♗e6 16 c4 c5 17 g4 ♘e7 18 ♘e1 ♗d7 19 ♘g3 g5!? and Black was okay.

Naturally one could try 10 ♗f4 immediately, as in Salai-Rogers, Senec 1998, but after 10...h6 11 ♖ad1 ♔c8 12 ♘e2 g5! 13 ♗d2

♗g7 14 ♗c3 ♖e8 Black had good pressure on the e-pawn. In fact after the further 15 g4 ♘h4 16 ♘xh4 gxh4 17 e6 ♖xe6 18 ♗xg7 ♖xe2 the ending offered Black the better chances.

Another sequence is 10 ♘e4 h6 11 ♗d2 aiming to put the bishop on c3, which led to a tense game in Dutreeuw-Jonkman, Mondariz Zonal 2000. After 11...c5!? 12 ♖ad1 ♚c8 13 ♖fe1 b6 14 ♗c3 ♘e7 15 ♘h4 ♗e6 16 f4 ♚b7 17 h3 ♚c6 18 a3 (18 g4 can be answered by 18...h5) 18...b5 19 ♘f3 ♘d5 Black eventually won.

If White wants to play f2-f4 and prefers not to have his queen's bishop exposed to attack, then b2 is the appropriate square.

Otherwise 10 ♖d1 (threatening e6 followed by ♘e5) 10...♚c8 11 ♘g5 ♗e8 12 e6 is aggressive, but after 12...fxe6 13 ♘xe6 ♗d6 only about equal.

10...h6 11 ♗b2 ♚c8 12 ♖ad1

Kasparov had to vary from game 1 of the London match, where he obtained no real opening advantage. That game continued 12 h3 b6 13 ♖ad1 ♘e7 (this knight often switches back and forth between f5 and g6 in this line, depending on circumstances) 14 ♘e2 ♘g6 15 ♘e1 h5 16 ♘d3 c5 17 c4 a5 18 a4 h4 (after this h-pawn advance, limiting the potential for a kingside pawn expansion, it's hard to see how White will progress) 19 ♘c3 ♗e6 20 ♘d5 ♚b7 21 ♘e3 ♖h5! 22 ♗c3 ♖e8 23 ♖d2 ♚c8 24 f4

24...♘e7! (coming back to f5 to construct an impenetrable blockade) 25 ♘f2 ♘f5 and a draw was agreed, Kasparov-Kramnik, London (1st match game) 2000.

12...b6

Kramnik varies from Shirov-Krasenkov, Polanica Zdroj 2000, which continued 12...a5 13 h3 b6 14 a4 ♗b4 15 ♘e2 ♖e8 16 ♘f4 g6 17 g4 (here White's majority is mobile) 17...♗g7 18 ♖d3 ♘e6 19 ♘xe6 ♗xe6 20 ♘d4 ♗d7 21 ♘e2 ♗d6 22 f4 and this time Shirov had maintained an opening initiative and went on to win.

13 ♘e2 c5

As the bishop on f8 cannot do much at present Kramnik first of all improves his light square control.

14 ♘f4 ♗c6 15 ♘d5 ♚b7 16 c4

Kasparov is using his space advantage to restrict the bishop on f8. So Kramnik uses an unconventional plan to activate his king's rook.

16...♘e7 17 ♖fe1

17...♖g8!?

Seeking to activate his kingside in an original manner.

18 ♘f4 g5

Although Black ultimately gets away with this thrust for freedom, one can't help feeling that White is better. This view may have been shared by Kramnik, who varied as early as move nine in their next Berlin encounter.

19 ♘h5 ♖g6 20 ♘f6 ♗g7 21 ♖d3

The outpost on f6 is annoying, so Kramnik simplifies to a position where he hopes his knight will be a match for his opponent's bishop.

21...♗xf3 22 ♖xf3 ♗xf6 23 exf6 ♘c6 24 ♖d3 ♖f8 25 ♖e4 ♔c8 26 f4 gxf4 27 ♖xf4 ♖e8 28 ♗c3 ♖e2 29 ♖f2 ♖e4

29...♖xf2 30 ♔xf2 favours White because his king quickly enters the fray, for instance after the further 30...♘d4 31 ♗xd4 cxd4 32 ♖xd4 ♖xf6+ 33 ♔g3, Black's isolated pawns and cut-off king will give him difficulties. Instead Kramnik heads for complications but these too seem to work out favourably for White.

30 ♖h3 a5 31 ♖h5 a4 32 bxa4!? ♖xc4 33 ♗d2 ♖xa4 34 ♖xh6

34...♖g8?!

34...♖xh6 35 ♗xh6 ♔d7! is a more solid alternative.

35 ♖h7! ♖xa2 36 ♖xf7 ♘e5 37 ♖g7

37 ♖e7 fails to 37...♖a1+ 38 ♖f1 ♘f3+ 39 ♔f2 ♖xf1+ 40 ♔xf1 ♘xd2+ etc.

37...♖f8 38 h3

Kasparov later claimed that 38 h4 was better.

38...c4 39 ♖e7 ♘d3 40 f7 ♘xf2 41 ♖e8+ ♔d7 42 ♖xf8 ♔e7 43 ♖c8 ♔xf7 44 ♖xc7+ ♔e6 45 ♗e3 ♘d1 46 ♗xb6 c3

The extra pawn is only a nominal advantage as the advanced c-pawn, when exchanged for either kingside pawn, will ensure the draw.

47 h4 ♖a6 48 ♗d4 ♖a4 49 ♗xc3 ♘xc3 50 ♖xc3 ♖xh4 51 ♔f3 ♖h5 52 ♔f2 ♖g5 53 ♖f8 ♔e5

½-½

Game 15
Svidler-Timman
Elista Olympiad 1998

1 e4 e5 2 ♘f3 ♘c6 3 ♗b5 ♘f6 4 0-0 ♘xe4 5 d4 ♘d6 6 ♗xc6 dxc6 7 dxe5 ♘f5 8 ♕xd8+ ♔xd8 9 ♖d1+

see following diagram

The advantage of this move is that it commits the Black king to e8 for the moment. The rook may however prove to better placed on e1 or f1 and Black, by playing an early ...♖d8, can often exchange a pair of rooks.

9...♔e8 10 ♘c3 ♘e7

A fashionable manoeuvre that can be seen in analogous positions in games 12, 13 and 14.

A popular alternative is 10...a5, a fairly non-committal move that gains space on the queenside. White can now play:

a) 11 h3 a4 12 a3 ♗d7 13 ♗f4 ♘e7 14 ♘g5 ♗f5 15 e6!? (Black's slow manoeuvring demands a vigorous reaction) 15...fxe6 16 ♖e1 ♘d5 17 ♘xd5 cxd5 18 g4 (if 18 ♘xe6 ♗xe6 19 ♖xe6+ then 19...♔d7 20 ♖ae1 ♗c5 is just equal) 18...h6 19 gxf5 hxg5 20 ♗xg5 ♖xh3 21 fxe6 ♗e7 and White's efforts had not yielded any advantage in Koch-Marciano, French League 2000.

b) 11 a4 ♗b4 12 ♘e2 ♘e7 13 h3 ♘g6 14 b3 h5 15 ♗b2 h4 16 ♘e1 (or 16 ♖ac1 ♖h5 17 c4 c5 18 ♘e1 ♗xe1 19 ♖xe1 ♗e6, Movsesian-Z.Almasi, Groningen 1998, where Black has a typical opposite-coloured bishop sponsored blockade on the light squares) 16...♗xe1 (Wedberg prefers 16...♗e7 17 ♘d3 c5) 17 ♖xe1 c5 18 ♘c3 ♗f5 (18...♗e6 is safer) 19 ♘e4 b6 20 e6! and White had the initiative, Asrian-Z.Almasi, Groningen 1998.

On the other hand 10...♗e6 is less popular these days as White can obtain a promising position by hitting this bishop. More recent tries involving some combination of ...a5, ...h6, ...♗d7, ...♗b4 or ...♘e7-g6 are more flexible. After 10...♗c6 we examine

three ideas, the third of which is the most logical:

a) 11 b3 a5 12 ♘g5 ♗e7 13 a4?! (13 ♘xe6 was better) 13...♗xg5 14 ♗xg5 h6 15 ♗c1 ♖d8 got nowhere for White in Herrera-Vera, Ubeda 1999.

b) 11 h3 ♗b4 12 ♗d2 ♖d8 13 a3 ♗c5 14 ♗g5 ♖d7 15 ♖xd7 ♗xd7 16 ♖d1 h6 17 e6!? (an aggressive try) 17...fxe6 18 ♗f4 ♗d6 19 ♘e5 and White had enough practical compensation in S.Kasparov-Romanov, Minsk 2000.

c) 11 ♘g5! h6 12 ♘xe6 fxe6 (this pawn structure must in principle favour White, but see Kasparov-Kramnik, {game 12, note to Black's 9th move} for an example of a successful defence) 13 ♘e4 ♗e7 14 g4 ♘h4 15 f4 gave White an edge in Zarnicki-Tempone, Argentine Championship 1996.

One consideration after 10...♗e7 is that White can offer the exchange of bishops with 11 ♗g5. Black then has more room for his pieces but arguably less potential for generating counterplay in a simplified position. Dervishi-Gorbatov, Cutro 2000, continued 11...♗xg5 12 ♘xg5 h6 13 ♘ge4 ♔e7 14 ♖d3 ♖d8 15 ♖xd8 ♔xd8 16 ♖d1+ ♔e7 17 b3 b6 18 f4 ♗b7 19 ♔f2 c5 20 g4 ♘d4 21 ♖d2 and Black had found good roles for his minor pieces. Perhaps now 21...♔e6, to hold up any future expansion, would give Black a reasonable game (whereas in the game 21...h5 22 gxh5 ♖h8 23 ♘g3 proved to be risky).

11 ♘d4 ♘g6

11...♘f5 has nuisance value, but after 12 ♘de2 ♗e7 13 b3 ♗d7 14 ♗b2 ♖d8 15 ♘e4 h5 16 c4 a5 17 ♖d3 ♗c8 18 ♖ad1, Matulovic-Karaklajic, Banja Vrucica 1991, White maintained some pressure.

12 ♘e4

Centralizing and covering the c5-square. Instead 12 f4 ♗c5 13 ♗e3 ♗xd4 14 ♖xd4 ♗f5, Ye Jiangchuan-Rausis, Lee Cup 1996, gave Black easy equality. Allowing opposite bishops eases Black's defensive task as the blockade will be nigh on impossible to shift.

12...♗e7

13 f4

After 13 ♖e1?! (maybe White already regrets the early check on d1?) 13...c5 (with his knight stationed on g6, this move is Black's typical method of ejecting the white knight from d4) 14 ♘b3 (or 14 ♘b5 ♔d7! {heading for the queenside after all} 15 ♗g5 ♖e8 16 a4 a6 17 ♗xe7 axb5 18 ♗xc5 ♖xa4 and Black stood well in Spasov-Zhang Zhong, Elista Olympiad 1998) 14...b6 15 ♘f6+? (15 ♘d6+ cxd6 16 exd6 ♗e6 17 dxe7 ♔xe7 is equal) 15...♔f8 16 ♘d5 ♗d8 17 ♘d2 c6 18 ♘e3 (18 ♘c3 ♗c7 19 ♘c4 ♗e6 20 ♘d6 ♖d8 also leads to the loss of a pawn) 18...♘xe5 Black had an extra pawn and went on to win in Leko-Z.Almasi, Budapest 1997.

13...♘h4

Now that White has played f2-f4 it's imperative to stop the further advance to f5. Another method is with 13...♗g4, which led to Black keeping the pawn majority under control after 14 ♖d3 (preparing to double) 14...♖d8 15 h3 ♗d7 16 ♗e3 c5 17 ♘e2 b6 18 c4 h5 19 ♖ad1 h4 and it's hard to see how White can make progress, Peng Xiaomin-Z.Almasi, Groningen 1997.

14 ♖e1

Not consistent as Black can now activate his king. A more recent try was 14 ♗e3 ♘f5 15 ♗f2 ♘xd4 16 ♖xd4 ♗e6 17 ♖ad1 b6 18 a3 ♖d8 19 ♖xd8+ ♔xd8 20 ♘g3 ♗h4?! (I like 20...h5!, intending to meet 21 f5?! with

21...♗c8 when the pawn on f5 is just weak) 21 ♘h5 ♗xf2+ 22 ♔xf2 and White has the better chances in view of his superior majority, Kundin-Postny, Litohoto 1999.

14...c5!

More routine is 14...♘f5 15 ♘xf5 ♗xf5 and if then 16 ♘d6+ ♗xd6 17 exd6+ ♔d7 White has nothing.

15 ♘b5 ♔d7 16 b4!?

Not wishing to allow Black to settle his king on c6, White tries to mix it.

16...♔c6!

Much better than the alternatives 16...a6 17 ♘bc3 cxb4 18 ♘d5 and 16...cxb4?! 17 ♖d1+ ♔c6 18 ♘d4+ ♔b6 19 ♗e3, both of which allow White a strong initiative.

17 a4 b6 18 bxc5 bxc5

The Black king is snug. White finds it hard to create any serious threats.

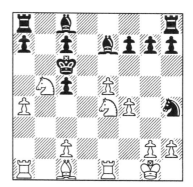

19 ♗a3 ♘f5 20 ♘f2

Wedberg points out that the aggressive try 20 g4 ♘h4 21 ♖e3, hoping for 21...♗xg4?! 22 ♖c3 is well met by 22...a6!.

20...a6 21 ♘c3 ♘d4 22 ♖ac1 g5!

Taking the initiative as White's units lack harmony.

23 ♘d3 gxf4 24 ♘xf4 ♗g5 25 ♘cd5 ♗f5 26 ♖e3 ♖ad8 27 c4 ♘e6 28 ♖f1?

28 g3 was the lesser evil. Black could then continue the minority attack with 28...h5 intending ...h4, but there is nothing concrete.

28...♘xf4 29 ♘xf4 ♖d4 30 ♗b2 ♖xc4

Or 30...♖xf4 31 ♖xf4 ♗xf4 32 ♖f3

♗xh2+ 33 ♔xh2 ♗e6 is promising, but presumably Timman decided that White then has reasonable drawing chances due to the presence of opposite bishops.

31 e6

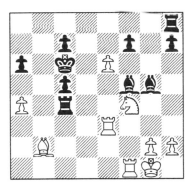

31...f6?!

Instead 31...♗xf4! should win easily against 32 ♖xf4, because of 32...♖xf4 33 ♗xh8 ♗xe6, or 32 ♖ef3, in view of 32...♖b8 33 ♖xf4 ♖xf4 34 ♖xf4 ♗xe6.

32 g3 ♖e8 33 e7 ♗e4 34 h4 ♗xf4 35 ♖xf4 ♖xe7 36 ♗xf6 ♖e6 37 a5 ♔d5 38 ♗c3 ♖xc3?!

Frustration. White's blockade on the dark squares should yield a draw, so Timman goes for a risky winning try.

39 ♖xc3 c4 40 ♖f7 c6 41 ♔f2 ♔d4 42 ♖e3 c3 43 ♖d7+ ♔c4 44 ♔e1 h5 45 ♖dd3 ♗xd3! 46 ♖xe6 ♔b3 47 ♖xc6 ♔b2 48 ♖c5 ♗g6 49 ♖c8 ♗d3 50 ♖c6

50...♗g6?? 1-0

A horrible blunder. Instead 50...♗b5 was necessary and, as Wedberg points out, leads to a draw after 51 ♖c7 ♗d3 52 ♔f2 ♗b5 53 ♔e3 ♗f1 54 g4 hxg4 55 h5 g3 56 h6 g2 57 ♔f2 ♗d3 58 h7 ♗xh7 59 ♖b7+ ♔a3 60 ♖xh7 c2 61 ♖c7.

Despite the result of this game it is clear that coming to c6 with the king is an interesting plan.

Game 16
Wahls-Ekström
Dresden Zonal 1998

---

1 e4 e5 2 ♘f3 ♘c6 3 ♗b5 ♘f6 4 0-0 ♘xe4 5 d4 ♘d6 6 ♗xc6 dxc6 7 dxe5 ♘e4!?

A provocative alternative to the usual 7...♘f5 (see Games 12-15).

8 ♕e2 ♗f5

Nobody plays 8...♘c5 these days, as the continuation 9 ♗e3 ♗g4 10 ♘c3 ♕e7 11 ♖fe1 ♕e6 12 h3, as in Gulko-Reshevsky, Vilnius 1978, yields White a comfortable edge.

9 ♖d1

It's not clear why 9 ♗e3 is so out of fashion, as White theoretically keeps an edge after both 9...♗e7 10 ♘d4 ♕c8 11 f3 ♘c5 12 ♕f2 ♘a4 13 b3 ♘b6 14 c4, as in Jiangchuan-Christiansen, Thessaloniki Olympiad 1988, and 9...♗g6 10 ♘e1 ♕d5 11 f3 ♘c5

12 f4 Van der Wiel-Timman, Tilburg 1988. Black's best is perhaps 9...♗c5 10 ♗xc5 ♘xc5 11 ♘c3 ♘e6 12 ♖ad1 ♕e7, with a rock-solid position.

9...♕c8

9...♕e7!? has been tried a few times. Black voluntarily blocks in his bishop but can react to 10 ♗f4 with 10...g5, and to 10 ♘d4 ♗g6 11 f4, with 11...0-0-0, which ECO suggests is unclear.

10 ♘d4

There are three alternatives, all having their points, but none of which lead to anything concrete:

a) I don't think that transferring the rook to the fourth rank leads to an advantage. So 10 ♖d4 ♘c5 11 ♘h4 (Sznapik-Hort, Thessaloniki Olympiad 1988, was about equal after 11 ♘c3 ♘e6 12 ♖d1 ♗e7 13 ♘e4 0-0 14 ♘g3 ♗g6 15 ♗e3 ♖d8 16 c3 c5) 11...♗g6 (even after 11...♗e7 12 ♗e3 g5!? 13 ♘f3 g4 14 ♘e1 ♕e6 15 ♗f4 ♖d8 16 ♖xd8+ ♔xd8 17 ♕e3 ♔c8, Giaccio-Ekström, Elista Olympiad 1998, Black had interesting chances) 12 ♘c3 ♗e7 13 ♘xg6 hxg6 14 b4 ♘e6 15 ♖g4 a5 16 b5 ♗b4 17 ♗b2 ♗xc3 18 ♗xc3 c5 was fine for Black in De Jong-Jonkman, Vlissingen 1999.

b) Dangerous, however, is the alternative 10 g4 ♗g6 11 ♘h4, as in Ulibin-Eslon, Benasque 1996. Now Black should try 11...♕e6 (rather than 11...♗c5? 12 ♘xg6 ♘xf2 13 ♘xh8 ♘xd1+ 14 ♔g2, which proved good

for White in the game) 12 f4 (12 ♘xg6 led to a solid game after 12...♕xg6 13 f3 ♘c5 14 ♘c3 h5 15 g5 ♘e6 16 ♕e4 ♗e7 in Fantin-Jonkman, York 2000) 12...♗c5+ 13 ♔g2 ♕e7 14 ♘f5 ♗xf5 15 gxf5 ♕h4, with mutual chances in a sharp position (analysis by Lobron).

c) Following the more solid continuation 10 ♗e3 ♗e7 11 ♘bd2 0-0 12 ♘d4 ♘xd2 13 ♖xd2 ♗g6 14 ♖ad1 c5 15 ♘b3 b6 16 ♗f4 ♕f5, as in S.Gonzalez-Eslon, Bilbao 2000, Black's bishop pair fully compensated his 'inferior majority'.

10...♗c5 11 b4!?

Playing directly to exploit Black's precariously placed minor pieces.

Instead 11 g4? rebounded badly after 11...♗xg4! 12 f3 ♗f5 in Jansa-Westerinen, Gausdal 1989, and then if 13 fxe4 Black has a powerful initiative after 13...♗g4 14 ♕f1 ♗xd1 15 ♕xd1 ♕h3 16 c3 0-0-0.

The quieter 11 ♗e3 is less critical. Play can then continue 11...0-0 12 f3 ♗xd4 13 ♗xd4 (13 ♖xd4!? is an interesting try, but in Hartman-Hjelm, Stockholm 1998, White quickly went astray and after 13...♘c5 14 ♗f4 ♘a6 15 ♖h4?! ♕e6 16 g4 ♕xe5! 17 gxf5 ♖fe8 18 ♔f2 ♕xb2 Black soon won) 13...♘g5 14 ♘c3 ♖e8 15 ♖d2 ♘e6, C.Hansen-Westerinen, Nordic Championship 1997, whereupon Black had a solid position.

11...♘b6

A clever move. In the past this had been dismissed as simply bad because Black's knight is denied a retreat square, but things are not so clear, as we shall see...

Instead taking on b4 may be playable: 11...♗xb4 12 e6! (after 12 ♘xf5 ♕xf5 13 ♖d4, Black wriggles out with 13...♘c3) 12...fxe6 (better than 12...♗g6?! 13 exf7+ ♔f8 14 ♕c4 and Black had serious problems in Sulskis-Westerinen, Gausdal 1995) 13 ♘xf5 exf5 14 f3 and although a piece is lost after 14...♕e6 15 fxe4 ♕e5 16 c3, Black has fair compensation. Most sources do, however, show a preference for White.

12 f3

If White tries 12 c4, then 12...c5 13 ♘xf5 ♕xf5 14 b5 (14 ♕f3 is answered by 14...♕xe5 and Black hits the rook and may even be better) 14...♗a5 15 f3 ♘c3 16 ♘xc3 ♗xc3 17 ♗b2, Magem-Eslon, Terrassa 1996, leads to solid equality.

12...♕d7 13 ♗b2

Allowing the knight to use the g5-square. Consistent is 13 ♗e3 0-0-0 14 fxe4 ♗g4 15 e6! ♕xd4! 16 ♖xd4 ♗xe2 17 ♖xd8+ ♖xd8 18 ♗xb6 cxb6 19 exf7 ♗h5 20 ♘c3 ♗xf7 and the ending is fine for Black. White has a passed pawn but his queenside is exposed to attack.

The first player can try to improve by first playing 14 c4 and after 14...c5, only now 15 fxe4. Black is not without resources; 15...♗g4 16 e6 ♗xe2! (now 16...♕xd4?! 17 ♖xd4 ♗xe2 18 bxc5 may leave White with an edge) 17 exd7+ ♖xd7 18 bxc5 ♗xd1 19 cxb6 axb6 20 ♘c3 ♗h5, with an unclear position as analysed by Wedberg.

13...♘g5 14 c4 ♗xd4+ 15 ♗xd4

15 ♖xd4 has the advantage of stopping long castling. However after 15...♕e7 16 a3 0-0 17 ♘c3 ♘e6 Black has no real problems, assuming he keeps an eye on any white kingside pawn expansion.

15...0-0-0

With this final developing move Black has achieved full equality.

16 ♘c3 ♘e6 17 ♗f2 ♕e7 18 ♕e3 b6 19 a3 ♖xd1+ 20 ♖xd1 ♖d8 21 ♖xd8+ ♕xd8 22 c5 g5 23 h3 ½-½

Black is well placed to restrain White's kingside pawn majority, and with the presence of opposite bishops the result is understandable.

Game 17
Rozentalis-Gorbitov
Saint Petersburg 1996

1 e4 e5 2 ♘f3 ♘c6 3 ♗b5 ♘f6 4 0-0 ♘xe4 5 d4 ♘d6 6 dxe5

A temporary piece sacrifice based on the point that the knight on b5 has no squares.

6...♘xb5 7 a4

The old 7 c4?! d6! 8 e6 fxe6 9 cxb5 ♘e7, as in Suetin-Faibisovic, USSR 1969, looks dubious for White. Compare this with the following note and it becomes clear that White should use his a-pawn.

7...♘bd4

The safest move, although 7...d6 hasn't been entirely worked out. White has free development and the initiative for his pawn after 8 e6 fxe6 9 axb5 ♘e7 10 ♘c3 ♘f5 11 ♘d4 ♕f6, as in Nunn-Romanishin, Mexico 1977. According to Maric, White then has the advantage after 12 b6! cxb6 13 ♘db5, but this requires testing. For instance *Fritz5* suggests 13...♔d8 14 ♘xa7 ♔e8, which remains far from clear.

8 ②xd4 ②xd4 9 ♕xd4 d5 10 ②c3

The simplifying 10 exd6 ♕xd6 11 ♕e4+ ♕e6 is given by Nunn as equal.

10...c6

Black constructs his centre and has a trump card in the bishop pair. White has a lead in development and a slight space advantage.

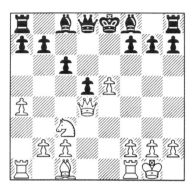

11 ②e2!?

After 11 a5 ♗f5 12 f4 ♕d7 (pawn grabbing with 12...♗xc2?! is too dangerous after 13 f5, as in Kindermann-Hickl, Bern 1990) 13 ♖f2 h5 14 ♗e3 ♖h6 15 ②a4 ♖g6 Black had a solid blockade on the light-squares, Nunn-Salov, Haifa 1989. So in order to avoid a similar scenario, White prepares to meet ...♗f5 with c2-c3 and ②g3.

11...h5

In order to harass the knight if it comes to g3, so White seeks an alternative square.

12 ♕c3 h4 13 h3 a5

It's instructive how Black competes for space on both wings, rather than aimlessly developing his pieces. With a fairly closed centre there isn't the same hurry to get one's pieces out and hide the king away, but time is still an important factor.

14 ②d4 ♗b4 15 ♕d3 ♖h5 16 ♗e3 g6 17 f4 ♗f5

Stopping any of White's attacking intentions on the kingside, so White switches his attention to the centre.

18 ②xf5 ♖xf5 19 c3 ♗f8 20 c4 ♗b4 21

♖ad1 dxc4 22 ♕xc4 ♕e7 23 ♗b6 ♔f8 24 ♖f3 ♖e8 25 ♗f2

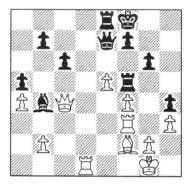

By keeping an eye on the h-pawn Black is denied the opportunity to play ...♕e6. White has the initiative but it's not clear that he can break through.

25...♖d8 26 ♖xd8+ ♕xd8 27 ♖d3 ♕e7 28 ♗b6 ♕e6?!

More practical was 28...g5 29 ♖d8+ ♔g7, allowing the black rook to come back into the game. Thereupon 30 ♖d4 gxf4 31 ♖xf4 ♖xf4 32 ♕xf4 would probably lead to a draw.

29 ♖d8+ ♔g7 30 ♕d4 ♗e7

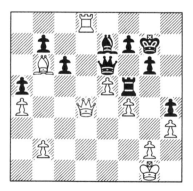

White now finds a way to complicate the struggle.

31 ♖d6!? ♗xd6?

No, this doesn't lead to perpetual check! Black was probably in time trouble, otherwise he would surely have been able to calculate that the precarious-looking 31...♕b3! is playable, for example 32 e6+ ♔h7! (but not 32...♗f6? 33 e7! etc.) doesn't get White anywhere, or 32 ♖d7 c5 33 ♕d2 and Black has a choice between 33...♗g5!? or immediately taking the bishop.

32 exd6+ f6 33 d7 ♕e1+ 34 ♔h2 ♕g3+ 35 ♔h1 ♖xf4

35...♕e1+ 36 ♕g1 also costs a piece.

36 d8♕ ♖f1+ 37 ♕g1 ♖xg1+ 38 ♗xg1 ♕b3 39 ♕e7+ ♔g8 40 ♕xf6 ♕xa4 41 ♗d4 1-0

Black's strategy was perfectly sound and thus we can conclude that he obtains a satisfactory game after 6 dxe5.

Game 18
Anand-Timman
Wijk aan Zee 1999

---

1 e4 e5 2 ♘f3 ♘c6 3 ♗b5 ♘f6 4 0-0 ♘xe4 5 d4 ♗e7

6 ♕e2

For 6 dxe5 see Game 20.

6...♘d6

Playable is the unusual 6...d5, giving Black a solid but unambitious set-up. After 7 ♘xc5 ♗d7 8 ♗xc6 ♗xc6 9 ♖e1 ♗d7 10 ♗f4 c6 11 ♘d2 (Keres) White has a small edge.

7 ♗xc6 bxc6

White obtains a strong attack after 7...dxc6, which must therefore be branded as dubious. Hübner-Vogel, Bundesliga 1986,

didn't last very long; 8 dxe5 ♘f5 9 ♖d1 ♗d7 10 e6 fxe6 11 ♘e5 ♗d6 12 ♕h5+ g6 13 ♘xg6 ♘g7 14 ♕h6 ♘f5 15 ♕h3 ♖g8 16 ♕xh7 ♖g7 17 ♕h5 ♕f6 18 ♘f4+ ♔e7 19 ♘c3 ♗xf4 20 ♗xf4 ♖h8 21 ♘e4! ♗e8 (if 21...♖xh5 then 22 ♖xd7+ ♔xd7 23 ♘xf6+ does the trick) 22 ♗g5! and Black resigned.

8 dxe5 ♘b7

9 ♘c3

The moves 9 c4 and 9 ♘d4 are covered in game 19.

After the important alternative 9 b3, Black's development strategy will be geared towards the timing of ...d7-d5 or ...f7-f6, in order to counter White's pre-eminence in the centre. After 9...0-0 10 ♗b2 there are three significant methods for Black:

a) Black failed to equalise after the continuation 10...f6 11 ♘bd2 fxe5 (or 11...♕e8!? 12 exf6 ♗xf6 13 ♕xe8 ♖xe8 14 ♗xf6 gxf6 as in Kirpichnikov-Bykov, USSR 1971; the ending is okay for Black, despite his ugly pawns, as White cannot really pressurise the four pawn islands) 12 ♘xe5 ♘d6 13 ♖ae1 ♗f6 14 f4 a5 15 ♘e4 ♘xe4 16 ♕xe4 d5 17 ♕e3 ♖a6 18 ♗c3 ♖e8 19 ♕d3 in Apicella-Payen, Cappelle la Grande 1999, as White's position was easier to play – Black had to cover various sensitive points.

b) The immediate 10...d5 can be met by 11 exd6 cxd6 12 ♖e1 ♗f6 13 ♗xf6 ♕xf6 14 ♘bd2, as in Psakhis-Fedorov, Nimes 1991, and now 14...♘c5 15 ♘e4 ♘xe4 16 ♕xe4

&xd7 gives a satisfactory game for Black. If White prefers not to capture the d-pawn he can instead try 11 ♘bd2 ♖e8 12 c4 (after 12 ♘d4 ♕d7 Black is ready to counter with ...c5 and/ or ...♘d8-e6) 12...a5 13 ♖fe1 ♗f8 14 ♗c3 a4 15 b4 c5! 16 b5 d4 17 ♗b2 c6! and Black took over the initiative, Renet-Sharif, France 1991.

c) By first playing 10...♖e8, and after 11 ♖e1 ♗f8 12 ♘c3, only now 12...d5, as in Vogt-Knezevic, Leningrad 1977, Black avoids the option of White capturing en passant and obtains a solid game.

In conclusion: To counter with ...d5 seems a better bet against 9 b3.

9...0-0 10 ♖e1

Less strong is 10 ♖d1, as this allows the freeing 10...d5.

10...♘c5

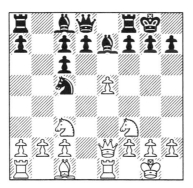

11 ♘d4

Geller twice played 11 ♗f4 ♘e6 12 ♗g3 ♖b8 13 b3 f5 (13...♗b4!?, as in the next note, is worth considering) 14 exf6 ♗xf6 15 ♘e5 ♗xe5 16 ♕xe5 and White's position is easier to play. It's not clear how Black handles his pawns and gets his pieces organised.

Instead 11 ♗e3 may be the most accurate of all. The continuation of 11...♘e6 12 ♖ad1 d5 does not solve all Black's problems as after 13 exd6 cxd6 14 ♘d4 ♗d7 (14...♕c7 has also been tried) 15 ♘f5 d5 16 ♘xe7+ ♕xe7 17 ♘a4 ♖fd8 18 ♕f3, as in Shamkovich-Lein, Tbilisi 1969/70, White

had nagging pressure. Another approach 12...♖b8 (instead of 12...♖b8) 13 b3 ♗b4 14 ♗d2 d5 15 exd6 cxd6 16 ♘e4 ♗xd2 17 ♕xd2 d5 18 ♕c3, as in Jansa-Knezevic, Namestovo 1987, isn't ideal either. The further 18...♕c7 19 ♘c5 (Jansa) leaves Black rather passive and White looking forward to his bind on the d4 and c5-squares.

11...♘e6 12 ♘xe6

The strategy of taking on e6 is not effective as it reinforces the opposing centre and opens the f-file. Again 12 ♗e3 eyes the isolated a-pawn, but here Black can get counterplay: 12...♖b8 13 b3 ♗b4 14 ♘xe6 fxe6 15 ♕d2 ♖b5!? 16 ♗xa7 ♖a5 (or 16...♖d5!?) and Black had interesting compensation for the pawn, Dvorecky-Lein, USSR 1974.

12...fxe6 13 b3 ♕e8

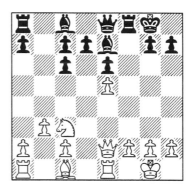

14 ♗e3

Instead 14 ♗b2 ♗b7 15 ♕g4 was prematurely agreed drawn in Spassky-Smyslov, Tilburg 1979.

14...♖f5!

Anand considers this stronger than 14...c5 15 ♘e4!? d6 16 ♖ad1, after which White has pressure on the centre.

15 ♘e4

15 f4 has the disadvantage of weakening various light squares, so Black would then switch his light-squared bishop to the long diagonal.

15...a5?!

15...♕f8! was the best way forward, for instance 16 ♗d4 c5 17 ♗b2 ♗b7 18 f3 and Black has organised his pieces and is ready for active play. Anand considers the resulting position to be equal.

16 ♗d4 a4 17 c4

With the option of playing c4-c5 to keep Black's bishop under wraps.

17...♗b7 18 ♘g3! ♖f4 19 ♗e3 ♖f7?!

Less accurate than 19...♖f8 20 c5 ♕g6, according to Anand.

20 c5 ♗a6 21 ♕d2 ♗h4 22 ♘e4 ♖f5 23 ♕d4 ♗e7?

Despite White maintaining his bind, 23...axb3 was objectively stronger. After the text White cheekily grabs a pawn and essentially has a winning position.

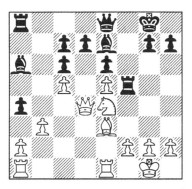

24 ♘g3 ♖f8 25 ♕xa4 h5 26 h3 ♗d3 27 ♕d4 ♕g6 28 h4!

The simplest.

28...♖fd8 29 ♗g5! ♗xg5 30 hxg5 ♖a3 31 ♕h4 ♖da8

In the complications that follow Black fights to the end but White is always well on top.

32 ♘xh5 ♗c2! 33 ♘f4 ♕h7 34 ♕g4! ♗xb3 35 ♖e3 ♖8a4 36 ♖h3! ♕f5 37 ♕xf5 exf5 38 g6! ♔f8?

The alternative 38...♖xa2 was apparently a better chance.

39 ♖h8+ ♔g8 40 ♖d1! 1-0

After 40...♖xf4 White plays 41 ♖xd7 and the unstoppable threat of ♖f7 and ♖xg8+ leads to mate.

> ## Game 19
> ## Markovic-Piket
> *Elista Olympiad 1998*

1 e4 e5 2 ♘f3 ♘c6 3 ♗b5 ♘f6 4 0-0 ♘xe4 5 d4 ♗e7 6 ♕e2 ♘d6 7 ♗xc6 bxc6 8 dxe5 ♘b7 9 ♘d4

Stopping any freeing attempt by Black based on ...d7-d5, as the c-pawn then hangs. Another way to restrain Black in the centre is with 9 c4 0-0 10 ♘c3 f6 (or even 10...d6 11 h3 ♕d7!? activating the queen; then after 12 ♖e1 ♖e8 13 ♗f4 ♕f5 14 ♗g3, as in Stein-Gipslis, Sousse 1967, Black should have played 14...♕h5, according to Keres and Olafsson, but they still prefer White) 11 ♖e1 fxe5 12 ♕xe5 (White had no advantage after 12 ♘xe5 ♗f6 13 ♗f4 ♗xe5 14 ♗xe5 d6 15 ♗d4 ♕h4 16 ♕d2 ♕f4 17 ♖e3 ♘d8 18 ♘e4 ♘e6 19 ♗c3 ♗d7 in Tal-Dorfman, USSR Championship 1976) 12...♗f6 13 ♕h5 g6 14 ♕h6 ♗g7, as in Ehlvest-Marciano, France 1992, where Black had a perfectly sound position. Ehlvest then tries to claim an edge with the continuation 15 ♕d2 d6 16 b3 ♘c5 17 ♗b2 a5 18 ♘e4? but this loses the exchange to 18...♗xb2 19 ♕xb2 ♘d3.

9...0-0 10 ♘c3

Yudasin has investigated the alternative 10 ♘f5 and the continuation 10...d5 11 ♘xe7+ ♕xe7 12 ♖e1 ♖e8 13 b3 ♕h4 14 ♘d2 ♕d4 15 ♖b1 ♗g4 16 ♗b2, whereupon the ending looks perfectly sound for the second player, for example 16...♕xb2 17 ♖xb2 ♗xe2 18 ♖xe2 ♘c5 19 ♖b1 ♘e6.

10...♗c5 11 ♖d1 ♖e8

Black can equally play 11...♕e8 12 ♗g5 ♗xd4 13 ♖xd4 d5, as in Uitumen-Bouwmeester, Tel Aviv Olympiad 1964. Then Keres and Olafsson give 14 exd6 ♕xe2 15 ♘xe2 cxd6 as equal.

12 ♗f4

It's decidedly risky to take the c-pawn with 12 ♘xc6?!, as 12...♕h4 13 g3 (or if 13 ♘d4 ♗xd4 14 g3 ♗xf2+ 15 ♕xf2 ♕h5 16 ♗f4 ♘d8, then after ...♘e6 and ...♗b7 Black stands well) 13...♕h3 14 ♘d4 d6 15 ♘f3 ♗g4 yields excellent compensation for the pawn.

In Yudovic-Maseev, correspondence 1966, White preferred 12 ♕h5, but after 12...♕e7 13 ♗f4 ♗xd4 14 ♖xd4 d5 15 ♘e2 ♘c5 16 ♖dd1 a5 17 ♘d4 ♗d7 Black had everything well covered.

12...♗xd4

This exchange, when combined with the follow-up 13...d5, allows Black to obtain some breathing space and a fair share of the centre.

13 ♖xd4 d5 14 ♕h5

14 ♘e4 only helps Black to obtain active play with 14...♕e7 15 ♘g5 ♘c5 16 ♖dd1 ♖b8 17 b3 f6.

14...♕d7 15 b4!?

Stopping the knight using c5, but there is

another route to e6. The downside of this move is that it facilitates quick counterplay with ...a5.

Otherwise White could try 15 ♗g3 ♘c5 (even 15...♕f5 is safe enough) 16 b4 ♘e6 17 ♖h4 ♘f8 and it's unclear if White has achieved anything positive with his aggressive approach.

15...♘d8 16 ♖d2

The continuation 16 ♘a4 ♘e6 17 ♘c5 ♘xc5 18 bxc5 is simply met by 18...♕f5 and the opposite bishops give the ending a drawish allure.

16...♘e6!?

Playing for more than a stodgy ending with 16...♕f5.

17 ♗e3 a5

Eliminating the b-pawn will free the way for Black's central pawns to advance.

18 ♕h4 ♕d8! 19 ♕g4

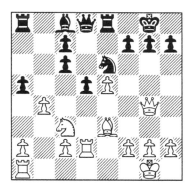

Unfortunately for White, 19 ♕xd8 ♖xd8 20 bxa5 d4 21 ♖ad1 c5 leads to the loss of a piece.

19...f5!

Deflecting the white queen and leading to a race where Black's queenside is by far the most dangerous majority.

20 ♕xf5?

The last chance to obtain a playable game was 20 exf6 ♕xf6 21 ♗d4 ♘xd4 22 ♕xd4 ♕xd4 23 ♖xd4 axb4 24 ♖xb4 c5 25 ♖b2, although Black is probably better after 25...c6.

20...axb4 21 ♘e2 c5 22 f4 g6 23 ♕g4
  23 ♕d3 fails to 23...♖a3.
23...♖a3 24 ♗f2
  24 ♖d3 loses on the spot to 24...♘d4.
24...♘d4 25 ♕h4 ♕xh4 26 ♗xh4 ♘xe2+
27 ♖xe2 ♗e6 28 h3 d4 29 ♖f2 h5

Prudently slowing down White's kingside majority before crashing through on the other wing.

30 ♔h2 ♔f7 31 ♗f6 ♖ea8 32 ♖g1 ♖xa2
33 g4 hxg4 34 hxg4 d3 35 f5 dxc2 36
fxe6+ ♔xe6 37 ♔g2 b3 38 ♗g5 b2 39
♖xc2 b1♕ 0-1

Game 20
Shirov-Kramnik
Linares 1998

1 e4 e5 2 ♘f3 ♘c6 3 ♗b5 ♘f6 4 0-0
  The direct 4 d4!? can be awkward for the unprepared. A sensible method of defence is as follows: 4...exd4 (possible is 4...♘xe4 which will transpose after 5 0-0, or 5 ♕e2, to later games in the chapter) 5 e5 (or 5 0-0 ♗e7 6 ♕e2 0-0 7 e5 ♘e8 8 ♖d1 d5, which is acceptable for Black) 5...♘e4 6 0-0 ♗e7 7 ♘xd4 0-0 8 ♘f5 d5!, with equal chances. This is analogous to a better-known variation of the Spanish where the bishop is on a4 and the Black pawn on a6.
4...♘xe4 5 d4
  White seems to get nothing much after 5 ♖e1, so it has been rather ignored of late.

After 5...♘d6 6 ♘xe5 ♗e7 7 ♗d3 (if 7 ♕h5 ♘xe5 8 ♕xe5, the straightforward 8...0-0! is comfortable and following 7 ♗f1 ♘xe5 8 ♖xe5 0-0 9 ♘c3 ♗f6 10 ♖e1, as in Gufeld-Klovans, Jurmala 1978, Keres's 10...b6 is about equal) 7...0-0 8 ♘c3 ♘xe5 9 ♖xe5 ♗f6 10 ♖e3 g6 (10...b6?? allows 11 ♗xh7+!) 11 b3 ♗d4 12 ♖e2 b6 13 ♗a3 c5, Sherwin-Bisguier, USA Championship 1962/3, an unusual position has arisen with both d-pawns on starters; White's temporary lead in development is about to fizzle out.
5...♗e7 6 dxe5
  There are a couple of interesting alternatives.
  a) Firstly 6 ♕e1!? (allowing the queen to later come to c3) 6...♘d6 7 ♗xc6 bxc6 8 dxe5 ♘b7 9 b3 0-0 10 ♕c3 c5 11 ♗b2 ♖e8 12 ♖e1 ♗f8 13 ♘bd2 d5 14 exd6 cxd6 gave an unclear position in I.Zaitsev-Yudovic, USSR 1972; Black has the bishop pair, White sensibly placed pieces. The black d- and c-pawns can either be strong (controlling some important squares) or weak (prone to attack), depending on who seizes the initiative.
  b) 6 d5 ♘d6 7 ♗e2 e4 led to drawish simplification in Rogers-Spassky, Wellington 1988 after 8 dxc6 exf3 9 cxd7+ ♗xd7 10 ♗xf3 0-0 11 ♘c3 c6, with equality.
6...0-0 7 ♖e1
  The most popular move has been 7 ♕d5, when after 7...♘c5 8 ♗e3 Black has two ideas:
  a) 8...♘e6 9 ♘c3 a6 10 ♗c4 d6 (10...b5!? might be preferable, for example 11 ♗b3 ♖b8! 12 ♖ad1 ♘a5 with equality, according to Sax) 11 exd6 ♕xd6 12 ♖ad1 is considered a shade better for White, Tringov-Filip, Havana Olympiad 1966.
  b) 8...a6 9 ♗xc5 (9 ♗e2 d6 10 exd6 ♕xd6, as in Apicella-Verat, Paris 1988, doesn't offer much at all) 9...axb5 10 ♗xe7 ♕xe7 11 ♘c3 (if 11 ♕xb5 Black counters with the move 11...♖a5) 11...b4 12 ♘b5 ♖a5 13 a4 b6

and standard theory prefers White slightly (a recent game Blehm-Pedzich, Koszalin 1999 continued with 14 ♘d2 ♗a6 15 ♘c4 ♗xb5 16 axb5 ♖xa1 17 ♖xa1 and seemed to confirm this).

7...d5 8 exd6 ♗xd6 9 ♘bd2

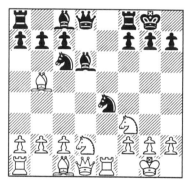

I get the impression that White's opening hasn't really yielded anything, as Black can now simply play 9...♘xd2 10 ♗xd2 ♕f6 11 ♗c3 ♕h6 with equality.

9...♗f5!?

White cannot capture twice on e4 as Black then wins the White queen with ...♗xh2+.

10 ♘c4 ♗b4! 11 c3 ♕xd1 12 ♖xd1 ♗c5 13 ♗e3 ♘e7 14 ♖e1

The threat to capture on c5 followed by e7 is best met by 14...♘g6 and it's hard to find any advantage to White.

14...♗xe3?! 15 ♘xe3 ♘d6

Or 15...♗g6 16 ♘e5 and White retains a

nagging edge.

16 ♘xf5 ♘exf5 17 ♗a4!

White's bishop controls the e8-square, stopping for the moment, a black rook from challenging for the e-file. If Black reacts with ...c7-c6 or ...b7-b5 then the pawn structure is slightly loosened. The advantage of bishop over knight is not significant except for this factor.

17...g6 18 ♖e2 b5

Another plan is to play ...♖fd8 and ...h7-h5, maintaining the knight in order to thwart any entry ideas into e7.

19 ♗c2 ♖fe8 20 ♖ae1 ♖xe2 21 ♖xe2 a5?

Too loosening, Shirov suggests instead 21...a6.

22 ♖e5 b4 23 ♖c5 bxc3 24 ♖xc3

The two isolated pawns are now a serious worry for Black.

24...♘b5 25 ♖c4 ♖d8 26 ♔f1 ♘e7?! 27 a4 ♘d6 28 ♖xc7 ♘d5 29 ♖c5 ♘b4 30 ♗b3 ♘d3 31 ♖xa5 ♘xb2 32 ♖d5!

White has to play accurately but the knight on b2 is fatally trapped.

32...♖b8 33 ♘d2 ♖b6 34 ♔e2 ♖a6 35 ♖d4 ♘b7 36 ♘e4! ♖b6 37 ♗d5 ♔g7 38 ♔d2 ♘d6 39 ♘c3 ♘f5 40 ♖f4 ♔f6 41 a5 1-0

Kramnik resigned because either the knight is lost (41...♖a6 42 ♖b4 etc.) or the rook's pawn runs for touchdown (41...♖b8 42 a6 and the pawn queens).

Game 21
Adams-Dautov
London 1996

1 e4 e5 2 ♘f3 ♘c6 3 ♗b5 ♘f6 4 d3

Leading to a closed game. White has a couple of other solid alternatives to avoid Black capturing on e4: 4 ♘c3, transposing to the Four Knights opening, and 4 ♕e2.

After 4 ♕e2 Black can play 4...a6 5 ♗a4 (on 5 ♗xc6 dxc6 6 ♘xe5 Black has 6...♕d4 winning back the pawn) 5...♗e7 (transposing from a Spanish with 3...a6 4 ♗a4 ♘f6 5 ♕e2 ♗e7) when a typical continuation is 6 c3 d6 7 d4 ♗d7 8 ♘bd2 exd4 9 ♘xd4 ♘xd4 10 ♗xd7+ ♕xd7 11 cxd4 0-0 12 0-0 ♖fe8 13 b3 ♗f8 14 f3 g6, as in Varnusz-Szily, Hungary 1958, which is pretty solid for Black.

If instead Black prefers to be more combative then I suggest 4...♗c5!? 5 c3 (5 ♗xc6 bxc6 6 ♘xe5 now wins a pawn but after 6...♕e7 7 f4 d6 8 ♘xc6 ♕xe4 9 ♕xe4+ ♘xe4 10 d4 ♗b6 11 c3 a5 Black has reasonable compensation as the white knight is short of squares) 5...♕e7 6 d3 0-0 7 ♗g5 d6 8 ♘bd2 ♘d8 (heading for e6 and then to f4 if given a chance) 9 d4 ♗b6 10 d5 c6 11 ♗d3 h6 12 ♗h4 ♔h8 13 c4 g5 14 ♗g3 ♗a5 15 0-0-0 b5

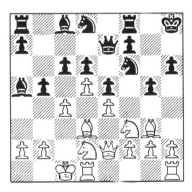

with sharp play, Ciocaltea-Campora, Timisoara 1981.

4...d6 5 0-0

The Maroczy-style 5 c4, aiming for a cen-

tral bind, is best met by 5...g6!, putting the bishop on an important diagonal. A typical continuation would then be 6 ♘c3 ♗g7 7 d4 exd4 8 ♘xd4 ♗d7 9 ♗xc6 bxc6 10 0-0 0-0 11 f3 (or 11 ♗g5 which was promising for Black after 11...h6 12 ♗h4 ♕b8 13 ♕d2 ♕b4 in Wolff-Kaidanov, USA Championship 1993) 11...♖e8 12 ♕d3 ♕b8 as proposed by Kaidanov, giving interesting counterplay.

5...g6

Pre-empting any White ideas of N-d2-f1-g3-f5, a typical manoeuvre in such closed positions.

6 c3 ♗g7 7 ♘bd2 0-0 8 ♖e1 ♗d7

A reasonable alternative would be 8...♘e7 intending to meet 9 d4 with 9...c6 10 ♗a4 ♕c7.

9 ♘f1

9 d4? looks silly after 9...♘xd4!.

9...♘h5 10 h3 h6

Preparing counterplay with ...♕e8 and ...f7-f5. Instead, the immediate 10...f5? would be premature after 11 exf5 gxf5 12 ♗c4+ ♔h8 13 ♘g5.

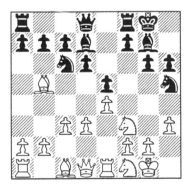

11 a4

Gaining space and getting ready for d3-d4.

11...a6 12 ♗c4 ♗e6 13 ♘e3 ♗xc4

Black could have tried 13...♘f4.

14 dxc4!?

An interesting try as the obvious 14 ♘xc4 is comfortably met by 14...d5.

14...♘f4 15 ♘d5 ♘c6 16 a5 f5

Black expands on the kingside, White on the other wing.

17 b4 ☒f7 18 ☒a2 ☖h7?!

Adams considers this to be the wrong plan. He judges it better to close the kingside with 18...f4.

19 ☒d2 ♛e8

White was intending c4-c5 so Black gets the queen off such a sensitive square.

20 exf5 gxf5 21 ♘h4 e4 22 f4 ♘e7 23 ☒de2!

Pressing against Black's edifice, for instance here White threatens 24 ♘xf5.

23...♘xd5 24 cxd5 ♘f8

Adams suggests the piece sacrifice 24...♗xc3!? 25 dxe6 ♛xe6, but after 26 ♗d2 Black's compensation is probably insufficient.

25 ♛c2 ♛d7 26 g4!

Unleashing the power of White's major pieces by cracking open the centre. Black now finds it impossible to contain the White initiative.

26...fxg4 27 ☒xe4 ☖h8 28 f5 gxh3 29 ☒e6! ♗f6 30 ♘g6+ ♘xg6 31 fxg6 ☒g8 32 ☖h1 ☒e7 33 ♗xh6 ♗e5 34 ☒xe7 ♛xe7 35 ♛f5 ♛f6 36 g7+ ☒xg7 37 ♗xg7+ ☖xg7 38 ☒g1+ ☖f8 39 ♛c8+ 1-0

Black decided to call it a day because the win is trivial after the continuation 39...☖f7 40 ♛xc7+ ♛e7 41 ☒f1+ ♗f6 42 ♛xe7+ ☖xe7 43 ☒f3.

Summary

The fashionable main line with 5...♘d6 has seen many recent developments. It is arguable that White maintains slightly the better prospects, but the resulting strategically complex positions are hard to handle, and even the world's best have problems to prove anything concrete. Best play in games 12-15 has yet to crystallise. Against 5...♗e7 theory suggests that White keeps an edge, but even here Black can obtain a satisfactory game.

The Berlin remains eminently playable even at the highest level, but queenless middlegames and intricate manoeuvres will not appeal to all club players. Tacticians would be well advised to study game 16 as a lively alternative to the standard 7...♘f5.

1 e4 e5 2 ♘f3 ♘c6 3 ♗b5 ♘f6 4 0-0
>   4 d3 d6 5 0-0 g6 6 c3 – *Game 21*

4...♘xe4
>   4...♗c5 - *Chapter 3*

5 d4 ♘d6
>   5...♗e7 *(D)*
>>   6 dxe5 – *Game 20*
>>   6 ♕e2 ♘d6 7 ♗xc6 dxc6 8 dxe5 ♘b7
>>>   9 ♘c3 0-0 10 ♖e1 – *Game 18*
>>>   9 ♘d4 – *Game 19*

6 ♗xc6
>   6 dxe5 ♘xb5 7 a4 – *Game 17*

6...dxc6 7 dxe5 *(D)* ♘f5
>   7...♘e4 8 ♕e2 ♗f5 9 ♖d1 ♕c8 10 ♘d4 ♗c5 11 b4 ♗b6 – *Game 16*

8 ♕xd8+ ♔xd8 *(D)* 9 ♘c3
>   9 ♖d1+ ♔e8 10 ♘c3 ♘e7 11 ♘d4 ♘g6 – *Game 15*

9...♔e8
>   9...♗d7 10 b3 – *Game 14*

10 h3 ♘e7
>   10...a5 11 g4 – *Game 13*

11 ♘e4 ♘g6 – *Game 12*

5...♗e7

7 dxe5

8...♔xd8

CHAPTER THREE

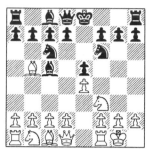

The Classical Berlin Defence

1 e4 e5 2 ♘f3 ♘c6 3 ♗b5 ♘f6 4 0-0 ♗c5

This chapter deals with the position, that can arise from 1 e4 e5 2 ♘f3 ♘c6 3 ♗b5 ♗c5 4 0-0 ♘f6, or alternatively 3...♘f6 4 0-0 ♗c5.

This constitutes a hybrid system, that can arise just as easily from the Berlin as from the Classical, hence my choice of name for this chapter. Those variations of the Classical that are distinct from the Classical Berlin are covered in Chapter Four.

Here Black opts for quick natural development. As we shall see below, this approach is sound and offers reasonable counter-chances for the second player, if he is well prepared!

White has two main plans, building up a pawn front, as in games 22-25, or an immediate tactical challenge in the centre, as in game 26-27.

Game 22
Bologan-Piket
Biel 1999

1 e4 e5 2 ♘f3 ♘c6 3 ♗b5 ♘f6 4 0-0 ♗c5

The other move-order is 3...♗c5 4 0-0 ♘f6. Against the Classical move-order

(3...♗c5 etc.) be aware of 4 c3, with the idea of meeting 4...♘f6 with the sharp 5 d4 as in game 28. Against 3...♘f6 then 4 d4!? is an interesting way to steer play away from the hybrid chapter. This is covered in the note to White's 4th move in game 20.

5 c3

5 ♘xe5 is discussed in Games 26-27.

5...0-0 6 d4

6...♗b6

Ceding the centre too early with 6...exd4?! is dubious; 7 cxd4 ♗b6 8 e5 ♘d5 9 ♗c4, Montero Martinez-Grau, Santiago 1998, and now in the game 9...♘de7?! 10 d5 turned out badly for Black, but after 9...♘ce7 10 ♕b3 c6 11 ♗g5, White still has strong pressure.

7 ♗g5

Logical, in view of the absence of Black's dark-squared bishop. 7 ♕d3 is seen in Game 24, while 7 dxe5 is discussed in Game 25.

7...h6 8 ♗h4 d6 9 a4

White's main try. The immediate 9 ♖e1 allows 9...exd4 10 ♗xc6 dxc3! (cheekily exploiting the position of the rook on a1) 11 ♘xc3 bxc6 12 ♕a4 ♕d7 13 ♗xf6 (13 ♖ad1!?) 13...gxf6 14 h3 (14 ♖ad1!?) 14...♔h8 15 ♘e2 ♖g8 16 ♘f4 ♗b7 and Black was much better, Kavalek-Spassky, Solingen 1977. White should have tried ♖ad1 on either his 13th or 14th move with ideas of e4-e5. However Spassky's trick is avoided by the text.

9...a5 10 ♖e1 exd4

10...♗g4 is analysed in the note to White's 9th move in game 23.

11 ♗xc6 bxc6

Forced, as unlike in Kavalek-Spassky above, 11...dxc3?? 12 ♗b5 cxb2 just loses a piece after 13 ♖a2.

12 ♘xd4

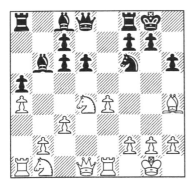

Now Black has two principal moves, both of which are probably sufficient for equality.

12...♖e8

Otherwise, 12...♗d7 also seems to be okay, for example 13 ♘d2 ♖e8 14 ♕f3 g5 15 ♗g3 h5! (an intended improvement on 15...♗g4 16 ♕d3 c5 17 ♘c2 d5 18 exd5 ♕xd5 19 ♕xd5 ♘xd5, Kaminski-Macieja, Warsaw 1991, where White could have kept an edge after 20 ♘a3; one could say that the

bishop on b6 doesn't inspire confidence!) 16 e5 dxe5 17 ♗xe5 (17 ♖xe5 is apparently inferior; 17...♖xe5 18 ♗xe5 ♘g4 19 ♗g3 h4 20 h3 hxg3 21 hxg4 gxf2+ 22 ♔xf2 ♗e6 23 ♕e4 ♕d5, with a better ending for Black in Dgebuadze-Macieja, Pardubice 1993) 17...♘g4 18 ♘c4 f6 19 ♗g3 h4 and Black has equalised according to Macieja.

13 ♘d2

A more prudent choice than 13 ♘xc6?!, when White comes under pressure after 13...♕d7 14 ♗xf6 ♕xc6 15 ♗d4 ♖b8 16 ♗xb6 ♖xb6 17 ♕c2 ♕b7 and it's difficult to imagine that White will be able to hold onto the pawn for long.

13...c5

Black had several weak points and White a firm hold of the centre after 13...g5 14 ♗g3 ♗xd4 15 cxd4 ♖b8 16 f3 ♗e6 17 b3 ♖b4 18 ♗f2, Spassky-Zuidema, Belgrade 1964.

14 ♘c2

Filip analyses 14 ♘4f3 ♗b7 15 ♕c2 (intending ♖ad1), as offering White an edge. This remains untested at a high level.

14...♗b7

In the more recent game Lanka-I.Sokolov, Batumi 1999, Black took the initiative with 14...g5 15 ♗g3 ♗b7 16 f3 d5 17 e5 (after 17 exd5 c4+ 18 ♗f2 ♗xf2+ 19 ♔xf2 Black has good play with 19...♕xd5, or even 19...♕d6!?) 17...♘h5 18 ♘f1 (18 ♗f2 f5 is unclear, according to Sokolov) 18...d4 19 ♘a3 ♕d5 20 c4 ♕c6. Black has the better of it despite his 'bishop' on b6. In fact the rest of his pieces are ready to spring into action and White has no real plan.

15 f4!?

A move that Piket considers to be an improvement on traditional theory. 15 f3 led to an interesting struggle in Ree-Knezevic, Kiev 1978, after 15...c4+ 16 ♘d4 g5 17 ♗f2 d5 18 exd5 ♕xd5 19 ♖xe8+ ♖xe8 20 ♕f1 g4! 21 ♘xc4 (21 ♕xc4?! is risky after 21...♕g5) 21...gxf3 22 ♘xb6 fxg2 23 ♘xd5 and a draw was agreed, as 23...gxf1♕+ 24 ♖xf1 ♘xd5 is equal.

15...c4+ 16 ♘d4

16 ♔h1 allows the freeing trick 16...♘xe4, as 17 ♗xd8? is then met by 17...♘f2+.

16...♖b8 17 ♖e3

Keeping the tension. Instead after 17 ♕c2 Piket intended to equalise as follows; 17...♕d7 18 ♗xf6 gxf6 19 ♘xc4 ♗xd4+ 20 cxd4 ♗xe4! 21 ♖xe4 ♖xe4 22 ♕xe4 d5.

17...♗a8 18 ♕c2

If 18 ♖b1 Black can generate enough counterplay with 18...♗xd4 19 cxd4 ♖b4.

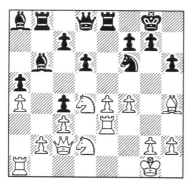

18...♘d5!

A queen sacrifice to liberate his position.

19 ♗xd8

White can refuse the offer with 19 ♖h3, but after 19...♘b4 20 ♕d1 ♗xd4+ 21 cxd4 ♕d7 Black is doing well. However, this is only because 22 ♗f6 is insufficient, Piket showing that after 22...gxf6 23 ♖xh6 ♔f8 24 ♕h5 ♘c2 25 ♖xf6 ♗xe4 26 ♘xe4 ♖xe4 27 ♕h8+ ♔e7 28 ♖xf7+ ♔xf7 29 ♕h7+ ♔f6 30 ♕xd7 ♘xa1 Black has a significant material advantage. Otherwise there is 22 ♖e3, but 22...d5 is comfortable for Black, who has a light square domination including the d3 outpost.

19...♘xe3 20 ♕b1 ♖bxd8 21 h3?!

Piket suggests instead 21 ♔f2, which could lead to an immediate repetition with 21...♘g4+ 22 ♔g1 ♘e3.

21...f5!

see following diagram

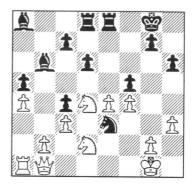

White is no longer able to keep the black horde at bay.

22 ♕a2

22 ♔f2 is now met by 22...♗xe4.

22...♗xe4 23 ♘xc4 ♗d5 24 b3 ♗xd4 25 cxd4 ♘xg2 26 ♕f2 ♖e6 27 ♘xa5 ♖de8 28 ♘c4 ♖g6 29 ♔h2 ♘xf4 30 ♖g1 ♖xg1 0-1

Game 23
Z.Almasi-Gulko
Pamplona 1996

1 e4 e5 2 ♘f3 ♘c6 3 ♗b5 ♘f6 4 0-0 ♗c5 5 c3 0-0 6 d4 ♗b6 7 ♗g5

If White tries the simplifying 7 ♗xc6 dxc6 8 ♘xe5 ♘xe4 9 ♖e1, as in Schmidt-O'Kelly, correspondence 1954, then 9...♘d6 gives equal chances, according to Keres.

A more important alternative is 7 ♖e1, when Black has two noteworthy replies: 7...exd4 and 7...d6.

a) 7...exd4 is the sharper try when 8 e5 (the 8 cxd4 d5 9 e5 ♘e4 10 ♘c3 ♗g4 of Unzicker-Fischer, Leipzig Olympiad 1960, led to a quick draw) 8...♘g4!? 9 h3 ♘xf2 10 ♔xf2 f6 is given as unclear by Keres. Black has only two pawns for the piece but White's king will remain exposed. Still, I have a feeling that it's not enough compensation.

b) 7...d6 is the more solid, when White has a choice between 8 h3 and 8 a4.

b1) 8 h3 ♘e7! (preparing an instructive

reorganisation) 9 ♘a3 (the naive 9 dxe5 dxe5 10 ♕xd8 ♖xd8 11 ♘xe5 is met successfully by 11...♘xe4 12 ♖xe4 ♖d1+) 9...c6 10 ♗f1 ♘g6 11 ♘c1 ♗c7 12 dxe5 dxe5 13 ♕c2 ♘h5, Robatsch-Van Geet, Beverwijk 1967, and Black has fine play.

2b) 8 a4 a5 9 ♘a3 exd4 10 cxd4 d5 (reacting in the centre only once the knight is decentralised) 11 e5 (after 11 exd5 then 11...♘b4!?) 11...♘e4 12 ♗xc6 bxc6 13 ♗e3 ♗g4 14 ♕c2 f5 (with ideas of ...f5-f4) 15 exf6 ♗xf3 16 gxf3 ♘xf6 17 ♕xc6, Rechmann-Winants, Belgium 1992, and now best is 17...♔h8, preparing ...♘h5. White has an extra pawn, but will be forced onto the defensive trying to hold everything intact.

7...h6 8 ♗h4 d6

9 ♗xc6

Aiming to leave Black with the inferior pawn structure in a static position where Black's bishops have little scope for active play. The mass exchanges following 9 a4 a5 10 ♗xc6 bxc6 11 dxe5 dxe5 12 ♕xd8 ♖xd8 13 ♖e1 ♗a6 gave no problems for Black in Sibarevic-Knezevic, Yugoslavia 1976. If instead 10 ♖e1 (which should probably be met by 10...exd4, the subject of game 22) 10...♗g4!? is risky but interesting. After 11 ♗xc6 bxc6 12 dxe5 dxe5 13 ♕xd8 ♖axd8 White has 14 ♘xe5 (grabbing a pawn as the bishop on g4 is hanging) 14...g5 15 ♗g3. Black doesn't seem to quite have enough compensation, for example:

a) 15...♘xe4 has been tried a few times by Ovod but without much success; 16 ♘xg4 f5 17 ♘a3 ♘xg3 18 ♘xh6+ ♔g7 19 hxg3 ♖d2 20 ♘c4 (or 20 ♖f1 ♖xb2 21 ♘c4 ♖b3 22 ♖fe1 ♔xh6 23 ♘xb6 ♖xb6 24 ♖e5, Aarthie-Ovod, Oropesa 1999, and again White has all the chances) 20...♗xf2+ 21 ♔f1 ♗e1 22 ♖xe1 ♖d3 23 ♖e6, Anand-Torre, Manila 1990, was slightly better for White.

b) 15...h5 16 ♘xc6 ♖de8 17 ♘d2! ♗d7 18 e5 ♘d5 19 c4, Re.Gonzalez-de la Paz, Santa Clara 1996, and now 19...♘f4 can be met by 20 c5, as suggested by Nogueiras, with an advantage to White.

9...bxc6 10 dxe5

Against the alternative 10 ♘bd2 Black should continue 10...exd4 11 ♘xd4 ♖e8, as in Game 22.

10...dxe5 11 ♘bd2 ♖e8

11...♗g4 was unsuccessful in Adams-Gulko, Hastings 1989/90, as after 12 ♕e2 g5 13 ♗g3 ♘d7 14 h3 ♗h5 15 ♕c4 ♔h7 16 ♕xc6 ♘c5 17 ♗xe5 f5 18 ♘d4 the complications clearly favoured White.

I prefer 11...♕d6! (unpinning without having to play the committal ...g5), when after 12 ♕a4 ♘d7 13 ♘c4 ♕e6 14 ♘fd2 ♘c5 15 ♕c2 ♗a6 16 b3 (Am.Rodriguez-Sariego, Bayamo 1991), despite the fact that White's knights were well installed, Black could challenge for equality with 16...♘b7! and on 17 ♖fe1, then 17...♘d6.

12 ♕c2!

The continuation 12 ♗g3 ♘d7 13 b4 ♕e7 14 ♘c4 f6 15 ♘fd2 ♕e6 was about equal in Hellers-Van der Wiel, Haninge 1990. The text move is more testing.

12...g5?!

Almasi prefers 12...♗g4, but after the simple 13 h3, Black still has to make a difficult decision. It's not ideal to play the text but it does release the pin.

13 ♗g3 ♘h5 14 c4!

14 ♗xe5? fails to 14...g4. The text threatens to put the bishop on b6 to the sword.

14...♘xg3 15 hxg3 ♕e7

Almasi proposes the manoeuvre 15...♗c5 16 ♘b3 ♗f8, as less damaging. In either case, however, the knights are superior to the bishops that are hemmed in by the characteristics of the pawn structure.

16 ♘b3 ♗c5 17 ♕c3 ♖b8 18 a3!

Heading for the a5-square with the queen, but first of all protecting the b4-square from any potential counterplay.

18...♗g4 19 ♘xc5 ♕xc5 20 b4 ♕d6 21 ♘h2!

Keeping the knight. An exchange of the last pair of minor pieces would ease the defensive task.

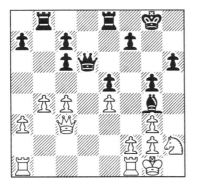

21...♗h5 22 g4 ♗g6 23 ♖fd1 ♕e7 24 f3 f6 25 ♕e3 a5!?

Tired of hanging around, Black tries to mix it.

26 bxa5 ♖a8 27 ♘f1 ♖xa5 28 ♖d3 ♗f7 29 ♕d2!

Hitting the rook and threatening invasion on d7.

29...♖aa8

Alternatively 29...♗xc4 30 ♕xa5 ♗xd3 31 ♘e3 would give White excellent play (c-file, a-pawn, f5-square) for a nigh on useless extra pawn.

30 ♘e3 ♖ed8 31 ♖xd8+ ♖xd8 32 ♕c3 ♗e6 33 a4 ♕c5 34 ♕a3!

A critical decision. The ending offers good chances due to the passed a-pawn.

34...♕xa3

34...♖d1+ is safely met by 35 ♔h2.

35 ♖xa3 ♗c8 36 ♔f2 ♖d2+?

Almasi suggests 36...♗a6 as more resistant.

37 ♔e1 ♖b2 38 ♖d3

According to Almasi 38 a5 ♗a6 39 ♖d3 would have won. Presumably the point is that after 39...♖a2 40 ♖d7 ♖xa5 41 ♖xc7 ♖c5 42 ♘d5!, all Black's pawns are under threat.

38...♔f7 39 ♖d8 ♗e6 40 ♖h8 ♔e7 41 c5!

The most precise, taking away d6 from the black king.

41...♖a2 42 ♖h7+! ♗f7 43 ♘f5+ ♔e6 44 ♘xh6 ♗e8 45 ♖xc7 ♗d7

Better than 45...♖xa4, because of 46 ♘g8 ♗d7 47 ♘xf6 ♔xf6 48 ♖xd7 winning easily.

46 ♘g8! ♖c2! 47 ♘xf6 ♔xf6 48 ♖xd7 ♖xc5

An instructive moment. The rook should go behind the passed pawn.

49 ♔d2?

Not good, nor for that matter is 49 ♖a7, because of 49...♖c2 with an active rook, but 49 ♖d2! is the key move, when after 49...♖c1+ 50 ♖d1 ♖c2 51 ♖a1 ♖xg2 52 ♖a3 White holds everything together and forces Black backwards. Then it's just a question of bringing up the king; 52...♖h2 53 a5 ♖h7 54 a6 ♖a7 55 ♔d2 ♔e6 56 ♔c3 ♔d6 57 ♔c4 and it's already zugzwang.

49...♖a5

Now Black should probably hold!

50 Rd6+ Kf7 51 Rxc6 Rxa4 52 Kd3
Rd4+ 53 Kc3 Ra4 54 Rb6 Rd4 55 Rb7+
Kf6 56 Rb6+ Kf7 57 Rb2 Ke6 58 Rc2
Rd1 59 Kc4 Rd4+ 60 Kc5 Rd1 61 Kc6
Rd6+ 62 Kc7 Rd7+ 63 Kc8 Rd6 64
Rb2 Rd1 65 Rb6+ Kf7 66 Rb7+ Ke6?

A mistake. Almasi points out a miraculous
defence starting with 66...Kf6! 67 Rd7 and
now not 67...Rg1? 68 Kd8 Rxg2 69 Ke8
Ra2 70 Rf7+ Ke6 (or 70...Kg6 71 Rf5 and
the e-pawn will soon fall) 71 Kf8! coming
round the back, but 67...Ra1! 68 Kd8 (68
Rd8 can be frustrated by 68...Kf7! stopping
the rook infiltrating to f5) 68...Ra8+, stopping
any progress whatsoever. Remarkable, but
because White cannot invade the two extra
pawns are insufficient to win!
67 Rg7 Kf6 68 Rg8 Rd2 69 Rf8+ Ke7
70 Rf5 Rc2+ 71 Kb7 Ke6 72 Rxg5
Rxg2 73 Kc7 Rd2 74 Kc6 Rc2+ 75 Kb5
Rc1 76 Rf5 Rc2 77 Kb4 Rc1 78 Kb3
Rc6 79 Kb2 Rc8 80 g5

80...Rh8
After 80...Rc7 Almasi intended 81 g6 Rg7
82 Rg5 Kf6 83 Rg4 Rxg6 84 Rxg6+ Kxg6
85 Kb3 Kf6 86 Kc4 Ke6 87 Kc5 etc.
81 Kc2 Rh2+ 82 Kd1 Ra2 83 Ke1 Rb2
84 Kf1 Ra2 85 Rf6+ Ke7 86 Rb6 Kf7
87 g6+ Kg7 88 Re6 Rb2 89 Rxe5 Kxg6
90 Ke1 Kf6 91 Rd5 Ra2 92 Rd2 Ra1+
93 Kf2 1-0
The two connected passed pawns will lead
to an easy win.

1 e4 e5 2 Nf3 Nc6 3 Bb5 Nf6 4 0-0
Bc5 5 c3 0-0 6 d4 Bb6 7 Qd3
Or 7 Bg5 h6 8 Bh4 d6 9 Qd3, which
transposes.

7...d6
Here Short has tried an interesting gambit
starting with 7...d5!?, when 8 Bxc6 bxc6 9
Nxe5 Nxe4 10 Nd2 (better than 10 Nxc6,
which allows useful counterplay with
10...Qd6 11 Ne5 c5) 10...Bf5 11 Qf3 Qf6
12 Nxc6 (Ehlvest suggests 12 Nxe4 dxe4 13
Qf4, judging it as edge to White) 12...Rae8
gave unclear play in Ehlvest-Short, Belgrade
1989, Black having sufficient activity for the
pawn. Perhaps 7...d5 is worth investigating
further, but note that White can avoid this
possibility by playing the 7 Bg5 move order.
8 Bg5 h6 9 Bh4 Bd7
After 9...Qe7!? 10 Nbd2, Suetin-Karasev,
USSR 1963, Black instigated an instructive
knight manoeuvre; 10...Nb8 11 Rfe1 c6 12
Bc4 Rd8 13 Nf1 Nbd7 14 Qc2 Nf8 15
Ne3 Ng6 and obtained a satisfactory position.
10 Nbd2 a6
10...exd4 should be compared with game
22, when White will capture on c6 and then
on d4 with the knight.

11 ♗c4

Simplifying with 11 ♗xc6 ♗xc6 12 dxe5 dxe5 13 ♕xd8 ♖axd8 leads nowhere for White.

11...exd4 12 cxd4 g5!?

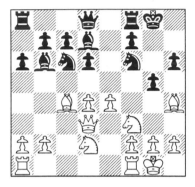

Highly provocative! Capturing on g5 is tempting and was indeed tested in a couple of Topalov-Leko encounters. Play continues with 13 ♘xg5!? hxg5 14 ♗xg5 ♔g7! (14...♗xd4?! is bad because of 15 e5 ♗xe5 16 ♕g6+ ♔h8 17 ♕h6+ ♔g8 18 ♘e4 and 14...♘xd4?!, Arnold-Wernelt, Bundesliga 1998, looks dubious after 15 ♕g3! as 15...♘h5? is then refuted by 16 ♕h4) and in this position White has several tries:

a) 15 ♕g3 is met by 15...♘h5! 16 ♕h4 f6! and Black is on top.

b) 15 ♘f3!? (Leko) requires testing.

c) 15 e5 dxe5 16 ♘e4, looks dangerous, but Svidler points out the defence: 16...♗f5! 17 dxe5 ♘xe4! 18 ♗xd8 ♖axd8 19 ♕f3 ♗g6, when three well-installed pieces should be worth more than a queen, especially as Black is ready to take the initiative.

d) The two encounters both continued with 15 ♘b3 when 15...♘e7 seems fine for Black: 16 ♗xf6+ (16 ♖ae1 ♘h7 17 ♗h4 f6, turned out badly for White in Topalov-Leko, Frankfurt {rapidplay} 1999) 16...♔xf6 17 f4 (Leko suggests 17 ♕g3 as an improvement) 17...♗e6!

see following diagram

and Black defended and went on to win in Topalov-Leko, Dortmund 1999. In any case, anyone intending to try this line with either colour should look very closely at these complications, which at present have come out in Black's favour.

13 ♗g3

13 e5 is safely met by 13...d5!, for instance 14 ♗b3 gxh4 15 exf6 ♕xf6 16 ♗xd5 ♘xd4 when Black is better.

13...♘h5 14 e5!? ♔g7 15 exd6 ♘xg3 16 dxc7 ♕xc7

After 16...♘e2+ 17 ♕xe2 ♕xc7 then 18 d5 is annoying.

17 fxg3!?

A sharp try, opening the f-file at the risk of compromising his pawns. Instead 17 hxg3 g4 18 ♘e5 ♘xd4 19 ♘xd7 ♕xd7 is given by Svidler as being only equal.

17...g4! 18 ♘h4 ♘e5!

Exploiting the pin on the a7-g1 diagonal, another problem with 17 fxg3.

19 ♘f5+

19 ♕c3 ♖ac8 20 ♖ac1 ♕d6 gives Black, if anything, slightly the better of it.

19...♗xf5 20 ♕xf5 ♗xd4+ 21 ♔h1 ♕d6 22 ♖ae1

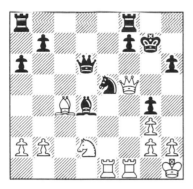

Black has the most exposed king and has to play precisely.

22...♖ad8?

Not good and in fact 22...♗xb2? is no better, failing to 23 ♗b3 ♕xd2 24 ♖xe5! ♗xe5 25 ♗c2. However, after 22...♖ae8! 23 ♘e4 ♕g6 24 ♘f6 ♕xf5! 25 ♖xf5 (or 25 ♘xe8+ ♔g6 26 ♖xf5 ♔xf5) 25...♖c8 26 ♗e2 the position is evenly balanced.

23 ♗b3!

This bishop is aiming to come to c2, creating serious threats on the diagonal.

23...♗xb2 24 ♘c4 ♘xc4 25 ♕xg4+ ♕g6?

Svidler feels that 25...♔h8 was the lesser evil, but even so, with such holes on the light squares Black has serious problems.

26 ♕xc4 b5 27 ♕b4 ♖c8 28 ♖e3! ♕g5 29 ♕d2 ♗f6 30 h4 ♕c5 31 ♖e4

A good illustration of the attacking potential of opposite bishops, in a middlegame, against an exposed king. The weak kingside light squares are indefensible.

31...h5 32 ♖ef4 ♖c6 33 ♖f5 ♕c3 34 ♕f4 ♖d8 35 ♖xh5 ♕d2 36 ♕g4+ ♔f8 37 ♖h8+ ♔e7

37...♔xh8 allows a drastic finish; 38 ♖xf7+ ♔e8 39 ♕g8 mate.

38 ♖h7 ♖f8 39 ♕e4+ ♔d7 40 ♗xf7 1-0

Game 25
Smirin-Weinstein
Israeli Championship 1992

1 e4 e5 2 ♘f3 ♘c6 3 ♗b5 ♗c5 4 0-0 ♘f6 5 c3 0-0

Here 5...♘xe4?! is dubious, for instance 6 ♕e2 f5 7 d3 ♘f6 8 d4 ♗e7 9 dxe5 ♘e4 10 ♘bd2 with a nice edge to White, Evans-Weinberger, USA Championship 1963.

6 d4 ♗b6 7 dxe5

Capturing on e5 before Black can reinforce his centre with ...d7-d6.

7...♘xe4 8 ♕d5

Stopping the freeing ...d5 break. Instead 8 ♗d3 d5 9 exd6 ♘xd6 10 ♗g5 f6 11 ♗f4 ♗g4, Bronstein-Spassky, Mar del Plata 1960, was fine for Black despite the slight concession in being forced to play ...f7-f6.

8...♘c5

9 ♗g5

After 9 b4 Black should play 9...♘e7 10 ♕d1 ♘e4 11 ♗d3 d5, achieving the freeing break. In the case of 9 ♘a3 Tolush suggests 9...a6 10 ♗e2 ♘e7 11 ♕d1 ♘e6 with equality. This was tested in D.Gross-Karolyi, Bundesliga 1998/9, which continued 12 ♘c4 ♗a7 13 ♗d3 b5 14 ♘e3 d5 15 exd6 ♕xd6 and Tolush's judgement was vindicated.

9...♘e7

After 9...♕e8 10 ♖e1 a6 11 ♗f1 ♕e6 12 ♕d1 ♕g6 13 ♗h4 White had some pressure in Shetty-Neelakantan, Calcutta 1994. If Black ever plays ...d5 White captures en passant and Black will end up with an isolani.

10 ♕d1 ♘e4 11 ♗h4

Best, retaining the pin. Inferior is 11 ♗f4 as after 11...d5 12 ♘bd2 (12 exd6 is met by 12...♘g6!) 12...c6 13 ♗d3 ♗f5 14 ♕c2 ♘xd2 15 ♗xf5 (in Polugaevsky-Boleslavsky, USSR 1963, Black took the rook and White had good compensation) Black has 15...♘xf3+ 16 gxf3 ♘xf5. Compared to the game continuation, Black's defence is eased without the pin on the e7-knight.

11...d5 12 ♘bd2

White also has 12 c4!?, as in Gi.Hernandez-Sariego, Havana 1991, to which Black replied with 12...c6. The game continued 13 ♗a4 ♗g4 (13...♗e6!?) 14 cxd5 cxd5 15 ♘c3 g5 (15...♘xc3 16 bxc3 ♕c7 or 15...♗xf3!? both look reasonable) 16 ♗g3 ♘xg3 17 hxg3 h6 leading to an unclear position. Black had several reasonable alternatives in this, so 12 c4 looks interesting, but weaker than the game continuation.

12...c6 13 ♗d3 ♗f5

In the game Bronstein-O'Kelly, Hastings 1953/4, White had a strong initiative after 13...f5 14 exf6 ♘xf6 15 ♕c2 g6 16 ♖ae1.

14 ♕c2 ♘xd2 15 ♗xf5

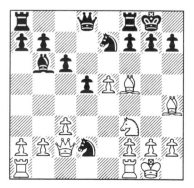

15...♘xf3+

15...♘xf1 wins material, but is not a good practical choice: 16 ♗xh7+ ♔h8 17 ♖xf1 ♕d7 18 ♖e1 ♕e6 19 ♗d3 ♖ae8 20 ♗g5 only yields one pawn for the exchange but Keres prefers White, who is more active. Black, it should be noted, has no counterplay and under-performing rooks.

16 gxf3 ♔h8

So that if White captures on h7 then the bishop will be trapped with ...g7-g6.

17 f4

More testing than 17 ♖ae1 ♕c7 18 ♗h3 ♖ae8 19 f4 f5 20 exf6 ♘g6!, which gave Black a fine position in Geller-Spassky, USSR 1962.

17...♕c7 18 ♔h1!

Keeping the bishop on f5, as otherwise after 18 ♗h3 Spassky's idea of 18...f5! 19 exf6 ♘g6 yields good counterplay.

18...♘xf5

Perhaps Black should consider 18...f6! at once (Flear), for example 19 ♗xh7 (19 exf6 ♘xf5 20 ♕xf5 g6 is okay for Black) 19...fxe5 20 fxe5 ♕xe5! 21 ♖ae1 ♕h5 22 ♗xe7 (not 22 ♖xe7?? as 22...♕xh4 gives Black a handy fork) 22...♕f3+ 23 ♔g1 ♕g4+, drawing immediately.

19 ♕xf5 f6!?

White is considered to be a little better, but if his initiative falters then Black would have the better pawn structure. An alternative is 19...♖ae8, but White then has tricks based on ♗f6, hence the choice in the game.

20 e6

20 exf6? would be met by 20...g6, leaving White with ugly tripled pawns.

20...♗c5

The bishop will be used to blockade the passed pawn and support the f6-square.

21 ♖g1 ♖g8 22 ♖ad1 ♗e7 23 ♖d3 g6

23...♖af8? would lose prettily to 24 ♖h3 g6 25 ♖xg6! ♖xg6 26 ♕xg6 hxg6 27 ♗xf6+ ♔g8 28 ♖h8 mate.

24 ♗xf6+ ♗xf6 25 ♕xf6+

So White wins a pawn, but Black has, to some extent, freed his position.

25...♕g7 26 ♕g5 ♖gf8 27 c4 ♖ae8

27...dxc4? allows the decisive invasion 28 ♖d7.

28 cxd5 cxd5 29 ♕xd5 ♖xf4 30 ♕c5?!

30 ♕d7!? would have retained winning chances, according to Weinstein.

30...♕f6! 31 ♖d7 ♕xe6 32 ♕c3+ ♕f6 33 ♖xb7 ♕xc3 34 bxc3 ♖xf2 35 ♖xa7

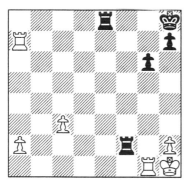

35...♖ee2 36 ♖d1 ♖xh2+ ½-½

Black has a draw by perpetual check but playing on with 36...♖xh2+ 37 ♔g1 ♖eg2+ 38 ♔f1 ♖d2 (but certainly not 38...♖xa2?? 39 ♖d8 mate) 39 ♖xd2 ♖xd2 40 a4 looks risky.

7 dxe5 is much less fashionable than 7 ♗g5, which suggests that White's edge here is insignificant or even non-existent (see the note to Black's 18th move).

> # Game 26
> ## Romero-Braga
> *Leon 1990*

1 e4 e5 2 ♘f3 ♘c6 3 ♗b5 ♘f6 4 0-0 ♗c5 5 ♘xe5 ♘xe5?!

How can such a natural move be dubious? In fact experience suggests that Black should prefer the alternative capture, 5...♘xe4, which has a solid reputation (see Game 27).

6 d4 c6

The alternative is 6...a6, when 7 ♗e2 ♗e7 (or 7...♗a7 8 dxe5 ♘xe4 9 ♕d5 ♘c5 10 ♗e3 with a clear advantage to White according to Pavlovic) 8 dxe5 ♘xe4 9 ♗f3! ♘c5 10 ♗f4

0-0 11 ♘c3 c6 12 ♖e1 (Kotronious-Co.Ionescu, Mangalia 1992) 12...f5 13 exf6 ♖xf6 14 ♗e5 gives slightly freer play for White.

7 f4!?

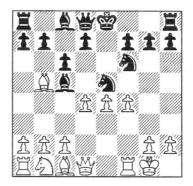

Very aggressive but not really necessary. White can keep an opening advantage without resorting to such violent means with 7 dxe5 ♘xe4 8 ♗d3. Experience has shown that Black cannot fully equalise:

a) 8...♘g5 9 ♘c3 d5 10 exd6 ♗xd6 (Velimirovic-Parma, Yugoslav Championship 1963) and after 11 ♖e1+ ♗e6 12 ♕h5 White has a useful initiative and the knight is very clumsily placed on g5 (analysis by Keres).

b) 8...d5 9 exd6 ♘f6 10 ♖e1+ ♗e6 11 ♘c3 ♕xd6 12 ♕f3 0-0! (12...0-0-0? 13 ♗f5 ♕d7 14 ♗xe6 fxe6 15 ♗e3 and White forces the win of either the black a- or e-pawn, Fedorowicz-Kaidanov, USA Championship 1993) 13 ♗f4 with an edge to White according to Kaidanov.

White also has the natural 7 ♗e2 but this is not so clear: 7...♗b6 8 dxe5 ♘xe4 9 ♘c3!? (ambitious, but Beliavsky wasn't keen on 9 ♗f4 d5 10 exd6 ♕f6 when Black has good play, while the routine 9 ♘d2 can be safely met by 9...d5) 9...d5 (Black could have tried 9...♘xc3 10 bxc3 ♗c5, intending ...d7-d5 and ...0-0 and White may live to regret his broken pawn-structure) 10 exd6 ♘xd6 11 ♗f4 ♘f5 12 ♕xd8+ ♗xd8 13 ♘e4 0-0 14 ♖ad1 ♗b6 15 ♗c4 with a nagging edge to White in Beliavsky-M.Gurevich, Groningen 1992, as Black cannot develop harmoniously.

7...♛b6

The main point of White's piece sacrifice can be seen in the line 7...♘g6 8 dxc5 cxb5 9 e5 ♘e4 10 ♛e2! ♘xc5 11 f5, with a strong initiative as compensation.

If instead 7...cxb5, then 8 fxe5 looks promising for White.

8 dxc5 ♛xc5+ 9 ♔h1 ♘eg4!?

Romero gives the line 9...♘xe4 10 fxe5 ♛xb5 11 ♘d2!? ♘xd2 12 ♗xd2 0-0 13 ♗c3 d5 14 ♛h5!? ♛c4 15 e6 ♗xe6 16 ♗xg7!, but I don't think that this is worth more than a draw by perpetual check after 16...♔xg7 17 ♛g5+ ♔h8 etc. Instead 14 exd6 must give White an edge; the passed pawn on d6 will prove annoying for Black.

10 e5! ♘f2+?

10...♘e4!? may be an improvement: 11 ♛xg4 ♛xb5 (11...♘f2+? 12 ♖xf2 ♛xf2 13 ♛e2 leaves White with two pieces for a sleeping rook) 12 ♛f3 with a lead in development for White but nothing catastrophic for Black. Romero suggests an alternative 10...♛xb5 as the best try, when the continuation 11 ♘c3 ♛c4 12 exf6 ♘xf6 13 ♖e1+ ♔d8 14 ♛d6 ♖e8 15 ♗e3 leads to White having pressure and a bind for the pawn, which he judges as slightly better for White.

11 ♖xf2 ♛xf2 12 exf6 cxb5 13 ♘c3

Black has the material advantage of the exchange. However his undeveloped pieces are of little help in defending his king and he is already in serious danger.

13...d5

see following diagram

The only hope was to seek relative safety by castling, but after 13...0-0 14 ♘d5 ♖e8 15 ♘e7+ ♔f8 16 ♗d2 Romero prefers White's attacking chances. He has a good point as following the plausible defence 16...gxf6 17 ♗b4 d6 18 ♛xd6 ♗e6 White crashes through in style with 19 ♘d5+ ♔g7 20 ♘xf6!.

14 ♗e3!

A strong move gaining time. If Black now takes the piece with 14...♛xe3, then after 15 ♘xd5, Black cannot cope with the threats.

14...♛h4 15 fxg7 ♖g8 16 ♘xd5 ♖xg7

After 16...♛d8, then 17 ♛d4, and Black is faced with ♘f6+.

17 ♘c7+ ♔f8

17...♗e7 loses the queen to 18 ♗c5+ ♔f6 19 ♛d8+.

18 ♛d6+ ♔g8 19 ♗f2! 1-0

A neat finish. Mate can be avoided with 19...♖g6, but playing on after 20 ♛xg6+ hxg6 21 ♗xh4 is pointless.

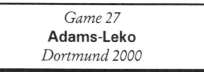

Game 27
Adams-Leko
Dortmund 2000

1 e4 e5 2 ♘f3 ♘c6 3 ♗b5 ♘f6 4 0-0

♗c5 5 ♘xe5 ♘xe4

This alternative to 5...♘xe5 (game 26) offers a fairly good chance of equalising.

6 ♕e2

The standard move, noting that 6 ♕g4 comes to the same thing after 6...♘xe5 7 ♕xe4.

The cheeky pawn grab 6 ♘xf7!?, is not favoured by theory as it helps Black take the lead in development after 6...♔xf7 7 ♕h5+ g6 8 ♕d5+ ♔g7 9 ♕xe4 d5 10 ♕a4 ♖f8!? (alternatives 10...♘d4, 10...♗d7, 10...♕d6 and 10...♕f6 are all reasonable enough) according to Keres and F.Olafsson, but White could then try and snatch a second pawn and hope to defend. Does Black have enough activity for his pawns? A question of taste in my opinion, but note that the world's top players avoid 6 ♘xf7, so they obviously believe Keres and Olafsson's analysis.

6...♘xe5 7 ♕xe4

White also has 7 d4, but following 7...♗e7 (7...♕e7!? probably transposes to the next note) 8 dxe5 ♘c5 9 ♖d1 c6 10 ♗c4 b5! (the elimination of the opposing light-squared bishop enables Black to play for the freeing ...f6) 11 ♗b3 0-0 12 ♘c3 ♘xb3 13 axb3 f6 14 exf6 ♗xf6 15 ♘e4 ♗e5, Matulovic-Knezevic, Yugoslavia Championship 1978, the players agreed to a draw in a rich position with chances for both sides.

7...♕e7 8 ♘c3

Less dangerous for Black is 8 d4 ♘c6 9

♕xe7+ (White can avoid the rather dull exchange of queens with 9 ♕g4, but not without risk as 9...h5! 10 ♕xg7 ♗xd4 11 ♕g3 ♗e5 12 ♕e3 ♘d4 13 ♗d3, Mikhalchishin-Legky, USSR 1978, followed by 13...d6 14 ♖e1 ♔f8 is unclear according to Mikhalchishin; Black's well centralised pieces mean that his king is not really exposed) 9...♗xe7 10 c3 a6 11 ♗d3 d6 12 ♖e1 ♗e6 13 f4 0-0 14 f5 ♗d7 15 ♗f4 ♖ae8 16 ♘d2 ♗d8 with an equal position in the game Kotronias-Skembris, Istanbul 1988.

8...♘g6 9 ♕xe7+

Another queen exchange with symmetrical pawns. This shouldn't be dismissed as simply drawish as White has a small lead in development. Indeed, accurate defence is required by Black.

Black has three captures and all have been played.

9...♘xe7!

Black's king tends to get in the way of everything else after 9...♔xe7, for instance 10 ♘e4 ♗b6 11 b3 a6 12 ♗c4 ♘e5 13 ♗b2 d6 14 ♖fe1 ♔f8 15 ♗d5, Marjanovic-V.Stoica, Kirovakan 1978, and Black is all tangled up.

9...♗xe7 doesn't equalise either: 10 ♘d5 ♗d6 11 ♖e1+ ♔d8 12 ♘e3 ♖e8 (or 12...♗e5 13 ♗c4 ♖f8 14 c3, Hulak-Knezevic, Yugoslavia Championship 1978, and now 14...d6 15 d4 ♗f4 {Keres and F.Olafsson} keeps White's edge in check) 13 ♗c4 ♖e7 14 d4 ♗f4 15 g3 ♗xe3 16 ♗xe3 d6 17 h4! (gaining space by harassing the knight) 17...h6 18 h5 ♘f8 19 f3 ♗f5 20 c3, Grünfeld-Salov, Haifa 1989, and White can use his bishop pair and slight space advantage to massage the position.

10 ♘e4 ♗b6 11 ♖e1 0-0

Leko's idea is that by castling he links his rooks and thus doesn't drop behind in development. Again after 11...♔f8 Black falls behind in development and following 12 b4 d5 13 ♘c5 c6 14 ♗d3 f6 15 ♗a3 ♔f7 16 b5 White had a persistent initiative, Howell-Macieja, Hastings 1990/1.

12 ♘d6

12 ♘f6+ 'damages' the Black pawns, but after say 12...gxf6 13 ♖xe7 ♗c5! (less precise is 13...c6 14 ♗f1 d5 15 d3 ♗c5 16 ♖e1 ♗d7 17 c3 ♖fe8 18 ♗e3 ♗xe3 19 ♖xe3 ♖e5, Howell-Bjornsson, Hafnarfirdi 1992, when White had a tiny edge but wasn't able to convert it into a win) 14 ♖e1 d5 15 d3 c6 16 ♗a4 ♗f5 17 ♗e3 ♗b6, Black has no problems to develop and the doubled f-pawns cannot be seriously put under pressure.

12...♘c6 13 ♘xc8 ♖axc8

So White has the bishop pair, but here Black has an advantage in development and Adams finds it hard to create any concrete

threats.

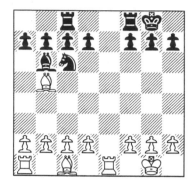

14 c3 ♖fe8 15 ♖xe8+ ♖xe8 16 ♔f1 ♘b8

Preparing to create a solid centre with ...c7-c6 and ...d7-d5.

17 d4 c6 18 ♗d3 ♗c7 19 a4 d5 20 a5 a6 21 ♗d2 ♘d7 22 g3 g6 23 b3 ♘f8 24 ♔g2 ♘e6 25 b4 f5 26 f4 ♔f7 27 ♔f3 ♔f6 28 ♖e1 ♗d6 29 h3 h5 30 ♖h1 ♖h8 31 ♖e1 ♖e8 32 ♖h1 ½-½

A very solid performance by Leko.

It looks as if capturing with the knight on e7 and quick castling gives Black a solid game. The inconvenience for Black is that creating winning chances may prove problematic.

Summary

The Classical Berlin is quite sound. After 5 ♘xe5 Black should play 5...♘xe4 which seems to lead to a playable, but dull ending. More interesting is 5 c3 but the main lines don't seem to offer White anything tangible and Black obtains good counterchances.

If you really want to play this hybrid variation then I recommend the Berlin move-order as 3...♗c5 is often met by 4 c3, whereas 3...♘f6 is almost always met by 4 0-0.

1 e4 e5 2 ♘f3 ♘c6 3 ♗b5 ♗c5 (3...♘f6 4 0-0 ♗c5) 4 0-0 ♘f6 5 c3
     5 ♘xe5 *(D)*
          5...♘xe5 – *Game 26*
          5...♘xe4 6 ♕e2 ♘xe5 7 ♕xe4 ♕e7 8 ♘c3 ♘g6 9 ♕xe7+ – *Game 27*
5...0-0 6 d4 ♗b6 *(D)* 7 ♗g5
     7 dxe5 ♘xe4 8 ♕d5 – *Game 25*
     7 ♕d3 d6 8 ♗g5 h6 9 ♗h4 ♗d7 10 ♘bd2 a6 11 ♗c4 – *Game 24*
7...h6 8 ♗h4 d6 *(D)* 9 a4
     9 ♗xc6 bxc6 10 dxe5 – *Game 23*
9...a5 10 ♖e1 exd4 11 ♗xc6 bxc6 12 ♘xd4 ♖e8 13 ♘d2 c5 – *Game 22*

    5 ♘xe5   *6...♗b6*   *8...d6*

CHAPTER FOUR

The Classical Defence

1 e4 e5 2 ♘f3 ♘c6 3 ♗b5 ♗c5

The move 3...♗c5 is a sensible developing move, but Black has yet to show his hand. White's logical plan is to react with 0-0 and c3 followed by d4, building a centre and hitting the bishop.

It's generally Black's fourth-move choice that sets the tone for the later stages. After 4 0-0 ♘d4, the exchange of a pair of knights quietens things down, whereas 4 0-0 ♕f6!? fishes in troubled waters, or 4...d6 5 c3 ♗d7 6 d4 ♗b6 7 ♗g5 f6 bolsters the central dark-squares.

After 4 c3, the Cordel Gambit with 4...f5 throws caution to the wind, 4...♘ge7 aims for ...d5, whereas 4...♘f6 tries to counter White's pawn centre with piece play.

So the Classical is a 'variation for all seasons', that is readily adaptable to counter your opponent's style.

Game 28
Short-Kamsky
Linares 1994

1 e4 e5 2 ♘f3 ♘c6 3 ♗b5 ♗c5 4 c3

For 4 0-0 see Games 31-33.

4...♘f6

This is the most solid and probably strongest continuation (for alternatives see

Games 29-30).

Now if 5 d3, play is analogous to d3-systems in the Italian, except that the bishop is on b5 rather than on c4 (see Game 21 for another early d3). Then a possible continuation is 5...d6 6 0-0 0-0 7 a4 a5 8 ♗g5 h6 9 ♗h4 ♕e7 10 ♕c1 ♗g4 11 ♘bd2 g5 12 ♗g3 ♘h5 13 ♗xc6 bxc6 14 d4 ♗b6 15 dxe5 ♘xg3 16 hxg3 dxe5, Vujovic-Godena, Formia 1994, and Black was okay.

5 d4

After 5 0-0 0-0 (5...♘xe4 should be met by 6 ♕e2 f5 7 d3 ♘f6 8 d4 ♗e7 9 dxe5 ♘e4 10 ♘bd2 with a clear advantage for White, Evans-Weinberger, USA Championship 1963) 6 b4!? (6 d4 transposes to Chapter Three, Games 22-25) is sharp, forcing the bishop to pick it's diagonal. Then 6...♗b6 (6...♗e7!?) 7 d3 ♖e8 (how about 7...♕e7!? 8 ♗g5 ♘d8, with ideas such as ...♘e6 or ...c7-c6 in the air) 8 ♗g5 a5 9 bxa5 ♗xa5 10 ♕c2, Barnes-Walker, Birmingham 1999, led to an interesting position.

5...exd4

A major alternative is 5...♗b6 when White has four main tries:

a) 6 ♗g5 h6 7 ♗xf6 ♕xf6 8 0-0 0-0 9 ♗xc6 ♕xc6 10 ♘xe5 ♕xe4 11 ♘d2 ♕f5 12 ♘dc4 d6 13 ♘e3 ♕e6 14 ♘5c4 d5 15 ♘xb6 axb6, Havlicek-Dückstein, Vienna 1998, was about equal.

b) 6 ♕e2 exd4 7 e5 0-0 8 cxd4 ♖e8 9 ♗e3 ♘g4 10 ♘c3 d6 11 0-0-0 ♘xe3 12 fxe3 ♗d7 13 ♖hf1 dxe5 14 ♗c4 ♖f8 (14...exd4 is too risky after 15 ♗xf7+ ♔xf7 16 ♘g5+ ♔g6 17 h4, S.Salov-Perov, correspondence 1994) 15 ♘xe5 ♘xe5 16 dxe5 ♕e8 with interesting complications (Van der Wiel).

c) 6 ♗xc6 dxc6 7 ♘xe5 0-0 8 ♗g5 ♕e8 9 ♕f3 can be met by 9...♘xe4! 10 ♕xe4 f6, as in Chandler-Gulko, Amsterdam 1989.

d) 6 ♘xe5!? leads to unclear complications: 6...♘xe5 7 dxe5 ♘xe4 8 ♕g4 ♗xf2+ and now:

d1) 9 ♔e2 ♕h4 10 ♕xg7 ♖f8 11 ♘d2 ♗c5!? (11...♘xd2 12 ♗xd2 ♗c5 13 ♖hf1 c6 14 ♗d3 d6 15 ♗h6 ♗g4+ 16 ♔d2 0-0-0 17 ♖f4 ♖g8 18 ♕f6, Short-Gulko, Linares 1989, left White with an edge) 12 ♘f3 ♕f2+ 13 ♔d1 ♗e7 14 ♖e1 ♕b6 was Beliavsky-Ivanchuk, Linares 1989. Now instead of the game continuation 15 ♖xe4 ♕xb5 16 c4 ♕c6 17 ♕xh7 d5 18 exd6 ♕xd6+ 19 ♖d4 ♕b6 20 ♕e4 ♖g8, when Black took over the initiative, Beliavsky recommends 15 ♗c4 ♕c6 16 ♗b3 d5 17 exd6 ♕xd6+ 18 ♕d4, giving it as unclear.

d2) 9 ♔d1!? may be best, as I like White after 9...♕h4 10 ♕xg7 ♖f8 11 ♘d2 ♗c5 12 ♘xe4 ♕xe4 13 ♖e1 ♕g6 14 ♕f6 ♗e7 15 ♕f3, as in Renet-Godena, Asiago 1994. The book suggests 'unclear', but this line was deeply analysed by Renet and the other members of the Clichy team and we concluded that White was better.

6 e5

Clearly better than 6 cxd4, after which 6...♗b4+ 7 ♗d2 ♘xe4! 8 0-0 0-0 9 d5 ♘xd2 10 ♘bxd2 ♘e7 11 a3 ♗xd2 12 ♕xd2 d6 (12...♘xd5! is even stronger) didn't look enough for the pawn, Baburek-Bojanic, Pula 1999.

6...♘e4

7 cxd4

7 0-0 is probably not as good as once thought, largely due to the third of Black's alternatives:

a) 7...0-0 8 cxd4 ♗b6 9 d5 ♘e7 10 ♗d3 f5 11 ♘bd2 ♘c5 12 d6! proved strong for White in Smyslov-Randvir, USSR 1947.

b) 7...d5 8 ♘xd4 0-0 9 f3 (or 9 ♗xc6 bxc6 10 f3 ♘g5 11 ♗e3 f6 12 ♔h1 ♗xd4 13 ♗xd4 fxe5 14 ♗xe5 ♗a6, Gligoric-Fischer, Buenos Aires 1960, was about equal) 9...♘g5 10 ♗e3 ♘e6 (Keres's 10...f6 is more active) 11 f4 f6 12 ♔h1 ♗xd4 13 cxd4 fxe5 14 dxe5 d4 15 ♗c1 gave a strong initiative for White in Nezhmetdinov-Valentinov, USSR 1963.

c) 7...a6! (Sokolov revitalises the line with some deep preparation) 8 ♗a4 dxc3 9 ♕d5 cxb2 10 ♗xb2 ♗xf2+ 11 ♔h1 ♘c5 12 e6 ♘xe6 (12...♘xa4 also looks promising; 13 ♗xg7 dxe6 14 ♕xd8+ ♘xd8 15 ♗xh8 ♗b6 and Black is better) 13 ♖xf2 0-0 14 ♘bd2 ♘e7 15 ♕h5 (Black has four pawns for the piece and although is behind in development,

it's not for long) 15...♘g6 16 ♗b3 ♘ef4 17
♕f5 d5 18 ♕c2 b6 19 ♘e5 c5 20 ♘xg6
♘xg6 21 ♖af1 ♗e6 22 ♘f3 f6 23 ♕d2 ♕d7
24 ♖e1 ♗f7 (Black is rock-solid) 25 ♖fe2 d4
26 ♖e4 ♖ae8 27 h4 ♖xe4 28 ♖xe4 ♗xb3 29
axb3 (exchanges have left White's remaining
pieces impotent as Black takes over the initiative) 29...♕d5 30 ♕c2 ♘e5 31 ♘d2 h5 32
♕d1 ♘d3 33 ♔g1 ♕f5 34 ♕b1 ♕f2+ 0-1
Wemmers-I.Sokolov, Amsterdam 2000.

Worth investigating is 7 ♕e2!?, when after
7...d5 (Ljublinsky-Karasev, USSR 1965) Hab-
erditz analyses 8 exd6 0-0 9 dxc7 ♕d5 10
♗c4, preferring White slightly. Taking this
further, 10...♕d7 11 0-0 ♘d6 12 ♗d3 dxc3
13 ♘xc3 ♕xc7 14 ♗f4 leaves White with the
freer piece play, so I have to agree with Hab-
erditz.

7...♗b4+ 8 ♘bd2 0-0 9 0-0 d5!

Black already has a healthy-looking position.

10 ♕a4

Ftacnik points out that 10 ♗xc6 bxc6 11
♕c2 can be met by 11...♗a6 12 ♖e1 c5, with
counterplay.

10...♗xd2 11 ♘xd2 ♗d7 12 f3 a6

12...♘xd2 13 ♗xd2 a6 comes to the same
thing.

13 ♗xc6

Not 13 fxe4? axb5 14 ♕xb5 ♘xd4 15
♕d3 c5, and Black is better, for example 16
exd5 ♗b5 17 ♘c4 ♕xd5 18 b3 ♗xc4 19
bxc4 ♕xe5.

**13...♗xc6 14 ♕a3 ♘xd2 15 ♗xd2 ♗b5
16 ♖fe1**

With opposite bishops and no attacking
prospects for either player the position
should be about equal, for instance 16...♕d7
17 f4 ♕f5 18 ♕f3 ♕d3 19 ♕f2 ♗d7, with
equality due to Black's hold on the light
squares.

16...♕h4 17 ♕e3 ♖ac8 18 ♖ac1 b6?!

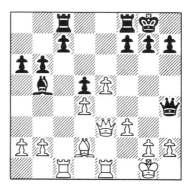

18...♖fe8 was more natural.

19 e6! fxe6?

Simplest was 19...♕e7!, holding everything
together. The text proves to be bad.

**20 ♕xe6+ ♔h8 21 ♕xd5 ♖fd8 22 ♕e4
♕xe4**

Even worse is 22...♖xd4 23 ♕xh4 (23
♖xc7 fails to the flashy 23...♖xe1+! 24 ♗xe1
♖xe4 25 ♖xc8+ ♗e8 and Black should hold
the ending) 23...♖xh4 24 ♖e7 ♖d4 25 ♗c3
♖d7 26 ♖ce1 and Black is in trouble due to
the weakness of g7.

**23 ♖xe4 ♖d7 24 ♗f4 ♔g8 25 ♖c3 c5 26
dxc5 ♖xc5**

After 26...bxc5 White plays 27 ♔f2 etc.

**27 ♖xc5 bxc5 28 ♔f2 ♔f7 29 ♗e3 ♖d5
30 h4**

see following diagram

White intends to probe away, create
threats and provoke concessions on all parts
of the board. In the meantime, Black is
somewhat tied down holding onto his loose
queenside.

30...h5?!

It's always a difficult choice; block the pawn, but give away a square, or hold onto the square but give up space. Here Ftacnik considers 30...h6 31 g4 to be a better try, but it's natural to avoid getting his pawns stuck on dark-squares.

31 ♗g5 ♖d4 32 ♖e7+ ♔g8 33 ♔g3 ♖d7

Ftacnik points out 33...♖b4!?, which is more active. The intention being to meet 34 b3 c4 35 ♗d2 with 35...cxb3! 36 ♗xb4 b2 37 ♖e1 ♗d3, which should be drawn.

34 ♖e5 c4 35 ♗f4 g6 36 ♖e6 ♔f7 37 ♖b6 ♖d5 38 ♗g5! ♖d7 39 ♗f6 ♖c7 40 ♗c3 ♖c6 41 ♖b7+ ♔e6 42 ♗f4 ♗a4 43 ♖a7 ♗c2 44 g4 hxg4 45 fxg4 ♗d1 46 ♔g5 ♗c2

46...♖c5+ loses a second pawn after 47 ♔xg6 ♗xg4 48 ♖xa6+.

47 ♖g7 ♔d5

How does White break through?

48 ♗f6! ♔e6 49 ♖xg6!

Sacrificing the exchange for two connected passed pawns.

49...♖c5+ 50 ♔h6 c3 51 ♗xc3!

Precisely played! 51 ♗xc3+ was rejected in view of 51...♗xg6 52 ♔xg6 ♖c4 53 ♔h5 ♔f7 (Ftacnik), when Short probably couldn't see how to push his pawns through.

51...♗xg6 52 ♔xg6 ♖a5 53 h5 ♖xa2 54 h6 ♖h2 55 g5 1-0

White wins the rook for the h-pawn and stops the black a-pawn with a timely c3-c4.

Game 29
Kavalek-Hase
Lucerne Olympiad 1982

---

1 e4 e5 2 ♘f3 ♘c6 3 ♗b5 ♗c5 4 c3 f5

The controversial Cordel Gambit.

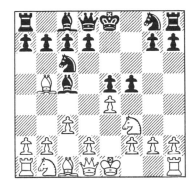

5 d4

5 ♗xc6 dxc6 6 ♘xe5 is not so precise as Black can play 6...♗d6 7 d4 (safer than 7 ♕h5+ g6 8 ♘xg6 ♘f6 9 ♕h4 ♖g8 10 e5 ♖xg6 11 exf6 ♗e6, which gives Black good development and the bishop pair) 7...♗xe5 8 dxe5 ♕xd1+ and it's more or less equal already, for example 9 ♔xd1 fxe4 10 ♗g5 ♘e7 11 ♘d2 ♘g6 12 ♘xe4 ♘xe5 13 ♖e1 0-0 14 ♔c2 ♗f5 and here a draw was agreed in Michel-Kohler, German Championship 1938.

Perhaps a bit more ambitious is 6...♕h4, which also seems adequate, for example 7 d4

(7 0-0 fxe4 8 d4 exd3 transposes to 5 0-0 below) 7...♕xe4+ 8 ♕e2 ♕xe2+ 9 ♔xe2 ♗d6 10 ♘c4 ♗e7 11 ♗f4 ♗e6 12 ♘bd2 0-0-0 with no problems for Black, H.Hunt-Hector, Isle of Man 1996.

After 5 0-0 fxe4 White has two principal continuations: 6 ♘xe5 and 6 ♗xc6 dxc6 7 ♘xe5.

a) 6 ♘xe5!? is possibly the best try for an opening edge. Following 6...♘xe5 7 ♕h5+ ♘f7 (7...♘g6 is more active according to Wedberg) 8 ♕xc5 ♘f6 9 d3 c6 10 ♗a4 b6? (10...d6 11 ♕e3 ♕b6 12 dxe4 ♕xe3 13 ♗xe3 ♘xe4 offers White a small but persistent edge, due to possession of the bishop pair and unbalanced pawns) 11 ♕e3 ♗a6 12 ♖e1 0-0 13 dxe4 ♕c7 14 ♕g3 Black had no compensation for the pawn, Barkhagen-Hector, Gothenburg 1999.

b) 6 ♗xc6 dxc6 7 ♘xe5 ♕h4 (otherwise 7...♘f6 8 d4 ♗d6 9 ♗g5 ♕e7 10 ♖e1 ♗xe5 11 dxe5 ♕xe5 12 ♗xf6 gxf6 13 ♘d2 ♗f5 14 ♕a4, Sakr-Gibbons, Genting Highlands 1998, gave good compensation for White, but 8...exd3 needs looking at) 8 d4 exd3.

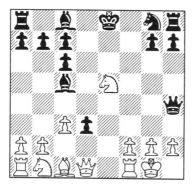

White has failed to prove any real advantage from the diagram position. After 9 ♕b3 (9 ♕xd3 ♘e7 10 ♘f3 ♕h5 11 ♘bd2 was prematurely agreed drawn in Yudasin-Rantanen, Tbilisi 1987 and 9 g3!? ♕h3 10 ♘xd3 ♗g4 11 ♕e1+ ♘e7 12 ♘d2 ♗d6 13 f3 ♗f5 14 ♘e4 ♗xe4 15 fxe4 ♘g6 yielded approximate equality in Akopi-

an-Rogers, New York 1998) 9...♕h5 10 ♘xd3 ♗d6 11 ♖e1+ ♘e7 12 ♗f4 ♗xf4 13 ♘xf4 ♕f7 14 ♕xf7+ ♔xf7 15 ♘d2 ♘d5 a draw was agreed in Mrdja-Rogers, Italy 1998, although White could try 16 ♘d3, keeping some tension.

5...fxe4

Milic-Kuprejanov, Yugoslav Championship 1962 varied with 5...exd4, but after the continuation 6 e5 dxc3 7 ♘xc3 ♘ge7 8 0-0 d5 9 exd6 ♕xd6 10 ♕a4 ♗d7 11 ♖d1 ♕e6 12 ♗c4 ♘d8 13 ♕b3 ♕b6 14 ♕c2 White had a strong initiative, as Black's king is dangerously stuck in the open centre.

6 ♘xe5

This is more dangerous than 6 dxc5 exf3 7 ♕xf3 ♘f6 8 0-0 0-0 9 ♗g5 ♕e7 10 b4 a5 11 ♘d2 axb4 12 ♗xc6 dxc6 13 cxb4 ♗e6 14 a3 ♗d5, as Black had good piece play to compensate for his slightly inferior pawn structure in the game Filipenko-Gavrilov, Piskov 1998.

Instead, another crucial move is 6 ♗xc6, when 6...exf3?! 7 ♗xf3 exd4 8 0-0 ♘f6 9 ♖e1+ ♗e7 10 ♗g5, as in Torre-Tatai, Haifa Olympiad 1976, gives White a pleasant edge, even after the best continuation 10...0-0 11 ♕xd4 c6 12 c4.

After the best move 6...dxc6, White has two important tries: 7 ♘fd2 and 7 ♘xe5.

a) 7 ♘fd2, when Black has no easy route to equality:

a1) 7...exd4?? 8 ♕h5+.

a2) 7...♗d6 8 dxe5 e3 9 exd6 (9 fxe3 ♗c5 10 0-0 is suggested by Fritz5 who prefers White) 9...exd2+ 10 ♘xd2 ♕xd6 11 0-0, as in Stean-Snyder, correspondence 1978, is better for White, but with opposite bishops it's a shade drawish.

a3) 7...♗e7 8 ♕h5+ g6 9 ♕xe5 ♘f6 10 ♘xe4 0-0 11 ♗g5 ♗f5 12 0-0 ♗xe4 13 ♗xf6 ♗xf6 14 ♕xe4 and Black had nothing for the pawn, Stanec-Trevelyan, European Club Cup 1996.

a4) 7...♗g5 8 dxc5 ♘f6 9 ♕e2 ♕xg2 10 ♕f1 ♕g4 11 ♘c4 ♕h5 12 ♗e3 ♗e6 13

♘bd2 0-0-0 14 ♕g2 didn't quite give Black enough compensation for the piece in de Firmian-Rogers, Philadelphia 1986.

b) Against 7 ♘xe5 the latter of Black's two options is the best:

b1) 7...♗d6?! 8 ♕h5+ g6 9 ♕e2 ♕h4 (9...♗f5 10 ♗f4 ♘f6 11 ♘d2 0-0 12 0-0 ♕e7 13 f3 was better for White in Mestel-Plaskett, Brighton 1984, while 9...♗xe5 has been known to be dubious since the famous game Smyslov-Vidmar, Groningen 1946, which continued 10 ♕xe4 ♘f6 11 ♕xe5+ ♔f7 12 0-0 ♖e8 13 ♕g5 ♗f5 14 ♗e3 ♕d7 15 ♘d2 ♘e4 16 ♕h6 and Black had nothing for the pawn) 10 ♘d2 ♗f5 11 g4! ♗e6 (11...♗xe5 left Black with a rotten ending in Davies-Speelman, Hastings 1987/8, after 12 gxf5 ♗f6 13 fxg6 hxg6 14 ♕xe4+ etc.) 12 ♘xe4 ♗xe5 13 h3! (threatening to trap the queen with 14 ♗g5 and thus leaving Black with no option except to head for a vastly inferior ending) 13...♗xg4 (13...♗f6? allows 14 ♘c5) 14 ♕xg4 ♕xg4 15 hxg4, Am.Rodriguez-Martin del Campo, Matanzas 1994.

b2) Precise is 7...♕d5! 8 ♗f4 (8 ♕h5+ g6 9 ♕e2 ♗d6 10 0-0 ♗f5 11 ♘c4, as in Hübner-R.Hess, Lugano 1989, gives nothing for White according to Hübner after 11...♘f6 12 ♘xd6+ cxd6 13 ♗h6 ♘g4 14 ♗g5 0-0; Hübner also gives 8 0-0 ♘f6 9 ♗f4 ♗b6, with ...c5 to follow, as unclear) 8...♗d6 9 c4 ♕e6 10 ♕h5+ g6 11 ♕e2 ♕f5! (inferior are 11...c5?! 12 ♘c3 cxd4 13 ♘xe4 ♘e7 14 ♘d3! 0-0 15 ♗h6 ♖f7 16 c5 ♘f5 17 cxd6 ♘xh6 18 dxc7 with a clear advantage to White in Arnason-Rantanen, Helsinki 1986, and 11...♘f6 12 ♘d2 with an edge to White according to Arnason as after 12...♕f5 White can try the annoying 13 ♗h6) 12 ♗g3 c5 13 ♘f3 ♘f6 14 ♗xd6 cxd6 15 dxc5 0-0 16 ♘fd2 and Black was fine, Pinter-Tompa, Hungarian Championship 1976.

6...♘xe5 7 ♕h5+

Keres's suggestion of 7 dxc5 c6 8 ♗e2 is worthy of note.

7...♘f7

Alternatively Black has 7...♘g6, when 8 ♕xc5 c6 9 ♗e2 d6 (perhaps Black should try 9...d5!? intending ...♘ge7 and ...0-0) 10 ♕g5 ♘f6 11 h4 ♕e7 12 ♘a3 ♗e6 13 h5 gives White a small but persistent initiative, as in Delchev-Buzimkic, Bosnia 1999.

8 ♗c4!

Better than 8 ♕xc5, which after 8...♘e7 9 ♗f4 c6 10 ♗c4?! (losing a tempo; better is 10 ♗e2) 10...d5 11 ♗e2 0-0 12 ♘d2 ♗f5 13 0-0-0 ♕f6 gave Black the better of it in Aparicio-L.Bronstein, San Luis 1990.

8...♕e7 9 dxc5 ♘f6 10 ♕xf7+!

If 10 ♗xf7+ then 10...♔f8! 11 ♕g5 ♔xf7 12 0-0, as in Suetin-Mukhin, USSR 1964, and now Keres gives 12...b6, with equality.

10...♕xf7 11 ♗xf7+ ♔xf7 12 ♗f4 ♘d5 13 ♗g3 b6 14 ♘a3

White maintains an initiative due to a superior pawn structure and Black's obligation to cover the various holes in his position.

14...♗a6

Experience suggests that 14...bxc5 is probably inferior, as after 15 0-0-0 ♘f6 16 ♘b5 d5 17 ♘xc7 ♗g4 18 ♖d2, White pressurises the centre.

15 0-0-0 ♗d3 16 f3 bxc5 17 fxe4

Kavalek suggests an alternative way to keep some pressure; 17 ♖he1!? ♘f6 18 fxe4 ♗xe4 19 ♘b5, but in that case Black would maintain his pawn advantage. The game continuation is more solid.

17...♗xe4 18 ♗xc7 ♖he8

After 18...♗xg2 White has 19 ♖hg1 ♗f3 20 ♖gf1 ♔g8 21 ♖xf3 ♘xc7 22 ♖xd7, threatening all manner of mischief on the seventh rank.

19 ♗d6

19 ♘c4 is adequately met by 19...♔g8.

19...♖ac8 20 ♘c4 ♘b6 21 ♘e3!

It's important to retain the knights, as otherwise the remaining opposite bishops would enhance Black's drawing chances.

21...♔g8 22 ♖hf1 ♖c6 23 c4 ♗g6 24 ♖f3 ♘c8 25 ♗f4

It's all a question of harmony. White's pieces have an active disposition, whereas Black's ragged queenside pawns require support, thus his pieces occupy awkward defensive posts.

25...♘b6 26 ♖d6

No doubt White had in mind that the exchange of one pair of rooks takes away a useful defender. Black should have buckled down to gritty defence with 26...♖cc8, instead he sees a tempting tactical trick, but Kavalek has seen further...

26...♖xe3?! 27 ♖xe3 ♖xd6 28 ♗xd6 ♘xc4 29 ♖e7!

Hase was surely expecting 29 ♗xc5 ♘xe3 30 ♗xe3 a6, which has 'draw' written all over it.

29...♘xd6 30 ♖xd7 ♘e4 31 ♖xa7

The distant passed pawn, supported by a rook, is too strong for a pair of minor pieces.

31...c4 32 ♖c7 ♘f2 33 ♖xc4 ♘d3+ 34 ♔d2 ♘xb2 35 ♖d4

Dominating the knight.

35...♗e8 36 ♔c3 ♘a4+ 37 ♔b4 ♗f7

A better practical try is 37...♘b6!?. Kavalek then suggests 38 ♖d6 ♘d7 39 a4, but the tricky 39...♘b8! requires 40 ♖b6! (rather than 40 a5? ♘c6+ 41 ♔b5 ♖xa5+!), so that 40...♘c6+ 41 ♔c5 ♘e5 is killed off by 42 a5! ♘d7+ 43 ♔d6.

38 ♖f4+ ♔g6 39 ♖e4 ♗d7 40 ♖d4 ♗e8 41 ♖d8 ♗f7 42 a3! ♘b2 43 ♖d4 ♔f5

If 43...♗e8, then 44 ♔b3.

44 ♖d2 1-0

After 44...♘c4 45 ♖f2+ ♔g6 46 ♖xf7 ♔xf7 47 ♔xc4 it's all over.

In conclusion; 4...f5 is an extremely complicated line. It's objectively risky, as White has a number of ways to keep an edge, often in a simplified position. However it engenders fascinating complications and with traps abounding, it certainly has surprise value.

Game 30
Sax-Kogan
Ljubljana 1999

1 e4 e5 2 ♘f3 ♘c6 3 ♗b5 ♗c5 4 c3

Here we deal with Black's fourth move alternatives.

4...♘ge7

a) The aggressive 4...d5?!, an idea championed by Konikowski, is dubious; I suggest three promising ways for White:

a1) 5 ♘xe5 ♕g5 6 0-0! (inferior is 6 d4 ♕xg2 7 ♕f3 ♕xf3 8 ♘xf3 dxe4 9 ♘fd2 ♗e7 10 ♘xe4 ♘f6, as in Pähtz-Lepelletier, Glorney Cup 1995, which is only about equal) 6...♕xe5 7 d4 ♕e6 8 dxc5 dxe4 9 ♖e1 ♗d7 (if 9...♘f6 then 10 ♗f4) 10 ♗g5! f6 11 ♘d2, as in Bitman-Konikowski, correspondence 1979, looks better for White.

a2) Surprisingly 5 ♕e2 is an unpleasant move to meet. In Velimirovic-Basagic, Yugoslav Championship 1984, Black found nothing better than 5...♔f8, when White can keep an edge in various ways such as 6 ♗xc6 bxc6 7 exd5.

a3) The critical 'refutation', in my opinion follows 5 0-0 dxe4 6 ♘xe5 ♕f6 7 d4 exd3 8 ♘xc6 bxc6 9 ♗g5! ♕g6 (following 9...♕d6, Konikowski and Filipowicz suggest the continuation 10 ♕f3 ♗d7 11 ♖e1+ ♔f8 12 ♗c4, yielding an advantage to White) 10 ♖e1+ ♔f8 11 ♕xd3 ♗f5 (11...♕xg5 is not good in view of 12 ♗xc6 ♗f5 13 ♕e2).

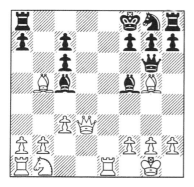

This position is judged as 'obscure' by Konikowski and Filipowicz, but after 12 ♕c4! it's clearly a big advantage to White (Flear and Kosten).

b) 4...♕e7?! is more solid but is equally unconvincing: 5 0-0 a6 6 ♗a4 b5 7 ♗b3 ♗b6 8 a4! ♖b8 9 axb5 axb5 10 ♘a3 (this position reminds me of some lines where Black has played the more useful ...♘f6 instead of ...♕e7; in that case Black is more or

less okay, but here Black's position proves to be difficult) 10...♘f6 11 d3 0-0 (11...♗a6 is a lesser evil, but White can play ♘c2-e3, heading for d5 or f5) 12 ♘db5 ♗xf2+ 13 ♖xf2 ♖xb5 14 ♗g5 h6 15 ♗h4 ♕d6 16 ♘d2! was Z.Almasi-Szurowszky, Hungary 1998. White was already close to winning as all his pieces are active and ready to pounce; Black's on the other hand are mostly badly placed.

c) A better try is 4...♕f6 when 5 d4! is critical. Instead 5 0-0 transposes to 4 0-0 ♕f6 5 c3 (game 33), which seems fine for Black, and 5 ♗xc6?! dxc6 6 d4 exd4 7 cxd4 ♗b6 doesn't impress, as in Stanojoski-Safin, Metz 2000, where the attempt to mix it with 8 d5?! looked fishy after 8...cxd5 9 ♘c3 ♕g6?! (why not 9...dxe4, I wonder?) 10 exd5 ♘e7 11 0-0 0-0 12 ♖e1 ♘f5 13 ♕a4 ♘d6, and Black had a solid position.

So after 5 d4, Black has to decide between two options:

c1) 5...♗b6 (this only puts off the moment when Black has to cede terrain in the centre) 6 0-0 exd4 7 e5 ♕f5?! 8 ♘xd4 (8 cxd4 is even more testing) 8...♘xd4 9 cxd4 ♘e7 10 ♘c3 h5!? 11 ♗e3 h4 12 g4!? ♕g6 13 d5 ♗xe3 14 fxe3 ♕g5 15 ♕f3 0-0 16 ♕f4 ♕xf4 17 exf4 d6 and White maintains his space advantage into the ending, Arizmendi Martinez-Campora, Algarve 1998.

c2) 5...exd4 6 e5 ♕g6 (6...♕d8?! {yuck!} 7 cxd4 ♗b4+ 8 ♘c3 ♘ge7 9 d5 ♘b8 10 0-0 0-0, and now 11 d6! yielded White a crushing position in Borge-Gretarsson, Copenhagen 1997) 7 cxd4 ♗b4+ (7...♘xd4 is really quite a clever trick, but White finds an answer with 8 ♘xd4 ♕b6 9 ♗e3 ♗xd4 10 ♕xd4 ♕xb5 11 ♘c3 ♕c6 12 ♘d5 ♘e7 13 ♘xe7 ♔xe7 14 0-0 ♕g6 15 ♖ac1, as in Rytshagov-Gretarsson, Excelsior cup 1997, where White's strong attacking chances proved to be a more important factor than his pawn deficit) 8 ♘c3 ♘ge7 9 0-0 d5! (it's necessary to obtain some solidity in the centre) 10 ♕b3 ♗xc3 11 bxc3 0-0 12 ♗a3 was the game A.Sokolov-Kharitonov, USSR Championship 1984. White is a little better but Black has a solid position. After the continuation 12...♖d8 13 ♗xe7 ♘xe7 14 ♖fe1 ♗g4 15 ♘h4 ♕h5 16 g3 ♘g6 17 ♘xg6 hxg6 18 ♖e3 White didn't have much advantage.

Black has experimented with early alternatives without much success, but Kharitonov's handling of 4...♕f6 suggests that this one at least is playable.

d) The experimentally-minded may like to investigate 4...♗b6!?, which is recommended by Van der Tak, who calls it Charousek's idea. The main point is that after 5 d4 (5 0-0 d6 6 d4 ♗d7 is examined in game 32 and 5 ♗xc6 dxc6 6 ♘xe5 ♕g5 is only equal) 5...exd4 6 cxd4, Black plays 6...♘ce7!?. Can White exploit this loss of time and Black's temporary abandoning of the centre? Black's unusual retreat is neither a misprint nor a slip of the hand, but preparation for ...c7-c6 and ...d7-d5. For instance after 7 ♗g5 c6 8 ♗a4, Black has 8...d5 9 e5 ♗g4, with interesting play.

So the most challenging is 7 d5!?, when White obtains a small edge against both of Black's main continuations:

d1) 7...c6 8 ♗a4 d6 9 ♘c3 ♘f6 10 ♗g5 ♘g4 occurred in Moberg-Hector, Gothenburg 1997, and now simplest is 11 0-0!, with a solid edge, rather than 11 dxc6?! ♗xf2+ 12 ♔e2 bxc6 13 ♗xc6+ ♘xc6 14 ♗xd8 ♗a6+, which led to a draw in the game after 15 ♔d2 ♗e3+ 16 ♔e1 ♗f2+ 17 ♔d2 ♗e3+ 18 ♔e1

♗f2+.

d2) 7...a6 8 ♗a4 ♘f6 9 ♘c3 0-0 10 d6! ♘g6 11 0-0 cxd6 12 ♕xd6 ♗c7 13 ♕d4 ♗b6 14 ♕d6 ♗c7 15 ♕d3 d6 16 ♗g5 ♗e6 was played in Franzen-Oim, correspondence 1996-7, when I think that White has a pull with 17 ♖ac1 ♖c8 18 ♖fd1.

5 0-0

5 d4 was played in a historically interesting game; 5...exd4 6 cxd4 ♗b4+ 7 ♗d2 ♗xd2+ 8 ♕xd2 a6 9 ♗a4 d5 10 exd5 ♕xd5 11 ♘c3 ♕e6+ 12 ♔f1 ♕c4+ 13 ♔g1 0-0 14 d5 ♘a7 15 ♖e1 ♘f5 with unclear play in Tal-Fischer, Curaçao Candidates 1962.

5...♗b6 6 d4 exd4 7 cxd4 d5 8 exd5 ♘xd5 9 ♖e1+ ♗e6 10 ♗g5 ♕d6 11 ♘bd2

Despite some interest over the years Black has not yet found a route to equality.

11...♕b4

No better is 11...0-0, for example 12 ♘c4 ♕b4 13 ♗xc6 bxc6 14 ♖c1, which is judged as clearly better for White by Vi.Ivanov. The c6-pawn is very weak and if then 14...c5? White wins a piece with 15 ♗d2 ♕b5 16 a4 and 17 a5.

12 ♗xc6+

A sensible and good move. However Euwe analysed 12 ♗a4 h6 (12...♕xb2!? doesn't work; 13 ♘c4 ♕b4 14 ♘ce5 0-0 15 ♘xc6 bxc6 16 ♗xc6 ♖ab8 17 ♗xd5 ♗xd5 18 ♗e7) 13 a3 ♕f8 (13...♕xb2? loses to 14 ♘c4 ♕c3 15 ♖c1) 14 ♗h4 g5 (what else?) 15

♗g3 0-0-0 16 ♗xc6, with a clear advantage for White, as Black's king is by far the most insecure.

12...bxc6 13 ♕c2 0-0 14 ♘c4

A couple of games at a lower level have continued 14 ♕xc6 h6? 15 ♖xe6 fxe6 16 ♕xe6+ ♚h8 17 ♕xd5, with a quick win in both cases. Clearly 14...♖ae8 (but not 14...♕xb2? 15 ♘c4 ♕c2 16 ♖xe6) is an obvious improvement, but after 15 ♘b3 I can't see any compensation for the pawn.

14...♕b5

14...♖ae8 is strongly met by 15 ♗d2 ♕e7 16 ♘g5.

15 ♘a3

The opening has clearly failed for the second player. Black can perhaps jettison the c-pawn and struggle on, but Kogan finds a more complicated continuation that loses the exchange for a pawn. However in either case he is in trouble.

15...♘b4 16 ♕d2 ♕a4 17 ♗e7 ♗a5 18 ♗xf8 ♖xf8 19 ♕d1

Or 19 ♘g5!? playing for an attack.

19...♕xd1 20 ♖exd1 ♗xa2 21 ♘c2 ♘xc2 22 ♖xa2 ♗b6 23 ♖a4

With a great ending for White. Black has only one broken pawn for the exchange.

23...a5 24 ♖c4 ♘b4 25 ♘e5 ♖e8 26 ♚f1

Better than 26 ♘xc6 ♘xc6 27 ♖xc6 ♗xd4!.

26...♖e6 27 ♖dc1 ♚f8 28 ♘xc6 ♘d3 29

♖b1 ♖f6 30 f3 ♖f5 31 g3 ♖h5 32 h4 g5 33 ♚e2 ♘b4 34 ♘xb4 axb4 35 ♖xb4?!

35 ♖h1! was the simplest way to keep excellent winning chances.

35...gxh4 36 ♖h1 h3 37 g4 ♖h6 38 f4 h2 39 ♚f3 ♖h3+ 40 ♚g2 ♖d3 41 ♖xh2

White has a clear exchange to the good, but against a well-played defence the win proves elusive.

41...♖d2+ 42 ♚g3 ♖d3+ 43 ♚h4 ♗xd4

Note how Kogan keeps his pieces active to frustrate any winning attempts.

44 g5 ♗c5 45 ♖c4 ♗d6 46 ♚g4 ♚g7 47 ♖h3 ♖d2 48 b3 ♖g2+ 49 ♚f5 ♖f2 50 ♖d3 ♖h2 51 b4 ♖b2 52 ♖dd4 ♖b1 53 ♖c6 ♖b2 54 ♖cc4 ♖b1 55 ♚e4 ♚g6 56 ♚d5 f6!

Exchanging a pair of pawns and creating an outside passed pawn.

57 gxf6 ♚xf6 58 ♚c6 h5 59 b5 h4 60 f5 h3 61 ♖xd6+ cxd6 62 ♖h4 ♖b3 63 b6 ♚g5 64 ♖h8 ♚xf5 65 b7 ♚g4 ½-½

Game 31
Bauer-Lepelletier
French championship 1997

1 e4 e5 2 ♘f3 ♘c6 3 ♗b5 ♗c5 4 0-0

A solid alternative to 4 c3.

4...♘d4

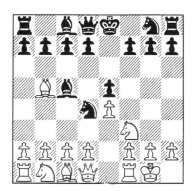

5 ♘xd4

The retreat 5 ♗c4 is not a particularly ambitious attempt at an opening advantage, for example 5...d6 6 c3 ♘xf3+ 7 ♕xf3 ♕f6 8 ♕xf6 ♘xf6 9 d3 ♗e6 was already equal in Guimaraes-De Souza Haro, Rio de Janeiro 1998.

On the other hand, the Evans-style 5 b4!? is quite a serious gambit, when 5...♗xb4 is the man's move. Instead 5...♗b6?! is a bit limp, as it leaves the d-pawn exposed, bearing in mind that White is getting his bishop to b2 'for free'. The game Gullaksen-Hector, London 1999 continued 5...♗b6 6 ♘xd4 exd4 7 ♗b2 c6 8 ♗d3 ♕h4 9 ♘a3 ♘f6 10 g3 ♕h3 11 ♕e2 0-0 12 ♘c4 d5 13 ♘xb6 axb6 14 ♗xd4 dxe4 15 ♗xe4 ♘xe4 16 ♕xe4 ♗f5 17 ♕e5 f6 18 ♕e2, when White had a clear extra pawn. The opposite bishops may present technical difficulties but this was hardly a successful opening experiment for Black.

So after the better 5...♗xb4, then 6 ♘xd4 exd4 7 ♗b2 ♕g5! (the best defence) 8 ♗d3 ♗c5 9 c3 d5! (9...dxc3 10 ♘xc3 is too dangerous, as White has an alarming lead in development for his pawn) 10 cxd4 dxe4 led to a double-edged position in Ghinda-Hector, Budapest 1986. After 11 ♕a4+ ♗d7 (11...♔f8!? is also playable; 12 dxc5 exd3 13 c6 ♘e7 14 ♗a3 b6 15 ♖e1 ♗e6 with an unclear position) 12 ♗b5 c6 13 dxc5 cxb5 14 ♕xe4+ ♘e7 15 h4 ♕g6 16 ♖e1, despite Ghinda's preference for White, Black is certainly okay following 16...0-0!.

5...♗xd4

5...exd4 transposes to a reasonable version of Bird's variation, normally arising via 3...♘d4 4 ♘xd4 exd4 5 0-0 ♗c5 (see Chapter Six).

6 c3 ♗b6 7 d4

7 d3 is hardly critical, being similar to a slow Giuoco Piano; 7...c6 8 ♗a4 ♘f6 9 ♗g5 (9 ♘d2 d5! 10 exd5 ♕xd5, is about equal), Vaculik-Konigova, Plzen 1998, and now I suggest 9...h6 10 ♗h4 g5! 11 ♗g3 d6 with good play for Black, exploiting the fact that White has castled but Black has yet to commit his king.

7...c6

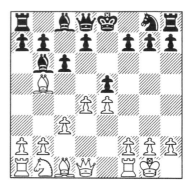

8 ♗a4

The normal move, maintaining the pin on the d-pawn.

White has on occasion opted for 8 ♗c4 when after 8...d6, there are three significant options:

a) 9 ♕b3 ♕e7 10 dxe5 dxe5 11 a4 ♘f6 12 a5 ♗c5 13 ♕c2 ♗e6 14 ♘d2 ♖d8 where Black, who has achieved harmonious development, was already at least equal in Kobalija-Adams, Las Vegas 1999.

b) 9 ♗e3 ♘f6 10 dxe5 dxe5 11 ♕xd8+ ♗xd8 is practically equal, but still requires some careful handling, for instance 12 ♘d2 0-0?! (more precise is 12...♗c7) 13 ♘f3 ♗c7?! (now the sequence 13...♘xe4 14 ♘xe5 ♗c7 should be preferred) 14 ♗c5 ♖e8 15 ♘g5, and White now had an edge in Manik-Turner, Litomysl 1997, as Black had to play 15...♗e6 allowing 16 ♘xe6.

c) 9 dxe5 dxe5 10 ♕xd8+ (old analysis of Suetin continues instead with 10 ♕h5 ♕e7 11 ♗g5 ♘f6 12 ♕h4 ♗e6 with equality) 10...♗xd8 11 a4 (11 f4!? has been tried, for example 11...exf4 12 ♗xf4 ♘f6 13 ♘d2 0-0 14 ♗d6 ♖e8 15 e5 ♘d5, Ricardi-Vives Cabau, Cala Galdana 1999, with chances for both sides) 11...a5 12 ♗e3 ♘f6 13 f3 ♘d7 14 ♖d1 ♗b6 15 ♔f2 ♗xe3+ 16 ♔xe3 ♔e7, Sylvan-Hector, Roskilde 1998, is about equal.

8...d6 9 ♘a3

9 d5 didn't lead to an opening advantage

after 9...♘e7 10 dxc6 bxc6 11 ♕e2 0-0 12 ♘a3 ♕c7 13 ♗e3 ♗e6 14 ♖fe1 ♘g6 15 ♘c4 f5 in Brynell-Christensen, Copenhagen 2000.

9...♘e7?!

A rare idea as Black normally captures on d4 first, but 9...♘f6 is also worth a closer look.

a) After 9...exd4 10 cxd4 ♘e7, White has three main options:

a1) 11 ♗g5 f6 12 ♗f4 0-0 13 d5 cxd5 14 ♗b3, and White keeps an initiative according to Berzinsh.

a2) 11 ♘c4 ♗c7!, keeping the bishop may improve on 11...d5 12 ♘xb6 axb6 13 exd5 ♘xd5 14 ♖e1+ ♗e6 15 ♗c2 0-0 16 ♕d3, Berzinsh-Sakovich, Riga 1995, where White maintained an edge.

a3) 11 d5!? 0-0 12 dxc6 bxc6 13 ♗g5 f6 14 ♗f4 d5 15 ♖e1 ♗b7 16 exd5 cxd5 17 ♘b5 ♘g6 18 ♗e3! (rather than 18 ♗g3 ♘e5 19 ♘d4 ♕d6 20 ♕d2 ♖ac8, Nadanian-Lybin, correspondence 1991-2, which allowed Black sufficiently active pieces to compensate for his isolani), challenging Black's most active minor piece, and leading to a White edge due to a superior pawn structure after 18...♗c6 19 ♘d4 ♗xa4 20 ♕xa4 ♖e8 21 ♖ad1 ♘e5 22 b3 g6 23 h3, as in Rasik-Sakovich, Pardubice 1997.

As Black has not been able to equalise with 9...exd4 then 9...♘f6 has become more popular and was recently the choice of Michael Adams.

b) 9...♘f6 and then two ideas for White: 10 ♗c2 and 10 ♗g5.

b1) 10 ♗c2 ♗e6 11 ♗g5 h6 12 ♗h4 (perhaps 12 ♗xf6 ♕xf6 13 d5 ♗d7 14 ♘c4 ♗c7 15 ♕d3, Portisch-Spassky, Budapest vs. Leningrad 1961, represents a better try) 12...g5 13 ♗g3 ♗g4 14 f3 ♗e6 15 ♗f2 ♘h5 and Black had full equality in Sulipa-Payen, Gonfreville 1999.

b2) 10 ♗g5 0-0! (an improvement on 10...h6?! 11 ♗xf6 ♕xf6 12 d5, when White keeps up the pressure; Todorovic-Petronic,

Yugoslavia 1992 continued 12...♗d7 13 ♘c4 ♗c7 14 dxc6 bxc6 15 ♕d3, and d6 and c6 are potential trouble spots) 11 dxe5 dxe5 12 ♕f3 h6 13 ♖ad1 ♕e7 14 ♗xf6 ♕xf6 15 ♕xf6 gxf6 with an acceptable ending for Black, Rowson-Adams, Southend 2000.

10 dxe5

Best might be 10 ♘c4!, when 10...♗c7 (10...exd4 is no better, as after 11 ♘xb6 ♕xb6 12 cxd4 d5 13 ♗g5 f6 14 ♗f4 White used the power of the bishops to obtain the initiative in Ravinsky-Cherenkov, USSR 1957) 11 dxe5 dxe5 12 ♕xd8+ ♔xd8 13 ♖d1+ is awkward for Black.

10...dxe5 11 ♕h5 ♗c7 12 ♖d1

White has pressure but can he find a weak point to attack?

12...♗d7 13 ♗g5 0-0 14 ♖d3 ♕e8 15 ♗b3 ♘g6 16 ♖ad1 ♗e6 17 g3 ♗xb3 18 axb3 ♕e6 19 ♖d7 ♖ac8 20 ♘c4

20...h6

Safer is 20...f6 21 ♗e3 b5.

21 ♗xh6!?

Risky, but otherwise he has nothing concrete. The fact that Black was already short of time was undeniably one of Bauer's reasons for his choice.

21...gxh6 22 ♘e3 ♘e7 23 ♘g4 ♖fe8 24 ♘xh6+ ♔f8 25 ♘f5 ♕g6 26 ♕h8+ ♘g8 27 ♔g2 ♕f6 28 ♕h7 ♖cd8?!

Lepelletier's most prudent course was 28...♕g6! 29 ♕h8 ♕f6, with a repetition. White has great activity as compensation (and in the actual game, a significant time advantage).

29 ♖1d3

29...♗b8??

Necessary was 29...♖xd7 30 ♖xd7 ♖c8, when it's hard to see how either side can make progress.

30 ♖xd8 1-0

Game 32
Brynell-Hector
Swedish Championship 2000

1 e4 e5 2 ♘f3 ♘c6 3 ♗b5 ♗c5 4 0-0 d6

4...♘ge7 is best met by 5 c3, as in game 30, where Black failed to solve his opening problems.

Instead 5 ♘xe5 doesn't impress; 5...♘xe5 6 d4 c6 7 ♗e2 (or 7 ♗a4 ♗d6 8 dxe5 ♗xe5 9 c4 0-0 10 ♗c2, Gaprindashvili-Koloty, USSR 1959, and now I suggest that Black should try 10...d6 11 ♘c3 f5, with equal chances) 7...♗d6 8 dxe5 ♗xe5 9 ♘d2 ♗c7 10 b3 0-0 11 ♗b2 d5 12 ♗d3 ♘g6 13 ♕f3 ♕h4 14 g3 ♕g5 15 ♕d1 ♗g4 and Black had already taken the initiative in Fressinet-de Vreugt, Lausanne 2000.

5 c3

Intending d2-d4 and sometimes a quick d4-d5. The immediate 5 d4 is also interesting, for example 5...exd4 6 ♘xd4 (after 6 ♗xc6+ bxc6 7 ♘xd4 ♘e7 8 ♘c3 0-0 9 ♘a4 ♗b6 10 b3 ♗d7 11 ♘xb6 axb6 12 ♗b2 c5 13 ♘e2

♘g6 14 ♘g3 f6, Antonio-Torre, Manila 1998, despite White's initiative Black's position proved to be rock-solid) 6...♘ge7 7 ♗g5!? f6 8 ♗e3 ♗xd4 9 ♕xd4 a6 10 ♗xc6+ ♘xc6 11 ♕c4 ♕e7 12 ♘c3 ♗e6 13 ♘d5 ♗xd5 14 exd5 ♘e5 15 ♕b3 0-0 16 ♖fe1 ♕d7 17 f4 and White had the superior minor piece and a nice space advantage in Shirov-I.Sokolov, Las Vegas 1999.

If this isn't satisfactory then Black can try 6...♗d7, whereupon White has two options:

a) 7 ♘b3 ♗b6 8 ♘c3 ♘f6 9 ♘a4 0-0 10 ♘xb6 axb6 11 f3 ♖e8 12 ♗d2 (if 12 ♗g5 then 12...♖e5) 12...d5 and Black has adequate activity to compensate for the bishop pair, Burnett-Ehlvest, Philadelphia 1999.

b) 7 ♘xc6 bxc6 8 ♗a6 ♘f6 9 c3 0-0?! (9...♗c8! is about equal according to Sokolov) 10 b4 ♗b6 11 a4 ♘xe4 12 ♕f3 f5 13 a5 ♗xf2+ 14 ♖xf2 ♘xf2 15 ♕xf2 f4 16 ♘d2, Nijboer-I.Sokolov, Rotterdam 1998, with complications that Sokolov judges to be better for White.

5...♗d7 6 d4 ♗b6

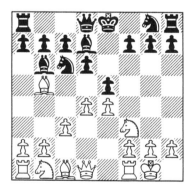

7 ♗g5

The most testing. Instead 7 dxe5 leads to heavy exchanges where Black is okay, despite having his king exposed on the e-file; 7...dxe5 8 ♗xc6 ♗xc6 9 ♘xe5 ♕xd1 10 ♖xd1 ♗xe4 11 ♖e1 f5 12 ♘d2 ♘f6 13 ♘xe4 ♘xe4 14 ♗e3 ♗xe3 15 ♖xe3 0-0 with an equal game, McShane-Plaskett, Southend 2000.

An interesting try is 7 ♘a3!?, when after

7...♗g(7 8 ♘c4 0-0 9 a4 exd4 10 cxd4 ♗g4
11 ♘xb6 axb6 12 d5! (12 ♖c3 d5 13 ♖e1
dxe4 14 ♖xe4 ♗f5 15 ♖e1 ♘g6 was only
equal in I.Polgar-Sax, Hungarian ch. 1970)
12...♘e5 13 ♗e2 ♘xf3+ 14 ♗xf3 ♗xf3 15
♕xf3 ♕d7 16 b3 f5 17 ♗b2 fxe4 18 ♕xe4
White had some pressure, but Black had
adequate defensive resources in Cherni-
aev-Paleologu, Geneva 1999.

7...f6

Not entirely forced, but after 7...♘f6?!
White can favourably simplify with 8 dxe5
♘xe5 9 ♘xe5 dxe5 (if 9...♗xb5 then 10
♕b3) 10 ♗xf6 gxf6 11 ♗xd7+ ♕xd7 12
♕f3! (12 ♕xd7+ ♔xd7 13 ♘d2 ♗e6, and
...f5 equalises) and Black has the worse
pawns and most exposed king.

8 ♗e3 ♘ge7

9 a4!

9 ♘bd2 is less annoying for Black; 9...0-0
10 ♖e1 ♔h8 11 a4 a6!? (Neiman avoids giving up his strong-point on e5, but that approach is also playable, for instance 11...exd4
12 cxd4 ♗g4 13 h3 ♗h5 14 ♗xc6 ♘xc6 15
d5 ♘e5 16 a5 ♗xe3 17 ♖xe3, Benja-
min-Gi.Garcia, New York 1994, is equal after
Benjamin's suggestion 17...c6) 12 ♗f1 ♗g4
13 h3 ♗h5 14 dxe5 ♗xe3 15 ♖xe3 fxe5 16
♗e2, with a reasonable game for Black,
D.Gross-Neiman, Clichy 1998.

After the text move the threat is a4-a5.

9...a6

More or less forced, but now White can

simplify and give Black a slightly crumpled
structure.

**10 ♗xc6 ♘xc6 11 d5 ♘e7 12 ♗xb6
cxb6 13 ♘fd2 ♕c7 14 ♘a3**

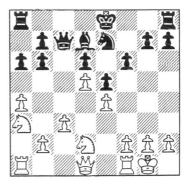

A knight will install itself on c4 bearing
down on b6 and d6. This will in turn force
...b5. The pawns will thus remain chronically
weak, but can Black obtain enough counterplay?

**14...0-0 15 ♕b3 ♖ac8 16 ♖fe1 ♕c5 17
♘dc4 b5 18 axb5 axb5 19 ♘e3 g6 20
♘b1 f5 21 ♘d2 f4?!**

Keeping the tension with 21...♖a8 is more
solid. Then it's not clear that White can progress on the queenside. Hector pushes his
kingside pawns in King's Indian-style but his
hoped for attack proves elusive.

22 ♘c2 g5 23 ♕b4 ♕c7 24 ♖a7

White has the option of forcing a superior
endgame with 24 ♘f3 h6 25 ♘xe5 ♘xd5 26
exd5 dxe5 27 d6 ♕c5 28 ♕xc5 ♖xc5 29
♘b4.

**24...♗e8 25 ♖ea1 ♕d7 26 ♖a8 ♖c5 27
♘e1 ♘c8 28 f3 ♘b6 29 ♖8a7 ♘c4 30
♘xc4 ♖xc4 31 ♕a5**

Intending to come to b6.

**31...♕c7 32 ♘d3 g4 33 ♕xc7 ♖xc7 34
♔f2 gxf3 35 gxf3 ♖f6 36 ♖g1+ ♔f7 37
♖a8 ♖h6 38 ♖g2 ♔e7 39 ♔g1 ♖h3?**

39...♖g6 would keep White down to a
small edge.

40 ♖g7+ ♗f7 41 ♘f2! ♖h4

The problem for Black is that 41...♖xf3

leaves the rook fatally out of play after 42
♖h8 ♚f6 43 ♖hxh7.

42 ♖h8 b4!

Counterplay.

**43 cxb4 ♖c4 44 ♖gxh7 ♖xh7 45 ♖xh7
♖xb4 46 ♘g4 ♚f8 47 ♖h6 ♚e7 48 ♖h7
♚f8 49 h4 ♖b3 50 ♚g2 ♗g6**

50...♖xb2+ can be met by 51 ♚h3 ♖b3 52
h5 ♖xf3+ 53 ♚h4, intending to use the king
as an attacking piece. Critical would then be
53...♖g3 54 ♖h8+ ♗g8 55 h6 ♖g1 56 ♚g5
♖h1, when the result is still in doubt.

51 ♖h6 ♗xe4

The point of Black's play, but this proves
to be insufficient.

**52 fxe4 ♖g3+ 53 ♚f2 ♖xg4 54 ♖xd6
♖xh4 55 ♖f6+! ♚g7 56 ♖f5**

The two connected passed pawns will rule
the day.

**56...♖h2+ 57 ♚f3 ♖h3+ 58 ♚g2 ♖b3 59
♖xe5 b5 60 ♖f5 b4 61 ♖xf4 ♖xb2+ 62
♚f3 b3 63 ♚e3 ♖c2 64 ♚d3 ♖c8 65 ♖f2
♖b8 66 ♚c3 ♖e8 67 d6 ♚g6 68 ♚xb3
♖xe4 69 ♖d2 ♖e8 70 ♚c4 ♚f7 71 d7
1-0**

Game 33
Pavlovic-Granados Gomez
Andorra 1999

---

1 e4 e5 2 ♘f3 ♘c6 3 ♗b5 ♗c5 4 0-0

Apart from 4 c3 (Games 28-30) others are
all clearly inferior: Both 4 ♗xc6 dxc6 5 ♘xe5

♗xf2+ 6 ♚xf2 ♕d4+ and 4 ♘c3 ♘d4 5 ♗c4
d6 don't pose any real problems. The cheeky
4 ♘xe5?! is dangerous only for White after
4...♘d4! 5 ♗c4 ♕g5. I don't like the speculative 4 b4?! either, as after 4...♗xb4 5 ♗b2 d6
6 0-0 ♗d7 7 d4, Petran-Lajos, Hungary 1971,
Black should play 7...♘f6! (7...f6? led to problems on the a2-g8 diagonal) and he is better.

4...♕f6

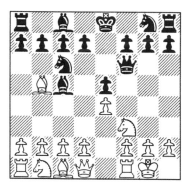

Showing something of a revival, this move
is better against 4 0-0 than against 4 c3 where
it fails to completely equalise (see the note to
Black's fourth move in game 30).

5 c3

White has other ways to handle the centre,
rather than c3 followed by d4.

a) 5 ♘c3 ♘ge7 and now a further split:

a1) 6 d3 h6 7 a3 a6 8 ♗c4 (a solid Ital-
ian-style position where the queen is not
badly placed on f6) 8...0-0 9 ♚h1!? d6 10
♘d5 (10 h3) 10...♘xd5 11 ♗xd5 ♘e7 12
♗b3 ♗g4, with a pleasant position for Black
in Chaves-Martins, Fortaleza 1997.

a2) 6 ♘d5 ♘xd5 7 exd5 ♘d4 8 ♘xd4
♗xd4 9 c3 ♗b6 10 d4 (given as slightly better for White in ECO, but read on) 10...0-0
(Fritz5 recommends 10...exd4!? 11 ♖e1+
♚d8, but this pawn-grab is decidedly risky)
11 dxe5 ♕xe5 12 ♖e1 ♕f6 13 ♗e3 c6!? (better than 13...d6 14 ♗xb6 axb6 15 ♕e2 when
White dominates the e-file) 14 ♗xb6 axb6 15
♗e2 d6 16 ♗g4 (16 ♗f3 ♗d7 is just equal)
16...♗xg4 17 ♕xg4 ♖a5 and Black has equal-

ised, Speck-Rogers, Melbourne 1998.

b) 5 d3 h6 6 ♗e3 ♗b6 and now·

b1) 7 ♗xc6 dxc6 (7...bxc6!? is more dynamic) 8 ♗xh6 axb6 9 d4 exd4 10 ♕xd4 ♕xd4 11 ♘xd4 ♘f6 12 ♘c3 ♔e7, Smirnov-Melnikov, St.Petersburg 2000, is nothing much for White. Compared to a Spanish Exchange pawn structure Black has use of the a-file.

b2) 7 c4! ♘d4 8 ♘xd4 exd4 9 ♗d2 c6 10 ♗a4 d6 11 f4 ♘e7 12 ♗e1,

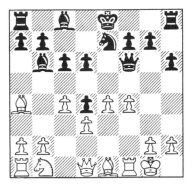

Ciric-Messing, Yugoslav Championship 1969, is judged as a shade better for White. This position is similar to something that can arise from the Bird's Defence, but Black is not in a position to play for ...f7-f5 here. 12...♘g6 13 ♗g3 h5 14 h3 h4 15 ♗h2 ♗d7 16 ♘d2 looks more comfortable for White and after 12...0-0 13 ♘d2 ♘g6 then 14 ♗g3 keeps some pressure. 12...♕g6?! loses time and leaves the knight on e7 poorly placed after 13 f5!. In the game Black played 12...g5!? 13 f5 ♗d7 14 ♗g3 c5 15 ♘d2 0-0-0? (15...♘c6 reduces White's edge to a minimum) 16 ♗xd7+ ♖xd7 17 e5 dxe5 18 ♘e4 and White was well on top.

5...♘ge7 6 d4

The continuation 6 b4!? ♗b6 7 ♘a3, Karpov-Mariotti, Ljubjana/Portoroz 1975, is best met by 7...a6.

A more popular move is 6 ♖e1, when it's best to avoid 6...h6 7 d4 ♗b6 8 ♘a3 0-0 9 ♘c4 d6 10 ♗xc6 ♘xc6 11 d5 ♘e7 12 a4 a6

13 ♘xb6 cxb6 14 ♗e3, as Black has some counterplay with ...♗g4 and ...♘g6 but not enough, Gufeld-Welling, USA 1998. So after the superior 6...a6 White has two tempting moves:

a) 7 ♗xc6 ♘xc6 8 d4 ♗a7?! (8...♗b6!) 9 ♗g5 ♕g6 10 dxe5 ♘xe5 11 ♗f4, Novita-Rogers, Bali 2000, and if the bishop were now on b6 then Black could equalise with capturing on f3 and then castling.

b) 7 d4 ♗a7 (7...exd4?! 8 e5 ♕g6 9 ♗d3 ♕h5 10 ♖e4 f5 11 exf6 gxf6 12 ♖h4 ♕f7 13 cxd4, P.Nielsen-Gretarsson, Gausdal 1996, leaves White with an aggressive set-up) 8 ♗a4 h6 9 ♔h1 0-0 10 dxe5 ♘xe5 11 ♘xe5 ♕xe5 12 f4 ♕f6 13 c4. This goes for the big space bind but after 13...d6 14 ♘c3 ♕h4 15 g3 ♕h3 Black had sufficient counterplay in Bologan-Shapiro, Philadelphia 1999.

6...exd4 7 ♗g5 ♕g6

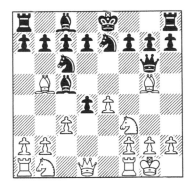

8 ♗xe7

Perhaps the best practical try is 8 ♕d2!?, an interesting gambit, as after the plausible 8...dxc3 9 ♘xc3 0-0 10 ♘d5 f6? (safer is 10...♘xd5! 11 exd5 ♘d4 12 ♘xd4 ♗xd4 13 ♖ae1 ♗f6 14 ♗f4 d6 when White has sufficient compensation, but no more) 11 ♗f4 d6 12 b4 ♗b6 13 ♗xc6 ♘xc6 14 b5, Kovalevskaya-Melnikov, St.Petersburg 1999, Black lost a piece.

8...♗xe7

Otherwise 8...♘xe7 9 cxd4 ♗b6 10 ♘c3 c6 11 ♗c4 (11 ♘e5!?) 11...d6 looks fine for

Black.

9 cxd4 0-0

Or possibly 9...a6!? 10 ♗d3 d6, Furdzik-Schwartz, New York 1999.

10 d5 ♘b8

Black loses time and is thus behind in development, but he avoids any weaknesses. He has a trump card in having the bishop pair in an open position.

11 ♕c2 c6 12 ♗d3 d6 13 ♘c3 ♕h6 14 ♖fe1 ♘d7 15 dxc6 bxc6 16 ♖ac1 ♗f6 17 ♗f1 ♘e5 18 ♘xe5 ♗xe5 19 g3 f5!?

This is an ambitious move. The bishops compensate for a slightly inferior pawn structure and Black has a comfortable position, where such moves as 19...♖b8, 19...♗d7 or even 19...g5!?, (holding onto the e5-outpost) come into consideration. The text leads to a general weakening of the Black camp and a surprising finish.

20 f4 ♗d4+ 21 ♔h1 fxe4 22 ♘xe4 c5

23 ♗g2 ♖b8 24 ♘g5 ♗a6

How does White win? Not by 25 ♗d5+ ♔h8 26 ♘f7+?, which fails to 26...♖xf7 27 ♗xf7 ♗b7+, but by...

25 ♕b3+!! 1-0

25...♖xb3 (or 25...♔h8 26 ♘f7+ ♖xf7 27 ♕xb8+) 26 ♗d5+ ♔h8 27 ♘f7+ mates or wins material.

Summary

In the Classical Defence, Black has to find a good continuation against each of White's two main moves: 4 c3 and 4 0-0.

Recent experience suggests that 4 c3 should be met by 4...♘f6, as in game 28, and 4 0-0 by either 4...♛f6 (game 33), or 4...d6 (game 32).

1 e4 e5 2 ♘f3 ♘c6 3 ♗b5 ♗c5 4 c3

> 4 0-0 *(D)*

>> 4...♛f6 – *Game 33*

>> 4...♘d4 – *Game 31*

>> 4...d6 5 c3 ♗d7 6 d4 ♗b6 7 ♗g5 f6 8 ♗e3 ♘ge7 9 a4 – *Game 32*

4...♘f6

> 4...♘ge7 – *Game 30*

> 4...f5 *(D)* 5 d4 fxe4 6 ♘xe5 ♘xe5 7 ♛h5+ ♘f7 8 ♗c4 – *Game 29*

5 d4 exd4 6 e5 ♘e4 7 cxd4 ♗b4+ 8 ♘bd2 0-0 9 0-0 d5 *(D)* – *Game 28*

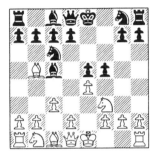

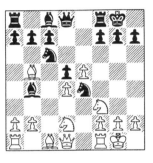

4 0-0   *4...f5*   *9...d5*

CHAPTER FIVE

The Steinitz Defence

1 e4 e5 2 ♘f3 ♘c6 3 ♗b5 d6

This has the reputation for being dull, passive and unambitious. The notes to the Alekhine-Capablanca game concentrate on those variations that earned the Steinitz it's dour image.

A modern approach, championed by Onischuk and Reinderman shows that Black can play the Steinitz with a more interesting game in mind. Black needs to capture on d4 and get his bishop to the a1-h8 diagonal.

Many of the hitherto book lines, claiming an edge for White, are often based on passive or incorrect play from Black and needed a fresh look. Furthermore, Black's set-up is certainly solid, even if White can hold onto a traditional opening pull based on space and more active pieces.

So, in my opinion, it's better than its reputation and worth the occasional try.

Game 34
Oral-Onischuk
Koszalin 1999

---

1 e4 e5 2 ♘f3 ♘c6 3 ♗b5 d6 4 d4

4 ♗xc6+ is akin to the 'Steinitz Deferred' (3...a6 4 ♗a4 d6 5 ♗xc6+) where Black's a-pawn is on a6 (this makes no real difference in practice). A model of how Black

should continue is 4 ♗xc6+ bxc6 5 d4 f6 6 ♗e3 ♘e7 7 ♘c3 ♘g6 8 ♕d2 ♗e7 9 h4 h5 10 0-0-0 ♗e6 11 dxe5 fxe5 12 ♘g5 ♗xg5 13 ♗xg5 (Ciocaltea considers 13 hxg5 ♕b8 14 ♖dg1 to be unclear) 13...♕b8 14 b3 ♕b4 15 f3 a5, with excellent play for Black, Ivkov-Smyslov, Yugoslavia vs. USSR 1956.

4...♗d7

For 4...exd4 see Game 35.

Instead 4...♗g4?! is sharp but probably not totally sound, for example 5 d5 a6 6 ♗a4 b5 7 dxc6 bxa4 8 c4 f5! (the best chance) 9 h3 ♗xf3 (9...♗h5?! 10 exf5 e4 11 g4 favours White) 10 ♕xf3 fxe4 11 ♕xe4 ♘f6 12 ♕c2 and White is better, although Black can inaugurate complications with 12...d5.

5 ♘c3

Defending the e-pawn and thus threatening to exchange on c6 followed by capturing twice on e5.

5...exd4 6 ♘xd4 g6

The modern way of handling the Steinitz. Black plays as in the Larsen variation of the Philidor (1 e4 e5 2 ♘f3 d6 3 d4 exd4 4 ♘xd4 g6) where the bishop takes up an active role on the long-diagonal.

7 ♗e3

There are three alternatives:

a) An interesting attempt to punish ...g6 is 7 h4!?, when perhaps Black should try 7...♘f6 8 ♗xc6 bxc6 9 ♗g5 h6. Instead 7...♗g7 allows 8 ♗xc6 bxc6 9 h5, which is troublesome for Black. A game Gusev-Zeliandinov, USSR 1976 continued 9...♕b8 (9...c5 is met by 10 ♘de2 keeping things solid in the centre) 10 ♕d3 ♕b4 11 ♘de2 a5 12 a3 and White had the better chances. Black had the unenviable choice of allowing h5-h6 or capturing on h5, leaving a fragile kingside.

b) 7 ♗xc6 bxc6 8 ♗f4 ♗g7 9 ♕d2 ♘f6 10 f3 (10 e5 ♘h5!? 11 exd6 ♘xf4 12 ♕xf4 ♕f6!? is double-edged but 10 ♗h6 is simplest) 10...0-0 11 0-0-0 ♕b8 with complications, Timman-Miles, Tilburg 1978.

c) 7 0-0 ♗g7 8 ♗xc6 bxc6 9 ♖e1, is another idea recommended by ECO, but then the continuation 9...♘e7 10 ♗f4 0-0 11 ♕d2 ♖e8 gives Black a flexible position where 12 e5 can be met by 12...♘f5 or 12...♕b8.

7...♗g7 8 ♕d2 ♘f6

8...♘ge7 is best met by 9 h4! (but even after 9 f3 0-0 10 h4 d5 11 0-0-0 dxe4 12 ♘b3 a6 13 ♗f1 ♗e6 14 ♕f2 ♕c8 15 ♘xe4, Pavlov-Papastopolu, Sofia 1967, White retained the better options).

9 f3

All sources suggest 9 ♗xc6 bxc6 10 ♗h6, as a safe way for an edge. However, whilst wondering about what Onischuk had prepared, I found that the quoted games were in fact not so well handled by Black. After 10...♗xh6 (10...0-0?! 11 ♗xg7 ♔xg7 12 0-0-0 ♖e8 13 f3 ♕b8 14 g4, Psakhis-Haik, Sochi 1985, made Black's kingside look too draughty) 11 ♕xh6 ♘g4 12 ♕d2 ♕h4 13 g3 ♕h3?! (the queen is out of play on h3 so 13...♕e7! is a clear improvement, keeping things 'tight at the back') 14 f4 0-0 15 0-0-0 and White had the better options in Kholmov-Kimelfeld, USSR 1970. Worth a try is the flexible 11...♕e7!?, with the idea of meeting 12 0-0-0 with 12...0-0-0, and if 12 0-0 only now 12...♘g4 followed by castling short.

9...0-0 10 0-0-0

Allowing a neat tactical trick that equalises.

10...♘xd4 11 ♗xd4

11...♘xe4! 12 ♘xe4

12 fxe4? is just bad after 12...♗xd4 13 ♕xd4 ♗xb5 14 ♘xb5 ♕g5+ 15 ♔b1 ♕xb5.

12...♗xb5 13 ♕c3

Possible is 13 ♗xg7 ♔xg7 14 ♕c3+ f6 15

♘c5 ♕c8 16 ♕b3 ♗d7 17 ♘xd7 ♕xd7 18 ♕xb7, analysed by Keres and Geller as yielding equality.

13...♗xd4 14 ♕xd4 f5 15 ♕d5+ ♔g7

Otherwise 15...♖f7 16 ♘xd6 ♕xd6 17 ♕xb5 ♕b6 18 ♕e2, Miklaiev-Niesman, Moscow 1968, is dead equal.

16 ♘xd6

This has already been seen in a number of games. The resulting ending is equal but with bishop against knight there is sufficient asymmetry for the stronger player to create winning chances. Perhaps now 16...♗a6! is the most precise reply.

16...♗c6 17 ♕e5+ ♕f6 18 ♘c4 b5!?

18...♖f7 is more solid but then 19 ♕xf6+ ♔xf6 20 ♘a5 allows White a nominal edge.

19 ♕xf6+

19 ♕xc7+?? loses on the spot to 19...♖f7.

19...♔xf6 20 ♘a5 ♗e8 21 ♖he1 ♖f7 22 b4 ♖d7 23 ♔b2

Threatening 24 ♖xe8. Onischuk avoids this and starts to get his kingside moving but he has some weaknesses on the other wing.

23...♖xd1 24 ♖xd1 h5 25 ♖d5 h4

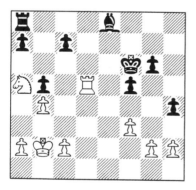

26 ♔c3?!

The solid 26 f4 g5 27 fxg5+ ♔xg5 28 ♔c3 was one improvement, but the most logical seems to be 26 ♖c5! ♖d8 27 ♔c1!, when White shouldn't be worse (but not 27 ♖xc7?! as Black is too active after 27...♖d2).

26...g5 27 ♘b3 h3 28 gxh3?

Definitely losing the thread. Instead 28

g4! was still unclear.

28...♗c6 29 ♖d3 ♖h8 30 ♘d4 ♗e8 31 f4 gxf4 32 ♔d2 ♗f7 33 ♖a3 ♗c4 34 ♖a6+ ♔e5 35 ♘f3+ ♔d5 36 h4 ♖e8 37 ♖f6 ♖e2+ 38 ♔d1 ♖e3 39 ♘g5 ♔e5 40 ♖f8 f3 41 ♘h3 ♖e4 42 ♖h8 ♔d4

43 ♖h5 0-1

Hastening the end as Black now wins immediately with the continuation 43...f2 44 ♘xf2 ♗e2+.

Game 35
Alekhine-Capablanca
Saint Petersburg 1914

This game looks at the 'old-fashioned' lines, as well as being a model of how to play against a premature ♘f5 by White.

1 e4 e5 2 ♘f3 ♘c6 3 ♗b5 d6 4 d4 exd4

The alternative plan of trying to avoid the capture on d4 fails to impress. After 4...♗d7 5 ♘c3 ♘f6?! (or 5...♘ge7?! 6 ♗c4!, when Black's best is the somewhat passive 6...♘xd4 7 ♘xd4 exd4 8 ♕xd4 ♘c6 9 ♕e3 ♗e6 10 ♘d5, Lasker-Steinitz, 5th match-game 1894; superior is 5...exd4! as in game 34) 6 0-0 ♗e7 7 ♖e1 Black should play 7...exd4, transposing back to the main game. Maintaining the tension with 7...0-0? constitutes a serious blunder; 8 ♗xc6 ♗xc6 9 dxe5 dxe5 10 ♕xd8 ♖axd8 11 ♘xe5 ♗xe4 12 ♘xe4 ♘xe4 13 ♘d3 f5 14 f3 ♗c5+ 15 ♘xc5 ♘xc5 16 ♗g5

and White was virtually winning, Tarrasch-Marco, Dresden 1892.

Even more troublesome is 6 ♗xc6! ♗xc6 7 ♕d3 ♘d7 (after 7...exd4 8 ♘xd4 ♗d7 9 ♗g5 ♗e7 10 0-0-0 0-0 11 f4, Spielmann-Maroczy, Gothenburg 1920, Black is cramped and White has all the chances) 8 ♗e3 (8 d5 ♘c5 9 ♕c4 ♗d7 10 b4 is not bad either, just playing for a space advantage), when Black has little option but to take on d4 anyway; 8...exd4 9 ♗xd4 f6 10 ♘h4 ♘e5 11 ♕e2 ♕d7 12 f4 ♘g6 13 ♕h5 with a promising position, I.Zaitsev-Smyslov, Moscow 1967.

5 ♘xd4 ♗d7 6 ♘c3 ♘f6

The modern move is 6...g6 (see Game 34).

7 0-0 ♗e7 8 ♘f5?!

A poor decision. Black is able to exchange a pair of minor pieces and weaken the White pawn structure. More testing is 8 ♖e1 0-0

and then White has three interesting options:

a) First of all 9 ♗f1 ♖e8 10 b3 ♘g4! 11 ♘xc6 bxc6 12 ♗b2 ♗f6 only leads to equality according to Kasparov.

b) After 9 ♗g5 h6 10 ♗h4 ♘h7 (or 10...♖e8!?, Keres's suggestion) 11 ♗xe7 ♕xe7 12 ♘d5 ♕d8, Black's position is not particularly dynamic, but he can relieve the pressure through exchanges, for example 13 c3 ♘f6 14 ♗f1 ♖e8 15 ♕f3 ♘xd5 and Black had more or less equalised, Wolf-Maroczy, Trenchianske Teplice 1922.

c) 9 ♗xc6! (gives Black some static pawn weaknesses to worry about) 9...bxc6 10 ♕d3 ♖e8 11 b3! (the bishop is well-placed on the long diagonal and Black has no play on the b-file) 11...♗f8 12 ♗b2 c5 13 ♘f3 ♗c6 14 ♖ad1 h6 and after 15 e5!, Nunn-Portisch, Budapest (6th matchgame), White kept a persistent edge due to his better pawns and more active pieces.

8...♗xf5 9 exf5 0-0

10 ♖e1

10 g4!? was suggested by Golombek. At least White has some space as compensation for a compromised structure.

10...♘d7 11 ♘d5 ♗f6 12 c3 ♘b6

Black's pieces have found reasonable squares and White will have to retreat or allow exchanges.

13 ♘xf6+

13 ♘e3 won't help White to complete his

development.

13...♕xf6 14 ♗xc6 bxc6 15 ♕f3 ♖fe8 16 ♗e3 c5 17 ♖e2 ♖e5 18 ♖ae1 ♖ae8

Instead 18...♖xf5? fails to 19 ♗d4!, and 18...♕xf5?! 19 ♕xf5 ♖xf5, leads to drawish simplification after 20 ♗xc5.

After the superior text move the f-pawn will inevitably fall and White is forced to seek counterplay by chasing far-off queenside pawns.

19 ♕b7

Unfortunately for White 19 g4 g6, leads to the loss of the f5-pawn anyway.

19...♕xf5 20 ♕xc7 ♕e6 21 ♕xa7 ♘d5 22 ♔f1?

Surely 22 g3! was correct, as if 22...♘f4 (not 22...♕h3?, as 23 ♗g5! exploits Black's back rank frailty) then 23 gxf4 leads to a draw by perpetual check. Has Black anything better than this?

22...♘f4 23 ♖d2 ♘xg2!

A blow that leads to a comfortable win for Black.

24 ♔xg2 ♕g4+ 25 ♔f1 ♕h3+ 26 ♔e2 ♖xe3+ 27 fxe3 ♕xe3+ 28 ♔d1 ♕xe1+ 29 ♔c2 ♕e4+ 30 ♔b3?

Objectively better is 30 ♔c1, but after the reply 30...h5! an extra pawn and the exposed white monarch, as well as owning the superior pieces, all suggest that Black is winning the game.

30...♕c6 31 a4 d5 32 a5 ♕b5+ 33 ♔a3 ♖b8 34 ♔a2 h6 35 a6

35...♕b3+ 0-1

Game 36
Timman-Reinderman
Rotterdam 1998

1 e4 e5 2 ♘f3 ♘c6 3 ♗b5 d6 4 d4 exd4 5 ♕xd4

In the game this position was reached via the Philidor move-order of 2...d6 3 d4 exd4 4 ♕xd4 ♘c6 5 ♗b5.

5...♘ge7

5...♗d7 can be made to look a bit passive by 6 ♗xc6 ♗xc6 7 ♘c3! (after 7 ♗g5?!, Black defends with the surprising 7...♗e7!, as 8 ♕xg7 ♗f6 9 ♕xh8 ♗xh8 10 ♗xd8 ♗xb2, only leads to equality) when White kept a bind on the centre after 7...♘f6 8 ♗g5 ♗e7 9 0-0-0 0-0 10 ♖he1 in Parma-S.Nikolic, Yugoslav Championship 1969. In many such positions the White central pawn on e4 (against a counterpart on d6) keeps Black cramped well into the game.

6 ♗g5

Otherwise 6 ♗e3 a6 7 ♗xc6+ ♘xc6 8 ♕d2 ♗e7 9 ♘c3 0-0 10 0-0-0 ♗f6 11 ♘d5 ♖e8 12 ♕d3 ♗g4, Kholmov-Vorotnikov, Moscow 1991, gave Black reasonable chances for equality. Another alternative 6 ♕c3 has been tried a few times recently, but it takes away the best square from White's knight and doesn't seem dangerous, for example 6...a6 7 ♗a4 ♗d7 8 0-0 ♘g6 9 ♗b3 ♘ge5 10 ♘xe5 dxe5 11 ♕g3 ♕f6 12 ♘c3 ♕g6 with equality, Kupreichik-Reinderman, Batumi 1999.

6...a6

At first sight 6...f6 followed by ...a6, suggested by Maroczy, looks ugly if you are sympathetic to the bishop on f8! However Reinderman shows how the idea actually seems playable, especially (as in the game) when Black can gain further time with a later ...g5.

7 ♗xc6+ ♘xc6

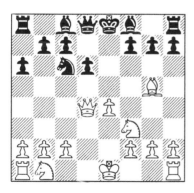

Taking on d8 gives nothing so White must move his queen.

8 ♕e3

This is seemingly more active than 8 ♕d2 but they both have points in their favour. The continuation 8 ♕d2 ♗e7 (8...f6 looks less good here in view of 9 ♗e3) 9 ♘c3 ♗xg5 10 ♘xg5 0-0 11 0-0-0 h6 12 ♘f3 b5

(more solid are 12...f5 13 e5 dxe5 14 ♕xd8 ♖xd8 15 ♖xd8+ ♘xd8 16 ♘xe5 and 12...♗g4 13 h3 ♗xf3 14 gxf3, when in both cases White's edge is kept to a minimum) 13 ♕f4 b4 14 ♘d5 f6 15 ♘h4, Ulibin-Adams, Halkidiki 1992, left White clearly on top as Black's pawn structure was a mess and he lacked any convincing counter to White's space advantage.

The disadvantage of the queen on e3 is that it provokes Black's continuation in the game.

8...f6!?

Playing for a more active game than the routine 8...♗e7.

9 ♗h4 ♗e6 10 ♘c3 g5 11 ♗g3 ♗g7 12 0-0-0 0-0

Black has played rather ambitiously and has found reasonable squares for his pieces, but his pawn on g5 is asking to be attacked!

13 h4

Hoping to loosen the Black structure.

13...g4 14 ♘d4 ♘xd4 15 ♖xd4 f5! 16 e5 ♖e8 17 ♕d3?!

If 17 ♖dd1? (unpinning) then 17...♗d7! (unpinning on the d-file but effectively pinning and winning the e-pawn!). Instead 17 f4 is a safer way to proceed but in any case Black seems to have enough counterplay with his bishops.

The text prepares an interesting exchange sacrifice.

17...♕c8 18 exd6! ♗xd4 19 ♕xd4 cxd6

20 h5!

Preparing a devilish attack with h5-h6 followed by ♖h1-h5.

20...h6 21 ♕f6

Timman forces the win of the h-pawn and at first sight seems to have compensation for the exchange, but Black now manages to organise an effective defence.

21...♗f7 22 ♕xh6 ♕e6 23 ♕g5+ ♔h7 24 ♖d1 ♕h6!

24...♖ad8?? is refuted by 25 ♘d5.

25 ♕xh6+ ♔xh6 26 ♖xd6+ ♔g5 27 ♖b6

And here 27 ♖d7? is not good after 27...♖ad8, as the forced exchange of rooks favours Black.

27...♖ad8 28 b3 ♗d5 29 ♗c7

The alternative 29 ♘xd5 ♖xd5 30 ♖xb7 fails to 30...f4.

29...♗xg2!

A better choice than 29...♖d7, as after 30 ♘xd5 ♖xd5 31 ♖xb7 ♖e2 White has 32 g3!.

30 ♗xd8+ ♖xd8 31 ♘e2 ♗c6 32 ♖b4 ♔xh5

With majorities on opposite wings the

bishop is powerful and so Black has winning chances, but Timman's experience saves the day.

33 ♘f4+ ♔h4 34 a4 ♖d6 35 ♘d3 ♔g5 36 ♔d2 f4 37 ♔e1 ♗f3 38 ♖c4 g3 39 fxg3 fxg3 40 ♖c8 ♖e6+ 41 ♔f1 g2+ 42 ♔g1 ♗c6 43 ♖g8+ ♔f6 44 ♔f2 ♖d6 45 ♘e1 ♔f7 46 ♖g3 ♖f6+ 47 ♔e2 ♖e6+ 48 ♔f2 ♖f6+ 49 ♔e2 ♖g6 50 ♖xg6 ♔xg6 51 ♔f2 ♗e4 52 ♘xg2 ♗xc2 53 a5 ♗xb3 54 ♔e3 ♔f5 ½-½

Summary

The Steinitz has the reputation of being solid but passive, which is certainly true of many lines in game 35. The modern way involves the fianchetto of the king's bishop, as examined in game 34, and Black certainly has more chances for counterplay. White can avoid ...g6 by recapturing on d4 with the queen (game 36). There Reinderman's plan of ...f6, ...g5 and ...♗g7 is double-edged.

The Steinitz with its modern interpretation is playable and surprisingly dynamic, but I suspect that White can keep a small space advantage.

1 e4 e5 2 ♘f3 ♘c6 3 ♗b5 d6 4 d4 exd4 *(D)* **5 ♘xd4**

     5 ♕xd4 ♘ge7 6 ♗g5 a6 – *Game 36*

5...♗d7 6 ♘c3 *(D)* **g6**

     6...♘f6 7 0-0 ♗e7 – *Game 35*

7 ♗e3 ♗g7 8 ♕d2 ♘f6 9 f3 0-0 10 0-0-0 ♘xd4 11 ♗xd4 *(D)* **♘xe4** – *Game 34*

    4...exd4   *6 ♘c3*   *11 ♗xd4*

CHAPTER SIX

Bird's Defence

1 e4 e5 2 ♘f3 ♘c6 3 ♗b5 ♘d4

At first sight the move 3...♘d4 seems to disobey a fundamental opening principal; moving the same piece twice before developing the remainder of the Black forces. There is a slight loss of time involved but on the plus side the reduction of White's central pressure is immediate.

There was a great surge in popularity for the Bird's in the mid-eighties, but now it is generally considered to be inferior. None of the world's elite have played it recently.

The e5-pawn, once displaced to the d4-square, has a cramping effect on the white position. White on the other hand is free to advance his e- and f-pawns, so Black reacts with ...d5 or ...f5 to limit their potential.

In the Bird's, there is no simple 'drawing-line' for White, nor is he ever totally in control of events. Black retains a certain flexibility with his king's knight coming either to f6 or e7, depending on circumstances, and the unusual pawn-structures set special problems to keep White on his toes.

The consensus of opinion is that after 4 ♘xd4 exd4 White should try 5 0-0 ♗c5 6 ♗c4, or 6 d3 c6 7 ♗a4, both of which require accurate play from Black. Can Black equalise? Possibly not, but it's a good practical choice that creates interesting chess and realistic winning chances.

Game 37
Kamsky-Ivanchuk
Tilburg 1990

1 e4 e5 2 ♘f3 ♘c6 3 ♗b5 ♘d4 4 ♘xd4

This is White's main move. For 4 ♗c4 see Game 42.

4...exd4 5 0-0 ♗c5 6 d3 c6 7 ♗a4!

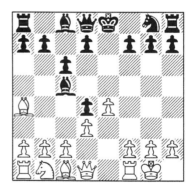

One of White's best systems against the Bird's. The pin along the a4-e8 diagonal is maintained and the ...d5-break is delayed and thus becomes less effective.

7...♘e7

The continuation 7...d6 8 f4 f5 is considered more accurate by ECO, but the weakness of the a2-g8 diagonal is still a problem. Critical is then 9 ♘d2 ♘f6 10 ♗b3 ♘g4! (10...d5 is similar to the main game) 11 exf5 (the provocative 11 ♖e1!? tempts Black into 11...♕h4 12 ♘f3 ♕f2+ 13 ♔h1 fxe4 14 dxe4 d3 15 h3 h5, which is given by Meister as unclear) 11...♗xf5 12 ♖e1+ ♔d7!

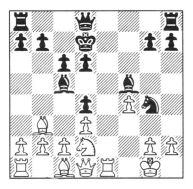

as in Novik-Meister, USSR Championship 1991, and after 13 ♘f3 ♕f6 14 h3 h5 it was Black who had the attacking chances. Meister won this game and ECO is convinced by Black's play, but the whole set-up looks somehow artificial and white players should be able to find something. However, at present it represents Black's best chance against the ♗a4 idea.

8 f4 f5

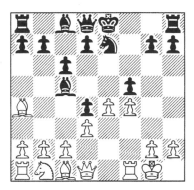

Virtually forced. After 8...d5?! 9 f5! the knight on e7 has no future and Black's position already looks dodgy, for instance

9...dxe4 10 dxe4 0-0 11 ♗b3 ♗d6 12 ♕h5 d3 13 cxd3 ♗e5 14 ♖f3, Spassky-Barua, New York 1987, when the ex-World Champion had an extra pawn plus an attack.

9 ♗b3!

Now White switches attention to the weakened b3-g8 diagonal. This is stronger than 9 ♕h5+, which was safely diffused in Blatny-Malaniuk, Warsaw 1989 with 9...g6 10 ♕h6 ♘g8 11 ♕g7 ♕f6, when the ending was equal.

9...d5 10 exd5 ♘xd5 11 ♖e1+ ♔f8 12 ♕h5 g6 13 ♕h6+ ♔g8 14 ♘d2

The knight is aiming for the e5-square whereupon it will dominate the battlefield.

14...♗f8 15 ♕h3 ♗g7 16 ♘f3 h6 17 ♘e5 ♕f6 18 ♗xd5+!

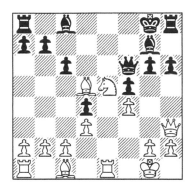

Leaving Black with static weaknesses everywhere.

18...cxd5 19 b3! ♔h7 20 ♗b2 ♕b6 21 ♕f3 ♖e8 22 ♕f2

Picking off a pawn and then, despite the presence of opposite bishops, the ending is probably lost for Black.

22...♗xe5 23 ♖xe5 ♖xe5 24 ♗xd4 ♖e2 25 ♗xb6 ♖xf2 26 ♗xf2 ♔g7 27 a4 ♗e6 28 a5 a6 29 ♗d4+ ♔f7 30 ♔f2 ♖c8 31 ♖a2 g5 32 ♗e5 ♔g6 33 ♔e3 ♔h5 34 ♔d2

34 ♔d4! looks more precise, intending to meet 34...♔g4, with 35 c3! gxf4 36 ♖f2.

34...♖g8 35 g3 ♔g4 36 ♔e3 ♔h3 37 c3 d4+

37...♖c8 38 ♔d4 ♖c6, just holding everything, is a more robust defence.

38 ♔xd4 ♖d8+ 39 ♔e3 ♗xb3 40 ♖b2 ♗d5 41 c4 ♗g2 42 ♖b6 ♗f1

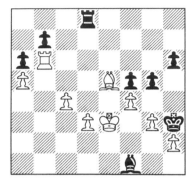

43 ♖xh6+

43 ♔f2! creates a mating net.

43...♔g2 44 d4 g4 45 c5 ♗c4 46 ♖f6 1-0

After 46...♔xh2 47 ♔f2! ♖h8 48 ♖xf5 ♖h3 49 ♖g5 it's all over.

Game 38
Hamarat-Burger
Correspondence 1990

---

1 e4 e5 2 ♘f3 ♘c6 3 ♗b5 ♘d4 4 ♘xd4 exd4 5 0-0

For alternative moves see Games 40-41.

5...♗c5

6 ♗c4

Because of a primitive threat Black doesn't have time for ...c7-c6 and ...d7-d5.

White has tried alternative ways to disorganise the black development plan:

a) 6 ♕g4 ♕f6! 7 b4?! ♗xb4 8 c3 ♗e7 9 cxd4 ♕xd4 10 ♘c3 c6 11 ♗a4 d5 12 ♕g3 dxe4 13 ♗b2 ♘f6 was clearly better for Black in J.Horvath-Flear, Zenica 1987.

b) 6 ♕h5!? (this is more promising) 6...♕e7 7 d3 ♘f6 8 ♕h4 c6 9 ♗a4 (9 ♗c4 is countered by 9...d5!) 10 exd5 ♘xd5 11 ♗g5 f6 12 ♗d2 ♗e6 with equal play, G.Kuzmin-Malaniuk, Trud vs. CSKA 1986) 9...a5 10 a3 b5 11 ♗b3 a4 12 ♗a2 d6, Fercec-Naumkin, Pula 1988. White's natural plan is to play ♗g5 and a timely ♗xf6, but in my opinion Black's space will compensate for his inferior structure, for instance, 13 ♗g5 can be met by 13...♗e6 14 f4 ♗xa2 15 ♖xa2 ♕e6 with a satisfactory position.

6...d6

Missing the point with 6...c6??, fails to 7 ♗xf7+ ♔xf7 8 ♕h5+.

7 d3 ♕h4?!

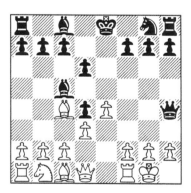

Aggressive but probably not quite adequate.

There are three alternatives worthy of note, of these 7...c6 has the best reputation:

a) 7...c6, after which 8 f4 can be met by 8...♘f6, intending to meet 9 e5?! with 9...♘d5, or by 8...f5. After the key continuation 7...c6 8 ♕h5 ♕e7, we obtain the following position.

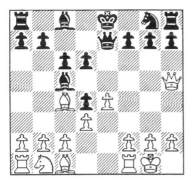

White may be able to squeeze a slight edge out of the position, but the two critical games are not that clear;

a1) 9 ♘d2 ♘f6 10 ♕h4 g5!? (10...♗e6 is more solid), Dvoiris-Ja.Meister, Russia 1992, when Dvoiris prefers White slightly after 11 ♕xg5 ♖g8 12 ♕f4 (12 ♕h4 ♖g4 13 ♕h6 ♖g6 repeats after 14 ♕h4 etc.) 12...♗h3 13 g3, as White has compensation for the exchange.

a2) 9 ♗g5 ♘f6 10 ♕h4 0-0 11 f4 h6 12 ♗xf6 ♕xf6 13 ♕xf6 gxf6 14 f5 ♖d8 15 ♘d2 d5 16 exd5 cxd5 (Black has enough space and central control to compensate his six(!) pawn islands) 17 ♗b3 a5 18 a4 ♗b4 19 ♘f3 (after 19 ♖ad1 ♗xd2 20 ♖xd2 it's not clear who has the 'bad' bishop) 19...♗xf5 20 ♘xd4 ♗c5 21 ♖xf5 ♗xd4+ 22 ♔f1 ♗xb2 was Serper-Naumkin, Tashkent 1987, which was eventually drawn.

b) Development with 7...♘e7 8 ♗g5 0-0 9 ♕h5 ♗e6 doesn't seem fully adequate as the continuation 10 ♕h4 ♖e8 11 ♗xe6 fxe6 12 f4! ♕d7 13 ♖f3! ♘g6 (13...h6? 14 ♗xh6!) 14 ♕h5 ♘f8 15 ♘d2 gave White the initiative in Brenke-Binder, correspondence 1994. However Black can then limit White to an edge by now playing the cautious 15...♕f7.

c) 7...♘f6?! allows an awkward pin with 8 ♗g5, about which Black needs to do something. Gelfand-Kupreichik, Sverdlovsk 1987, then continued 8...h6 9 ♗h4 g5 10 ♗g3 ♘g4 11 h3 ♘e5 12 ♗b3 ♗e6 13 ♕h5 ♗xb3 14

axb3 and, with f4 in the air, White had excellent prospects.

8 ♘d2 ♘f6 9 f4 ♗e6 10 ♘f3 ♕h5 11 ♗b3 ♗xb3 12 axb3 ♗b6 13 h3 0-0-0 14 ♗d2!

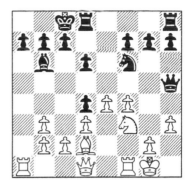

An improvement based on the presumption that White should be better in a middle-game scrap. Instead 14 ♘g5 ♕xd1 15 ♖xd1 ♖de8 16 ♗d2 a6 17 ♘xf7 ♖hf8 18 ♘g5 h6 19 ♘f3 d5 gave Black enough play for the pawn in Cheshkovsky-Klaric, Moscow 1989.

14...h6 15 ♗e1!

Hamarat also suggests 15 ♖a4!? d5 (perhaps 15...♘d7!?) 16 e5 ♘d7 17 ♗a5! g5 18 ♗xb6 ♘xb6 19 ♖xa7 gxf4 20 ♕d2 with a clear advantage to White.

15...♖dg8

Black doesn't have an easy choice, as 15...g5 16 fxg5 hxg5 17 ♘h2! gives White a strong initiative on the f-file, while 15...d5 16 e5 ♘d7 17 ♗f2 c5 allows 18 b4, breaking up the Black centre. He could have tried the cunning 15...♔b8!? 16 ♗f2 c5 17 c3 dxc3 18 bxc3 and now that White hasn't the same play on the f-line, the plucky 18...g5!. In all cases however, White is still better.

16 ♗f2 g5?!

After 16...c5, White intended 17 ♗c1, stopping 17...g5?, because of 18 fxg5 hxg5 19 ♘xd4! etc.

17 ♘xd4 g4 18 ♘f5 gxh3 19 g3! ♘g4!?

Following the natural 19...♗xf2+ 20 ♖xf2 ♕xd1+ 21 ♖xd1 ♔d7, White just pockets the lose h-pawn with 22 ♖h2 ♘h5 23 ♔f2.

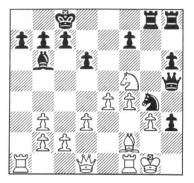

20 ♗xb6 axb6 21 ♘e7+ ♔b8 22 ♘xg8 ♖xg8 23 b4!

Stopping the opposing queen coming to c5.

23...c6 24 ♕f3 ♕b5

After 24...h2+ 25 ♔h1 ♕h3, White has 26 ♖fe1!, preparing to consolidate with ♕g2.

25 c3 c5 26 ♖ac1 h5 27 ♔h1 ♕a4 28 bxc5 bxc5 29 ♖fe1 ♕b3 30 ♖e2 f6 31 d4 ♕c4 32 ♖d1 ♕a4 33 ♖ed2 ♕c6 34 dxc5 f5!

Creating some tricks, but as the game took place over a three or four year period, White probably had sufficient time 'on the calendar' to find a way to transpose to a winning ending!

35 ♕d3! ♕xc5 36 b4! ♕c6

36...♘f2+ 37 ♖xf2 ♕xf2 fails dismally to 38 ♕xd6+, picking up the rook on g8 with

check.

37 b5 ♕xe4+ 38 ♕xe4 fxe4 39 ♖xd6 ♔c8 40 b6! ♘f2+ 41 ♔h2 ♘xd1 42 ♖xd1 h4 43 gxh4 ♖g4 44 ♔xh3 ♖xf4 45 ♖d4! ♖f3+ 46 ♔g4 ♖xc3 47 ♖xe4 ♔d7 48 h5 ♔c6

After 48...♖c6 the move 49 ♔g5! leads to a win, for instance 49...♖xb6 50 h6 ♖b5+ 51 ♔g6 ♖b1 52 ♖e5 b5 53 h7 ♖h1 54 ♖h5.

49 ♖e6+ ♔d7 50 ♖g6 ♔e7 51 ♖g7+ ♔f8 52 ♖xb7 ♖c6 53 ♔f5 ♔e8

54 ♖b8+ 1-0

Game 39
Zulfugarli-Najer
Bydgoszcz 1999

1 e4 e5 2 ♘f3 ♘c6 3 ♗b5 ♘d4 4 ♘xd4 exd4 5 0-0 ♗c5 6 ♗c4 d6 7 b4

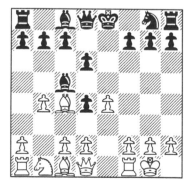

An interesting Evans-style thrust.

The game Khalifman-Kupreichik, Minsk 1986 continued 7 c3 ♕f6 8 ♘a3 ♗xa3 9 ♕a4+ ♗d7 10 ♕xa3 ♘e7 11 ♗e2 0-0 12 d3 ♖fe8 13 cxd4 ♕xd4 14 ♗e3 and was better for White, who has the bishop pair and interesting options in the centre. Instead 7 c3 is best met by 7...c6!, for example 8 cxd4 ♗xd4 9 ♘c3 ♕h4! 10 ♘e2 ♗b6 11 d3 ♗g4 12 ♕e1 ♘e7 13 ♗e3, Liang Jinrong-Ye Rongguang, China 1990, with an interesting position offering balanced chances.

7...♗b6

Tempting is 7...♗xb4 but it allows the manoeuvre 8 ♕h5 ♕d7 9 ♗xf7+ ♕xf7 10 ♕b5+ ♕d7 11 ♕xb4 c5 12 ♕b3, which is more comfortable for White.

8 a4 a6

8...a5 9 bxa5 ♖xa5 10 d3 ♕h4, Ciocaltea-Markovic, Romania 1969, looks equally unclear.

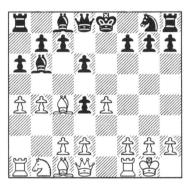

9 ♖a3!?

The more routine 9 d3 ♘e7 10 ♕h5 0-0 11 ♗g5 (11 f4 is best countered by 11...♗e6) 11...♗e6 12 ♘d2 ♗xc4 13 ♗xe7 ♕xe7 14 ♘xc4 ♗a7 15 ♕d5 ♖ab8 was only equal in Kasparov-Kupreichik, USSR 1978.

9...♘f6 10 ♖g3 ♘xe4 11 ♖e1 d5 12 ♖xg7

White should have contented himself with 12 ♗xd5! ♕xd5 13 d3 0-0 (to be avoided are the continuations 13...♗f5?? 14 dxe4 ♗xe4 15 ♘c3 and 13...f5? 14 ♖xg7!) 14 dxe4 ♕c6 15 a5 with a slight initiative.

12...♕f6

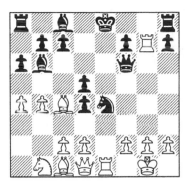

This is the best, as 12...♔f8 looks too dangerous after 13 ♖xf7+! ♔xf7 14 ♕h5+ ♔g7 15 d3, with a vicious attack.

13 ♖xe4+?

This seems to play into his opponent's hands. Instead 13 ♗xd5!? sacrifices the exchange under more favourable circumstances; 13...♕xf2+ 14 ♔h1 ♔f8 15 ♖xf7+ ♕xf7 16 ♗xe4, when Black's king lacks cover.

13...dxe4 14 ♖xf7 ♕g6

Funnily enough the rook is badly placed on f7, getting in the way of any white attacking ideas.

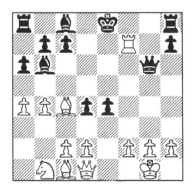

15 a5 ♖g8 16 g3 ♗e6

16...♗a7 was possible, as 17 ♖xc7 ♖f8 18 d3 ♔d8! wins back the exchange.

17 ♗xe6 ♕xe6 18 ♖f4 ♗a7 19 ♕h5+ ♖g6 20 ♕h4

20 ♕xh7 0-0-0 leaves Black with all the trumps.

20...♖h6

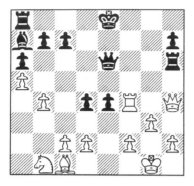

21 ♖xe4

If 21 ♕g5, then 21...e3! is too strong.

21...♖xh4 22 ♖xe6+ ♔f7 23 ♖e5 ♖h6 24 d3 ♖e6 25 ♖xe6 ♔xe6 26 ♘d2 b6 27 ♘b3 ♔d5

With two pawns for the exchange material is equal. However Black's king is well centralised and his rook will create play from afar, so he has the better chances.

28 ♗f4 c5! 29 bxc5 bxa5

A passed pawn is an important asset here.

30 ♘xa5 ♗xc5 31 h4 ♗b4 32 ♘c4 ♔c6 33 ♗e5 ♖d8 34 g4 a5

The race is easily won by Black.

35 g5 a4 36 h5 a3 37 ♘xa3 ♗xa3 38 g6 h6 39 ♗f6 ♖c8 40 ♗xd4 ♔d5 41 c3 ♔e6 42 g7 ♔f7 43 ♔f1 ♗b2 0-1

Game 40
Ljubojevic-Salov
Rotterdam 1989

Black has been generally successful in the main line which involves Black having doubled d-pawns (on d4 and d5), cramping and limiting the White forces. If White obtains play against these pawns Black can usually organise counter-pressure on the e- or c-files.

1 e4 e5 2 ♘f3 ♘c6 3 ♗b5 ♘d4 4 ♘xd4 exd4 5 d3

As we've seen before, 5 0-0 is considered the most precise. After 5...c6 6 ♗c4 d5 7 exd5 cxd5 Black's plan is compromised by 8 ♖e1+, when all the Black replies are uncomfortable. The game Geller-Klaman, USSR 1949 continued 8...♗e7 9 ♗f1 ♗e6 10 c3 ♕d7 11 ♘a3 ♘c6 12 ♕a4 ♗e7 13 ♘c2 when Black has nothing better than 13...dxc3 14 dxc3 allowing White good chances against the isolated d-pawn.

So after 5 0-0, Black's most consistent reply is 5...♗c5, when 6 d3 c6 7 ♗c4 (for 7 ♗a4 see Game 37) 7...d5, gives Black a respectable version of the 'doubled d-pawns' position.

Instead 5 ♕h5!? is simply met by 5...♘f6! 6 ♕e5+ ♕e7 7 ♕xd4 ♕xe4+ which is just equal.

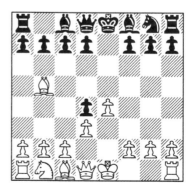

5...c6

After 5...♗c5 White can try 6 ♕h5!? ♕e7

7 ♗g5, but 7...♕d6!? (I prefer this to 7...♘f6?! 8 ♗xf6 gxf6 9 f4 which looks promising for White) 8 ♗c4 ♕g6 offers a solid enough game for Black.

So therefore 6 0-0 c6 7 ♗c4 d5 is analogous to the main game, but here 8 exd5 cxd5 9 ♗b5+ can, with this move-order, be met by 9...♚f8!? giving us the following position.

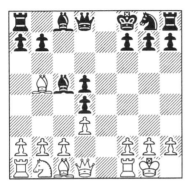

At the cost of a misplaced king, Black retains the light-squared bishops, hoping that White's will be locked out of play. This strategy was more or less successful in Hennigan-Flear, Oakham 1988, which continued 10 ♗a4 ♗e6 11 ♘d2 ♘e7 12 h3 ♘f5 13 ♘f3 f6 14 ♗f4 h5 15 ♖e1 ♗f7 16 h4 ♚g8 17 ♕d2 a6 18 ♖e2 ♚h7 19 ♖ae1 b5 20 ♗b3 a5 21 a3 a4 22 ♗a2 ♖c8 and Black was doing well. Note that White's e-file pressure is hitting empty space whereas Black has a real target on c2.

White has also tried 10 c3 to open up the centre and compete for space, but without great success, for example 10...♘e7 11 cxd4 ♗xd4 12 ♘c3 g6 13 ♗h6+ (13 ♘e2 ♗g7 14 d4 is about equal) 13...♚g8!? 14 ♖e1 ♗e6 15 ♗g5 h6 16 ♗e3 (after 16 ♗xe7 ♕xe7 not 17 ♘xd5? in view of 17...♕c5) 16...♘f5 17 ♗xd4 ♘xd4 18 ♗a4 ♕g5 19 ♚h1 ♖c8 20 ♗b3 ♚g7 21 ♕c1 a6 22 ♕e3 ♕f6 23 ♗d1 ♘c2! 24 ♗xc2 d4 25 ♕e2 dxc3 26 bxc3 ♕xc3 27 ♗b3 ♗xb3 28 axb3 ♖he8 29 ♕f1 ♕xb3 30 ♖eb1 ♕d5 31 ♕d1 ♖c3 0-1 Sigurjonsson-Kupreichik, Winnipeg 1986.

These examples suggest that 9...♚f8 is a worthwhile ambitious alternative to 9...♗d7.

6 ♗c4 d5 7 exd5 cxd5 8 ♗b5+

Experience has shown that keeping too many pieces on is not advantageous for White as the doubled d-pawns have a significant cramping effect. So following 8 ♗b3 ♗c5 9 0-0 ♘e7 10 c4 (Black was doing well after both 10 ♗g5 f6 11 ♗f4 0-0 12 ♘d2 ♚h8 13 ♖e1 a5 14 a4 ♗b4 15 h3 g5 16 ♗h2 ♖a6, Beliavsky-Cheshkovsky, USSR Championship 1986 – pleasant initiative – and 10 ♖e1 0-0 11 ♘d2 a5 12 a4 ♗b4 13 ♕f3 ♖a6 14 ♕f4 ♖f6! 15 ♕xd4 b6, Anand-Cheshkovsky, Calcutta 1986 – strong attack for the pawn) 10...0-0 11 cxd5 ♘xd5 12 ♘d2

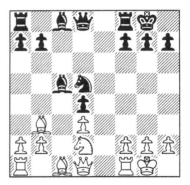

12...♘e3! (simplifying to an equal position) 13 fxe3 dxe3 14 ♕h5 exd2+ 15 ♕xc5 dxc1♕ 16 ♖axc1 ♗e6, Dvoiris-Balashov, USSR Championship 1986, Black had no complaints.

8...♗d7 9 ♗xd7+ ♕xd7 10 0-0 ♗c5 11 ♘d2 ♘e7 12 ♘b3 ♗b6 13 ♗g5 f6

Or 13...0-0 14 ♗xe7 ♕xe7 15 ♖e1 ♕f6 16 ♕h5 ♖ac8, Chandler-Wolf, Germany 1985, when play was about equal.

14 ♗d2 a5 15 ♕h5+!?

Lanc-Cheshkovsky, Trnava 1986 varied with 15 a4 0-0 16 ♖e1 ♘g6 17 h3 ♖fc8 and was also satisfactory for Black.

15...g6 16 ♕f3 0-0 17 ♖fe1 ♘f5

17...a4?! is strongly met by 18 ♗b4!.

18 a4 ♘h4 19 ♕g3 ♘f5 20 ♕g4

A winning try, rather than just repeating.

20...♔g7

It's hard to see how White can improve without c2-c3 coming in somewhere.

21 ♘c1 ♖ac8 22 c3 ♖f7 23 ♕h3 h5!

Maintaining the rock-solid knight on f5.

24 ♘e2 g5!?

Stopping the intended 25 ♘f4. Now, after the text move, if White tries 25 ♕xh5 ♖h8 26 ♕f3 (but not 26 ♕g4? ♖h4 27 ♕f3 g4 28 ♕f4 ♗c7 and Black wins) 26...♘h4 27 ♕g3 ♘f5 28 ♕f3 the game is drawn by repetition.

25 ♘g3 ♘xg3 26 ♕xd7 ♖xd7 27 hxg3 ♔f7 28 ♔f1 ♖h8

Despite Black's slightly inferior queenside pawns, he is not really in danger.

29 cxd4

After 29 ♖ac1 (intending c4) Salov suggests 29...g4 to obtain counterplay. Then

after 30 c4 dxc4 31 ♖xc4 h4 32 gxh4 ♖xh4, despite Black's 'bad' bishop, White cannot increase the pressure.

29...♗xd4 30 ♗xa5 ♗xb2 31 ♖ab1 ♗d4 32 ♖b5 h4 33 gxh4 ♖xh4 34 ♖eb1 ♖e7!

Defending by tactical means.

35 ♔g1 ♖f4 36 ♗b6

If 36 ♗e1 then 36...♖xe1+! would be Black's reply.

36...♗xb6 37 ♖xb6 ♖xa4 38 ♖xb7

38...♖a3 39 d4 ♖d3 40 ♖xe7+ ♔xe7 41 ♖b4 ♖c3 42 g4 ♖c4 43 ♖xc4 dxc4 44 ♔f1 ♔e6 45 ♔e2 ♔d5 46 ♔e3 c3 ½-½

Game 41
Anderssen-Lange
Breslau (2nd matchgame) 1859

This is the sort of game Black dreams of playing when venturing 3...♘d4.

1 e4 e5 2 ♘f3 ♘c6 3 ♗b5 ♘d4 4 ♘xd4 exd4 5 ♗c4

Stopping 5...♗c5?, as this loses a pawn to 6 ♗xf7+, and 7 ♕h5+.

5...♘f6

Still considered to be the best move.

A couple of recent experimental ideas are playable but less convincing; 5...h5!? (slightly committal but preparing ...♗c5) 6 d3 ♗c5 7 ♘d2 c6 8 ♘f3 d5, as in the encounter Am.Rodriguez-Arencibia, Cienfuegos 1996, and 5...g6 6 c3 ♗g7 7 cxd4 ♗xd4 8 0-0 ♘e7 9 d3 0-0 10 ♘c3 ♗g7 11 ♗g5 h6 12 ♗h4 c6, as in Mainka-Moreno, Bayamo 1995, and White is better in both cases.

6 e5

The modern move is 6 0-0, when Black should play 6...d5! (the alternative 6...♘xe4?! has been discarded as dubious in view of 7 ♗xf7+ ♔xf7 8 ♕h5+ g6 9 ♕d5+ ♔g7 10 ♕xe4 ♕f6 11 d3 ♗c5 12 ♘d2 ♖f8 13 ♘f3 h6 14 b3!, Jandemirov-Pandavos, Athens 1994, with pressure building against d4 and along the long diagonal) 7 exd5 ♘xd5 8 ♕h5 c6 9 ♕e5+ ♘e7 (a loss of time but in this way Black is able to keep everything intact) 10 ♖e1 f6 11 ♕f4 ♕b6 12 d3 ♗d7 13 ♕d6 c5 14 ♗f4 ♔d8!, Novikov-Sulman, USSR 1987, a little eccentric perhaps, but after the exchange of queens chances are equal.

Short's innovation 6 ♕e2?! was met vigorously by 6...♗c5 7 e5 0-0! 8 0-0 d5! which led to a Black advantage in Short-Ivanchuk, Linares 1989. The game continued 9 exf6 dxc4 10 ♕h5 b6 11 fxg7 ♖e8 12 d3 cxd3 13 cxd3 ♗a6 14 ♕f3 ♕e7 15 ♗f4 ♕e2, when the bishops were king in the ending.

6...d5! 7 ♗b3

Black has the better centre and development after 7 exf6 dxc4, and 7 ♗b5+ is met simply by 7...♘d7, when the plausible continuation 8 f4 c6 9 ♗e2 ♗c5 10 d3 ♕h4+ 11 g3 ♕e7 12 0-0 0-0 13 ♘d2 f6 looks better for Black.

7...♗g4?

Highly optimistic! Instead 7...♘g4! 8 ♕e2

♕g5 9 0-0 d3! gives Black a promising initiative.

8 f3 ♘e4 9 0-0

Not 9 fxg4?, as this allows 9...♕h4+ 10 g3 ♘xg3.

9...d3 10 fxg4

10 ♕e1! would have made Black's attacking scheme look dubious; 10...♗c5+ 11 ♔h1 ♘f2+ 12 ♖xf2 ♗xf2 13 ♕xf2 dxc2 14 ♘c3 ♗e6 15 d4 clearly favours White.

10...♗c5+ 11 ♔h1 ♘g3+! 12 hxg3 ♕g5 13 ♖f5

Black's next move probably came as a shock.

13...h5!

Mate on the h-file is rather difficult to stop.

14 gxh5 ♕xf5 15 g4 ♖xh5+! 16 gxh5 ♕e4 17 ♕f3 ♕h4+ 18 ♕h3

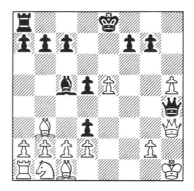

18...♕e1+ 19 ♔h2 ♗g1+ 0-1

> ### Game 42
> ### S.Pedersen-T.Wall
> *Wrexham 1998*

1 e4 e5 2 ♘f3 ♘c6 3 ♗b5 ♘d4 4 ♗c4!?

After the typical 4 ♘xd4 exd4 the pawn on d4 can cramp White's development (see Games 37-41). However retreating the bishop is not generally considered the best try for an advantage.

After the other main retreat 4 ♗a4 Black has a number of options;

a) 4...♘xf3+ (the danger inherent in this simplifying continuation is that Black is behind in development) 5 ♕xf3 ♕f6 6 ♕g3 ♗c5 (after 6...c6 7 ♘c3 d6 8 0-0 ♕g6 9 ♕e3 ♗e7 10 d4 ♗d8!, Lopez-Moreno, Cuba 1996, Black implements a manoeuvre known from the Philidor and despite his cramped position he has counterchances based on ...♗b6) 7 d3 h6 8 ♘c3 c6 9 0-0 ♘e7 10 ♗e3 with a pleasant initiative for White in Papapostolou-Trifunovic, Bad Wildbad 1997. The game continuation 10...♗xe3 (10...♗b6!? is best met by 11 f4) 11 fxe3 ♕g5 12 ♗b3 f6?! (perhaps 12...0-0 13 ♕xg5 hxg5 14 ♖f2 d6 15 ♖af1 ♗e6 was a better defence) suggests that all is not right in the black camp.

b) 4...b5?! is too loosening, as after 5 ♗b3 ♘xb3 6 axb3 ♘f6 7 0-0 d6 8 d4 ♗b7 9 ♖e1 a6 10 ♘c3 Black had problems to complete his development and maintain his centre in

Kr.Georgiev-Hector, Haifa 1989.

c) 4...♕f6!? is perhaps less effective here (than against 4 ♗c4) due to the annoying pin on the d-pawn. This is noticeable on move 8 in the following variation; 5 ♘xd4 exd4 6 0-0 ♗c5 7 d3 ♘e7 8 f4 ♘c6 (now with the white bishop on c4 rather than a4 then 8...d5 would be tempting; here it's illegal) 9 a3 0-0 10 b4 ♗b6 11 ♘d2 d6 12 ♘f3 a6 13 h3 ♗a7 14 ♕e1, Lanc-Shuetz, Slovak Championship 1999, when White had more options. In fact he won quickly due to a blunder; 14...b5?! (14...h6!) 15 ♗b3 ♗e6?? (15...h6) and 16 f5 won a piece as 17 ♗g5 was threatened.

d) Sensible development with 4...♗c5 is the best of the bunch, as if White now captures on e5 then Black reacts with 5...♕g5. The Evans-like 5 b4 can be met by 5...♗xb4! 6 ♘xd4 exd4 7 0-0 ♘e7 8 ♗b2 0-0 9 ♗xd4 d5 10 a3 ♗a5 11 exd5 ♕xd5, Kosten-Flear, Gausdal 1987, with unclear play. White can play the more restrained 5 c3 ♘xf3+ 6 ♕xf3, when the game Mokry-Agdestein, Gausdal 1987 continued 6...♕f6 (both 6...♘e7!? and 6...♘f6 look reasonable) 7 d3 ♕xf3 8 gxf3 ♘e7 9 f4 exf4 10 ♗xf4 ♗b6 11 ♘d2 0-0 12 ♘c4 d6 yielding a marginal edge for White, who has more options, for instance 13 ♗b3 ♔h8 14 a4, as in the game.

After 5 0-0 ♘xf3+! 6 ♕xf3 ♘e7, we have the following position;

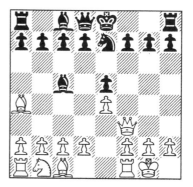

White has three continuations, but none of them give anything significant.

d1) 7 ♗b3 0-0 8 d3 a5!? (8...d6 followed by ...♗e6 is solid) 9 ♗e3, Schallopp-Bird, Nuremberg 1883, when Black had interesting play after 9...♗xe3 10 fxe3 ♕e8 11 ♘c3 ♖a6!.

d2) 7 d3 0-0 8 ♗e3 ♗b6 9 ♘c3 d6 10 ♖ad1 f5! with counterplay, Reti-Spielmann, Budapest 1914.

d3) 7 ♕g3 ♘g6 8 d3 0-0 9 ♘c3 d6 10 ♗b3 a6 gives Black a solid enough position.

4...♗c5

Black has four main alternatives, the first two being inferior, the latter couple being very playable.

a) The wild 4...b5?! provokes 5 ♗xf7+ (the simple 5 ♗b3 is probably worth an edge, as in Kr.Georgiev-Hector, Haifa 1989, see note to White's fourth move) 5...♔xf7 6 ♘xd4. However 6...♕h4! (not 6...exd4?, as 7 ♕h5+ wins for White) is not so clear after 7 ♕f3+!? (otherwise 7 ♘e2 ♕xe4 8 0-0 ♗b7 9 f3 ♕h4, looks about equal) 7...♘f6 8 ♘xb5 ♗c5, with a dangerous initiative for his brace of pawns, Zaitsev-Timoschenko, Moscow 1956.

b) Yet again 4...♘xf3+ helps White's development; 5 ♕xf3 ♕f6 (perhaps 5...♘f6 could be considered) 6 ♕g3 ♗c5 (or 6...d6 7 ♘c3 c6 8 d3 ♗e6) 7 ♘c3 ♘e7 8 ♖f1! (8 d3 is routine, with the slightly better options for White, but the text plays for more with a quick f2-f4 in mind) 8...0-0 9 d3 ♗b4 10 ♗g5 ♕d6 11 f4 ♘c6 12 f5! ♘a5 13 ♗e7! and White was already winning, Schweber-Benko, Buenos Aires 1982.

c) 4...♕f6, an ancient continuation not mentioned in ECO, is actually one of the best ways to equalise; 5 ♘xd4 exd4 6 d3 (no better was 6 0-0, Rohl-Ginzburg, San Felipe 1998, when 6...♗c5 7 e5 ♕g6 8 d3 ♘e7 9 ♘d2 0-0 10 ♘e4 ♗b6 11 ♘g3 d5 12 exd6 ♕xd6 led to equality) 6...♗c5 7 0-0 ♘e7 8 f4 d5! 9 exd5 h5 10 ♘d2 ♗g4 11 ♕e1 0-0-0, Mason-Bird, 1876, and Black was doing well.

d) Otherwise 4...♘f6!? is an entertaining continuation.

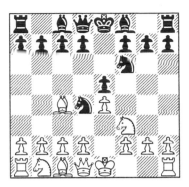

There are two reasonable replies: 5 ♘xe5!?, which looks to be a rather double-edged pawn grab, and the stodgy 5 c3:

d1) 5 ♘xe5!? d5 6 exd5 ♗d6 7 ♘f3 (or 7 ♘d3 ♕e7+ 8 ♔f1 b5) 7...♕e7+ 8 ♔f1 ♗g4 9 h3 may appeal to some, but White could just be made to suffer for his greed.

d2) 5 c3 ♘xf3+ 6 ♕xf3 c6! (a good flexi-move) 7 ♕c2 (after 7 0-0 d5 8 exd5 cxd5 9 ♗b5+ ♗d7 10 ♗xd7+ ♕xd7 11 ♕g3 Tseitlin suggests the pawn sacrifice 11...♗d6 12 ♕xg7 ♔e7 13 ♕h6 ♖ag8 with good compensation) 7...♗e7 8 d4 d6 9 0-0 0-0 10 dxe5 (rather limp) 10...dxe5 with equality, Godes-Tseitlin, correspondence 1988.

5 ♘xd4

Kopisch-Payen, Budapest 1996 continued with 5 c3 ♘xf3+ 6 ♕xf3 ♕e7 7 d3 ♘f6 8 ♘d2 d6 9 h3 ♗e6 10 b4 ♗b6 11 0-0, with a satisfactory game for Black. He even felt sufficiently confident to play the ambitious 11...g5!? and subsequently obtained a good game.

5...♗xd4 6 c3 ♗b6 7 d4

7...♕f6

Two other queen moves have been played;

a) 7...♕e7 8 0-0 ♘f6 9 a4 a6 10 ♗e3 ♘xe4! (10...d6 is less accurate as 11 dxe5 dxe5 12 ♗xb6 leaves White with an edge) 11 ♖e1 0-0 12 ♗d5 ♘f6 13 dxe5 ♘xd5 14 ♕xd5 ♗xe3 15 ♖xe3 ♖b8 16 ♘d2 b5 17 ♕d4 bxa4, Romanishin-Malaniuk, Tbilisi 1986, and now White should play 18 ♘c4 to hold the balance.

b) 7...♕h4!? 8 0-0 ♘f6 9 ♘d2 d6 10 ♘f3 ♕h5 11 ♘g5 ♕xd1 12 ♖xd1 h6 13 ♘xf7 ♖f8 14 dxe5 ♘g4! 15 exd6 ♘xf2 16 ♖f1, Böök-Prins, Munich 1936, and Black took the repetition starting with 16...♘g4+ 17 ♔h1 ♘f2+.

Both alternatives seem reasonable.

8 0-0!?

8 ♗e3 looks more natural.

8...♘e7

Black could have considered accepting the gambit with 8...exd4 as 9 e5 ♕c6! (9...♕h4 looks dangerous after 10 ♕f3 ♕e7 11 ♗g5, with a strong attack) 10 ♕b3 ♕g6 is hardly clear compensation for White.

9 ♗e3 0-0 10 ♘a3 ♘g6

10...d6 is the most solid as 11 ♘b5 can then be met by 11...c6.

11 ♕d2 c6 12 ♗b3 h6 13 f4 exf4 14 ♗xf4 ♘xf4 15 ♖xf4

White maintains a lead in development, but has no obvious targets in the Black camp.

15...♕g5 16 ♘c4 d5

After 16...♗c7, then 17 e5 keeps Black tangled-up.

17 ♘xb6 axb6 18 exd5 cxd5 19 ♖e1 ♗e6 20 ♖e5 ♕d8

The better pawn structure, superior minor piece and more active rooks obviously give White an advantage, but Black is still able to resist.

21 a3 ♖e8 22 ♕d3 g6 23 ♕e2 ♖a5 24 ♖f1 ♔g7 25 ♕f3 f6 26 ♖e3 ♗f7 27 ♖xe8 ♗xe8 28 ♖e1 ♗f7 29 ♕e2 ♕d7 30 ♕e7

The ending is favourable for White and perhaps the only way to make progress.

30...♕xe7

30...♕b5? fails to 31 ♖e6 ♕xb3 32 ♖xf6 ♕d1+ 33 ♖f1.

31 ♖xe7 ♔f8

With 31...♖b5, Black prepares to blunder after 32 ♗a2, with 32...♖xb2?? (33 ♗xd5).

32 ♖xb7 ♖b5 33 ♗a4 ♖xb2 34 ♗c6 ♖b1+!

More natural looking is 34...♖c2 (not 34...♖b3?? 35 ♖xf7+!), trying to play actively with the White king still on the first rank. White can however keep the advantage with 35 ♖xb6 ♖xc3 36 a4 ♖c4 (36...♖a3 37 ♖b7! when Black is going nowhere and White intends 🏰a7 followed by advancing the a-pawn) 37 a5 🏰xd4 38 a6 🏰d1+ 39 ♔f2 🏰a1 40 ♗b5!, as White's a-pawn will make the difference.

35 ♔f2 🏰b2+ 36 ♔e3 ♗e6

Or 36...g5!?, but not 36...🏰xg2??, due to 37 🏰xf7+.

37 a4 🏰xg2

38 c4!

A much stronger continuation than 38 🏰xb6 🏰xh2 39 a5 🏰a2 40 a6 h5, which is unclear.

38...🏰xh2

38...🏰g5!? looks a better try but 39 c5 leads to a race where White is favourite.

39 cxd5 🏰h3+ 40 ♔d2 ♗f5 41 🏰xb6

🏰d3+ **42 ♔e2 ♔e7**

Or 42...🏰xd4 43 a5 🏰d3 (43...♔e7 44 a6 etc.) 44 a6 🏰a3 45 🏰b8+ ♔e7 46 🏰b7+ ♔d6 47 a7 and wins.

43 d6+! ♔xd6 44 ♗e4+ ♔c7 45 🏰b7+ ♔c8 46 ♔xd3 ♗xe4+ 47 ♔xe4 ♔xb7 48 d5 f5+

There is nothing to do, as the three connected pawns can be stopped by the White king whereas the two isolated pawns will queen for example 48...h5 49 a5 h4 50 d6 h3 51 ♔f3 ♔c6 52 a6, or 48...♔b6 49 a5+ ♔xa5 50 d6 ♔b6 51 ♔d5 h5 52 ♔e6 h4 53 d7.

49 ♔f4 ♔b6 50 a5+ ♔xa5 51 d6 ♔b6 52 ♔e5 f4 53 ♔e6 1-0

White queens with check.

Summary

The Bird's Defence has the advantage of creating unusual problems for White, but the loss of time for Black's development is an important factor. Capturing on d4 and playing as in game 37 is the most awkward way of upsetting Black's normal development. Retreating the bishop to c4 at various stages is a popular counter to this defence, perhaps 5 0-0 ♗c5 6 ♗c4 d6 7 d3, as in game 38, being the most likely to give an edge.

All in all the Bird's Defence is a useful weapon as it gives winning chances and (even if White is booked-up) gets close to fully equalising.

1 e4 e5 2 ♘f3 ♘c6 3 ♗b5 ♘d4 4 ♘xd4

> 4 ♗c4 ♗c5 – *Game 42*

4...exd4 (D) 5 0-0

> 5 ♗c4 – *Game 41*
>
> 5 d3 c6 6 ♗c4 d5 7 exd5 cxd5 8 ♗b5+ – *Game 40*

5...♗c5 6 d3

> 6 ♗c4 d6 (D)
>
>> 7 b4 – *Game 39*
>>
>> 7 d3 ♕h4 – *Game 38*

6...c6 7 ♗a4 ♘e7 8 f4 f5 (D) 9 ♗b3 – *Game 37*

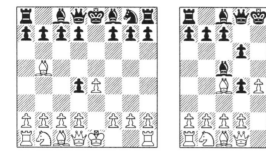

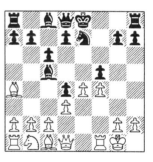

| *4...exd4* | *6...d6* | *8...f5* |

CHAPTER SEVEN

The Cozio Variation

1 e4 e5 2 ♘f3 ♘c6 3 ♗b5 ♘ge7

The solid-looking knight move 3...♘ge7 is often called the Cozio Variation. By defending his other knight, Black consolidates the e5-pawn, but, on the negative side, he temporarily blocks in his own dark-squared bishop. Black has yet to commit his d-pawn, the point being that d7-d5 (countering in the centre and activating his pieces) is often an interesting option. Black can continue by preparing the king's bishop's development with ...♘g6 (see Barczay-Sydor) but these lines are generally considered inferior. So most games continue with an early ...g7-g6, intending to develop the bishop actively on the long diagonal. Hence lines starting with 3...♘ge7 are analogous to 3...g6 (see chapter eight) as the king's bishop fianchetto is a major feature of both.

Game 43
Tiviakov-I.Sokolov
Wijk aan Zee 1995

---

1 e4 e5 2 ♘f3 ♘c6 3 ♗b5 ♘ge7 4 0-0

4 c3 is examined in game 45, while 4 ♘c3 is the subject of games 46-47.

4...g6

Alternatives for Black are studied in the notes to Black's 4th move in game 46.

5 c3

5 d4 is studied in Game 44.

5...♗g7

The actual move-order in the game was 3...g6 4 c3 ♘ge7 5 0-0 ♗g7, an example of the closeness of Chapter 8, covering 3...g6, to the present one.

Instead 5...d6?! 6 d4 ♗d7, looks reasonable at first sight, but was refuted in Ciric-Nikolai, Dortmund 1976, with 7 dxe5! ♘xe5?! (7...dxe5 8 ♗c4 ♘c8, looks a better try for Black) 8 ♘xe5 dxe5 9 ♕b3 ♘c6 10 ♗c4 ♕e7 11 ♕xb7.

6 d4 exd4

Otherwise 6...0-0?! 7 d5 a6 8 ♗e2 ♘a7 9 c4 d6 10 ♘c3 leads to a King's Indian-style position, where Black has a silly knight on a7,

Grünfeld-Sanz, Buenos Aires Olympiad 1978.

7 cxd4 d5 8 exd5 ♘xd5 9 ♗g5

Another important line starts with 9 ♖e1+ ♗e6 10 ♘e5 (after 10 ♘g5, then 10...♕d6 holds everything together, and if 10 ♘c3 0-0 11 ♗xc6 ♘xc3 12 bxc3 bxc6 13 ♗g5 ♕d5 14 ♕c1 ♖fe8 15 ♗h6 ♗g4, as in Parma-Ostojic, Yugoslav Championship 1969?, things are about equal) 10...0-0 and now there are two ways to capture on c6: a) 11 ♘xc6, when 11...bxc6 12 ♗xc6 ♖b8 13 ♘c3 ♘b4 14 ♗e4 ♗xd4 was about equal in Dely-Mechkarov, Riga 1968.

b) 11 ♗xc6!?, is critical; 11...bxc6 12 ♘xc6 ♕d6 13 ♘e5 c5.

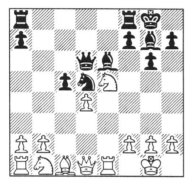

This position is given by Filipenko as better for Black, by ECO (after the further 14 ♘a3 ♘b4, Garcia Gonzalez-de Grieff, Cienfuegos 1973) as equal, and by Fritz5 (after 14 ♘c3) as better for White! So what on earth is really happening? I suggest the following simplifying line; 14 ♘c3 cxd4 (14...♘b4 is met by 15 a3) 15 ♕xd4 ♖fd8 16 ♘xd5 ♕xd5 17 ♕xd5 ♖xd5 18 ♗f4 g5 19 ♗g3 ♖d2 and Black has adequate play for his pawn, so 'equal' is closest to the mark.

9...♕d6 10 ♖e1+ ♗e6 11 ♘bd2

Less dangerous is 11 ♘c3, as Black can obtain a reasonable game by simplifying, for instance 11...♘xc3 12 bxc3 0-0 13 ♕d2 ♘a5 (13...♗d5 is a solid alternative) 14 ♗h6 ♘c4 15 ♗xc4 ♗xc4 16 ♗xg7 ♔xg7 17 ♘e5 ♗e6

18 ♖e3 ♖ad8 19 ♕b2 ♕b6, and chances were balanced in Khomullo-Shiliaev, correspondence 1990.

11...0-0

Too provocative is 11...h6?!, as after 12 ♘e4 ♕b4 13 ♗xc6+ bxc6 14 ♗d2! ♕xb2 15 ♕a4 White has a strong initiative, as analysed by Filipenko.

12 ♘e4

Promising is 12 ♘c4!?, a recent try, when after 12...♕b4 13 a4 a6 14 ♗xc6 bxc6 15 ♘fe5 ♖fe8 16 ♖c1 ♕b7 17 ♗d2 ♘e7 18 b4, Palac-d'Amore, Mitropa cup 1999, Black complicated the struggle with the enterprising 18...c5!?, and the game was eventually drawn. Palac seemed to be doing well, so perhaps 12 ♘c4, avoiding the heavily analysed main lines, is worth further investigation.

12...♕b4 13 ♗xc6 bxc6 14 ♕c1

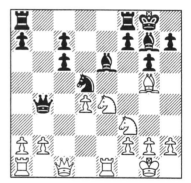

A complicated struggle is in prospect. White has weakened the Black pawn structure and has fine outposts for his knights on c5 and e5. On the other hand, Black has a firm grip on d5 (in front of the isolated d-pawn), the bishop pair and play on both the b-file and the long black diagonal.

14...♖fe8

There is little doubt in my mind over the fact that 14...♗xd4?!, is simply dubious. Here is the evidence; 15 ♘xd4 ♕xd4 16 ♕xc6 ♕xb2 17 ♖ad1 ♕b6 18 ♕c4!? (18 ♕c1 f6 19 ♗h6 ♖fe8 20 h3, Minic-Dely, Belgrade 1968, gave White excellent compensation for the pawn) 18...♕b4? (18...c6 is Black's best chance, but even so his kingside is frankly too weak to hold) 19 ♘f6+ ♔g7

20 ♕c1 ♘xf6 21 ♕a1 ♕e7 22 ♖d7! and Black resigned, Vul-Arkhangelsky, Moscow 1999.

After 14...♗f5?!, which also looks suspicious, 15 ♕xc6 ♗xe4 16 ♖xe4 ♕xb2 17 ♖ee1 ♘c3 18 ♗c7 (Sion Castro-I.Sokolov, Léon 1995) White seems to be better in all lines:

a) 18...♖fc8 19 ♕c4 c6 20 ♘e5 just about forces 20...♗xe5, when White keeps the initiative as Black's king is lacking defenders.

b) 18...♘e2+ 19 ♔h1 (19 ♖xe2, however, yields no advantage after 19...♕xa1+ 20 ♖e1 ♕xa2 21 ♗xf8 ♖xf8 22 ♕xc7 a5) 19...♖fe8 20 ♗c5 ♕c3 is given by Sokolov as unclear, but after 21 ♖ad1 Black has some problems; his pawns are weaker and his pieces are awkwardly placed.

c) 18...♖fe8 (the game continuation) 19 ♗c5 ♘e4?! (19...♘e2+) 20 ♘d2! ♕xd2 21 ♖xe4 and Black was in trouble and should have lost.

15 h3

Stopping any counterplay with ...♗g4.

Also popular is 15 ♗d2 ♕b5 (or 15...♕b6 16 ♘c5 ♗f5 17 ♘e5 ♖ad8 18 a3 h5 19 b4, and White has consolidated his knight outposts) 16 ♘c5 ♗f5 17 ♘e5 ♖ad8 and Black completes his development and has

well-placed pieces, but White has the most options so is objectively slightly better. After the further 18 a4!? (18 a3, intending b4, is also reasonable) 18...♕b6 19 ♖a3 ♗xe5 20 ♖b3!? ♗xd4 21 ♖xe8+ ♖xe8 22 ♖xb6 cxb6 23 ♘b3 ♗f6 24 ♕xc6 ♖d8, Filipenko prefers White slightly.

Another idea for White, 15 a3, was tried out in Grünfeld-d'Amore, Haifa 1989, which after 15...♕b6 16 ♕d2 f6 17 ♘c5!? ♗g4 18 ♗h4 ♗f8 19 b4 ♗xf3 20 ♘d7!? led to interesting complications.

15...♖ab8 16 b3 ♗f5 17 ♗d2

Otherwise there is 17 ♘c5!?, when after 17...♖xe1+ 18 ♕xe1 ♗xd4 19 ♘a6 ♕b6 20 ♘xd4 ♕xa6 21 ♘xf5 gxf5 (in view of Black's six pawn islands!), White with 22 ♕e5, must have good compensation for his pawn.

17...♕f8

17...♕b6 is the alternative. Then the continuation 18 ♘c5 h5 19 ♘e5 ♖bd8 20 ♕a3 ♖e7 21 ♖ac1 ♖de8 22 ♕b2 occurred in Wolff-I.Sokolov, Biel Interzonal 1993, where Black should have considered 22...f6 (instead the game continued with 22...♕b5?! 23 a4 ♕b6 24 b4 f6 25 ♘c4 ♖xe1+ 26 ♗xe1 ♕b8 27 ♘a5 with advantage to White).

18 ♘g3

Naturally the knight could also go to c5.

18...♖xe1+ 19 ♗xe1 ♗d7 20 ♘e5 ♕e8

Just about the only way to hold onto the c6-pawn.

21 ♕c5! ♗xe5 22 dxe5 ♕xe5 23 ♖d1 ♖a8

Perhaps Black should try and play more actively with 23...♖e8 24 ♕xa7 h5.

24 f3!?

Hoping to bring the knight to e4 where threats against the f6-square and indeed the long dark-squared diagonal in general are dangerous. After 24 ♗a5 ♗e8 25 ♖e1 ♕d6 26 ♕xd6 cxd6 27 ♘e4, Cheshkovsky Dreev, Moscow 1992, White won back his pawn with an advantageous ending (which he eventually won).

24...f5 25 &f2 ♕d6?!

More active is 25...a5, intending ...a4, as pointed out by Tiviakov.

26 ♕a5

Now Black is tangled up and the rook is very passive on a8.

26...&e6 27 ♘e2 ♕e5 28 ♘d4 &d7 29 ♘c2!

Heading for c4. White takes his time as Black cannot undertake anything positive. Instead the impatient 29 ♖c1 ♕d6 30 ♕a6 is met by 30...c5.

29...♖e8

The best try.

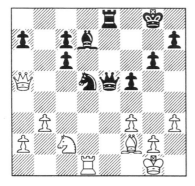

30 ♘a3

The best of various options. Instead 30 &xa7 is met by the annoying pin 30...♖a8, 30 ♕xa7 loses control to 30...♕e2 and 30 ♖e1 ♕b2 31 ♖xe8+ &xe8 is less clear after the exchange of a pair of rooks.

30...f4

After 30...♕e2 then 31 ♖d2 keeps Black's ambitions in check.

31 ♘c4 ♕g5 32 h4

32 &h2? allows 32...&xh3! 33 gxh3 ♖e2 34 ♖d2 ♕g3+.

32...♕f5 33 ♕xa7 ♘c3 34 ♖d2 g5 35 hxg5?

A time trouble error. White could keep the advantage after 35 ♕xc7 ♘d5 36 ♕a7 g4 (36...gxh4 37 &xh4) 37 fxg4 ♕xg4 38 ♕d4.

35...♘e2+! 36 ♖xe2 ♖xe2 37 ♕xc7 ♕d5! 38 ♘d6

38...♖xf2?

Missing his chance! Necessary was 38...♖e6!, when 39 ♘e4 ♖xe4 40 fxe4 ♕d1+ 41 &h2 ♕h5+ forces a draw.

39 ♕d8+ &g7 40 ♕xd7+ &g6 41 ♕e8+ &g7 42 ♕e7+ &g8 43 ♕d8+ &g7 44 ♘e8+ 1-0

The resulting pawn ending is won for White.

The whole variation is complex but White seems to keep a small but persistent edge deep into the game. Black's pieces are however well entrenched and his position is difficult to crack, which explains the continued popularity of the variation.

> ## Game 44
> ## Tiviakov-Scherbakov
> *Odessa 1989*

1 e4 e5 2 ♘f3 ♘c6 3 &b5 ♘ge7 4 0-0 g6 5 d4 exd4 6 ♘xd4

The gambit idea 6 &g5?! &g7 7 c3 dxc3 8 ♘xc3 doesn't impress; 8...h6 9 &h4 0-0 10 ♖e1 d6 11 e5 g5 12 exd6 ♘f5 and White hasn't enough compensation, Van Mechelen-Duhagin, Belgium 1999.

6...&g7 7 &e3 0-0 8 ♘c3

This type of position can arise from other openings, and if Black were to now play the routine ...d6 he could count on having a fairly solid position as in a Philidor's Defence, Larsen variation (1 e4 e5 2 ♘f3 d6 3 d4 exd4

4 ♘xd4 g6 etc.). However he can obtain an interesting game by striking in the centre immediately:

8...d5!?

If the text move proves to be inadequate then Black can fall back on 8...d6 against which nothing seems convincing for White; 9 f4!? (quieter tries lead to equality, for example 9 ♘d5 ♘xd5 10 exd5 ♘e7 11 c4 ♘f5, Ilyin-Zhenevsky - A.Kubbel, USSR Championship 1920, or 9 ♗e2 f5 10 ♘xc6 ♘xc6 11 exf5 ♗xf5, Kolbaek-Larsen, Grenada 1973) 9...f5! 10 ♕d2 fxe4 11 ♘xe4 ♘f5! 12 ♘xc6, Sax-Sanz, Las Palmas 1978 and now 12...bxc6! 13 ♗xc6 ♘xe3 14 ♗xa8 (14 ♕xe3 ♖b8 is fine for Black) 14...♘xf1 15 ♗d5+ ♔h8 16 ♖xf1 c6 17 ♗b3 d5 18 ♘c3 ♗a6 yields sufficient compensation according to Keres and Geller.

9 exd5

Following 9 ♗xc6 bxc6 10 exd5 then 10...♘xd5! seems adequate, for instance 11 ♘xc6 ♘xe3 12 ♕xd8 (after 12 fxe3 ♕e8 13 ♘d5 ♗b7 White risks getting his knights tangled up) 12...♖xd8 13 fxe3 ♖e8 and Black's active bishops are worth a pawn.

9...♘xd5 10 ♘xc6 bxc6 11 ♘xd5

11 ♗xc6 ♘xe3 12 fxe3 ♖b8 again gives Black excellent compensation, particularly due to his pressure on the dark squares.

11...cxb5 12 ♗c5 ♖e8 13 ♘e7+

Drawish opposite bishops occur after 13 ♗e7 ♕d7 (13...♖xe7?? is busted by 14 ♘f6+)

14 ♘f6+ ♗xf6 15 ♗xf6 ♕xd1 16 ♖axd1 ♗f5 17 c3 ♖e6, when the dark-squared pressure will soon be neutralised and equality is on the cards.

13...♔h8 14 ♕f3 ♗e6 15 ♖ad1 ♕b8

16 ♘c6?!

I'm not convinced by this move. The knight is better left on e7 for the moment, as Black cannot then organise himself that easily. The sensible 16 b3 was played against me, and the position after 16...a5 17 h3 a4 18 ♖d2 ♖a6 19 ♖fd1 ♕a8 20 ♕f4 turned out to be very unpleasant for Black in Prié-Flear, Oakham 1994.

In fact, 16 ♖fe1! may be even more dangerous; 16...a5 (16...b4 17 ♕f4 ♕b5?! proved inadequate for Black after 18 ♕xc7 ♖ab8 19 ♕d6 ♖b7 20 ♘c6 ♖c8 21 ♘d8 in Boey-Castro Rojas, Nice Olympiad 1974) 17 h4 (after 17 ♖xe6 fxe6 18 ♕h3 ♖a6 19 ♘xg6+ ♔g8 20 ♘e7+ ♔h8 21 ♘g6+ White took a repetition in Gesos-Vul, Ano Liosia 1997) 17...♖a6 18 h5 with a dangerous initiative, Pichler-Zach, Germany 1983.

The theory up to now tends to give the whole line as unclear, but ignores other moves, concentrating only on 16 ♘c6. My feeling is that White's position is easier to play as the knight on e7 restricts Black's freedom of movement. If White has a draw (see Gesos-Vul above) and can even safely play for more, then Black would do best to stick to 8...d6.

16...♕b7 17 ♗d4 b4!

Dvoiris-Filipenko, Rezh 1988, continued with 17...a5, but after 18 ♕c3 ♗xd4 19 ♖xd4, White had attacking chances.

18 ♗xg7+

Otherwise, 18 ♖fe1 ♗xd4! (not 18...♗c4??, Dvoiris-Filipenko, Katowice 1992, losing on the spot to 19 ♘d8!) 19 ♖xd4 ♗f5 20 ♖ed1 ♖e6 is given as unclear by Filipenko.

18...♔xg7 19 b3

19 ♕e4 a5 20 ♖fe1 is suggested as an improvement by Filipenko, who judges the position as unclear.

19...h5 20 h3 a5 21 ♖fe1 ♖a6 22 ♘d4 ♕xf3 23 ♘xf3

A quiet ending arises. With White's pawns fixed on light squares, the bishop is the superior minor piece and Black has an edge.

23...a4 24 ♘d4 ♗d7 25 ♔f1 ♖xe1+ 26

♔xe1 c5 27 ♘e2 ♗f5 28 ♔d2 g5

A nice technical move, moving the pawn to a dark-square, thus improving his bishop's scope. The f4-square is now 'out of bounds' for White's knight and Black just increases his space and extra pressure on the white camp. The idea of ...h5-h4 is always in the air but can be reserved for later.

29 ♘c1 ♔f6 30 ♘d3 ♗xd3!

31 cxd3

The pure king and pawn ending after 31 ♔xd3 axb3 32 axb3 ♖d6+ 33 ♔e2 ♖xd1 34 ♔xd1 ♔e5 35 ♔d2 ♔e4 is very unpleasant for White, but might be tenable. White decided on an inferior rook ending, as in general, if in doubt, keeping the rooks on is a better drawing try.

31...♔e5 32 ♖e1+ ♔d6 33 h4

This proves to be inadequate, but 33 ♔e3 ♔d5 34 ♖c1 axb3 35 axb3 ♖a3 36 ♖b1 would be woefully passive.

33...axb3 34 axb3 ♖a2+ 35 ♔e3 gxh4 36 ♖h1 ♖b2 37 ♖xh4 ♖xb3 38 ♔d2 ♖b2+ 39 ♔e3 ♖c2 40 ♖xh5 b3 41 ♖h6+ ♔c7 42 ♖f6 b2 43 ♖xf7+ ♔c6 44 ♖f6+ ♔b5 45 ♖f8 ♔b4 46 g4 ♔c3 47 ♖b8 ♖c1 48 g5 ♖e1+ 49 ♔f4 b1♕ 0-1

Game 45
Gdanski-Ye Rongguang
Manila Olympiad 1992

---

1 e4 e5 2 ♘f3 ♘c6 3 ♗b5 ♘ge7 4 c3

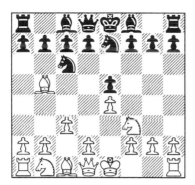

4...d5

I came to dislike this move after losing to Hauchard. Best in my opinion is 4...g6, aiming to transpose to game 43 which White cannot profitably avoid; 4...g6! 5 d4 (for 5 0-0 ♗g7 6 d4 exd4 7 cxd4 d5 8 exd5 ♘xd5 see Game 43) 5...exd4 (not 5...♗g7?!, as 6 d5, is promising for White) 6 cxd4 d5 (again 6...♗g7?! is met by 7 d5, for example 7...♘b8 8 ♘c3 a6 9 ♗a4 b5 10 ♗b3 d6 11 ♗e3, which gave White the better game in Spassky-Lehmann, Solingen 1974) 7 ♗g5 ♗g7 (7...dxe4?! looks suspicious after 8 ♗f6 ♖g8 9 ♘g5) 8 exd5 (now, unlike in the main line examined in game 43, Black is unable to recapture on d5 with his knight; however this doesn't seem to be a major problem) 8...♕xd5 9 ♘c3 (Filipenko judges the position as better for White, but Radulov has shown that Black is fine) 9...♕d6 10 0-0 0-0 11 d5 (after 11 ♘e4 ♕b4 12 a4 ♘d5 13 ♖e1 ♗g4 14 ♗d2 Black took on b2 and White never had enough compensation in Iljin-Radulov, Biel open 1989) 11...♘e5 12 ♘e4 ♕b4 13 ♘f6+ (13 ♘xe5 ♗xe5, Geller-Radulov, Palma de Mallorca 1989, offered no advantage either) 13...♗xf6 14 ♗xf6 ♘g4 15 ♗xe7 ♕xe7 16 ♖e1 ♕d6, Dobrev-Radulov, Bulgaria 1991, and a draw was agreed.

So 4 c3 can be met by 4...g6, aiming for transposition to 4 0-0 g6 5 c3 etc. (see Game 43).

Another idea, 4...a6, is not bad; 5 ♗a4 (5 ♗c4?! d5 6 exd5 ♘xd5 7 0-0 ♘b6 8 ♗b3 ♗d6 9 d4 0-0 10 ♗g5 ♕d7 11 dxe5 ♘xe5 was only equal in Psakhis-Sydor, Naleczow 1980) 5...d6 (5...b5!? 6 ♗b3 d5 can be met actively by 7 d4! exd4 8 exd5 ♘xd5 9 0-0 ♗e6 10 ♗g5 ♗e7 11 ♗xe7 ♕xe7 12 ♖e1, with an edge to White, Kurajica-Klaric, Yugoslavia 1978) 6 d4 ♗d7 7 ♗e3 ♘g6, transposing to a Steinitz deferred (1 e4 e5 2 ♘f3 ♘c6 3 ♗b5 a6 4 ♗a4 d6 5 c3 ♗d7 6 d4 ♘ge7 7 ♗e3 ♘g6) where White can try 8 h4, or 8 d5 ♘b8 9 ♗xd7+ ♘xd7 10 c4, with a small but pleasant edge for White due to his better bishop and space advantage.

5 ♘xe5

I remain impressed by the immediate 5 ♕e2!?, as the natural 5...♗g4 6 d3 ♕d6 7 ♘bd2, is awkward for Black who has problems to satisfactorily complete his development. Hauchard-Flear, French League 1996, continued 7...0-0-0!? (enterprising but not quite good enough for equality) 8 exd5 ♕xd5 9 ♗c4 ♕d7 10 ♗xf7 ♘f5 11 ♗b3 ♘h4 12 ♖g1!? ♗e7 13 h3 ♗h5 14 ♗c2 ♖hf8 15 g4 ♗g6 16 ♖g3 h5 17 ♘e4 hxg4 18 hxg4 ♘xf3+ 19 ♖xf3 ♕xg4 20 ♖xf8 ♕g1+ 21 ♕f1 ♕xf1+ 22 ♔xf1 ♖xf8 23 ♗e3, and White had the better pawn structure and was able to squeeze a win out of the ending.

Unconvincing is the alternative 5 d4, for example 5...exd4 6 ♕xd4 ♗d7 7 ♕d3 dxe4 8 ♕xe4 ♗f5 9 ♕e2 ♕d6 10 0-0 0-0-0, with equal chances.

5...dxe4 6 ♕e2!

Clearly the best way forward.

The complications starting with 6 ♕a4!? are fascinating, but give Black too much play; 6...♕d5 7 f4 (7 ♘xc6, just helps Black's development; 7...♘xc6 8 0-0 ♗d6 9 ♖e1 0-0 10 ♗xc6 bxc6 11 ♕xe4 ♕h5 and Black was better, Lutt-Keres, correspondence 1933) 7...♗d7 8 ♘xd7 ♔xd7 9 ♗c4 ♕h5 10 b4 (10 ♕b3 grabs a pawn, but 10...♘f5 11 ♗xf7 ♕h4+ 12 g3 ♕f6 offers Black enough compensation according to Filipenko) 10...♘f5

11 0-0 a5 12 ♕b5 axb4 13 ♗d5 b3 14 ♗xe4 ♘g3 and Black is doing fine, Biakov-Shiliaev, correspondence 1988.

6...♕d5 7 ♘xc6!

Alternatively 7 f4 exf3 8 ♘xf3 ♗g4 9 0-0 0-0-0 10 d4 is complex but probably fine for Black after 10...♘f5.

7...♘xc6 8 d4 ♗f5 9 ♗f4

Hachian-Vul, Moscow 1992 varied with 9 0-0 0-0-0 10 ♘d2 ♗g6 11 ♖e1 f5 12 ♕c4, and was also rather better for White. The text is accredited in ECO to the Brazilian Milos.

9...0-0-0 10 ♘d2 ♗g6 11 0-0 ♗d6 12 ♗xd6 ♖xd6 13 ♖ae1 ♗h5 14 ♕c4 f5 15 ♕xd5 ♖xd5 16 ♗xc6 bxc6 17 ♘c4

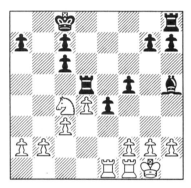

White has the better minor piece and superior pawn structure and thus has a comfortable advantage. Black in turn hopes to activate his rooks but this proves to take a long time.

17...♖b5 18 b4 ♗f7 19 ♘d2 a5 20 a3 ♖e8 21 ♖e3 ♗g6 22 g3 ♖b8 23 f3 axb4 24 axb4 ♖a8 25 fxe4 ♖a2 26 ♖f2 fxe4 27 ♘c4 ♖a1+ 28 ♔g2 ♔b7 29 g4 h5

Black ditches a pawn as after 29...♖e7 30 ♘e5 ♔b6 the e-pawn will soon drop off anyway after 31 h4 etc.

30 ♘e5

From this square the knight will dominate the bishop.

30...♖e6 31 gxh5 ♗xh5 32 ♖xe4 ♗e8 33 ♖g4 ♖e7

With such an ugly position, a pawn down,

Black's position, despite his valiant resistance, must be judged as objectively lost.

34 ♖h4 ♖a3 35 ♖h8! c5

Giving some breathing space to his long-suffering bishop. Instead after 35...♖xc3, then 36 ♖ff8 traps the unfortunate piece.

36 bxc5 ♖xc3 37 ♖b2+ ♔a7 38 ♖f8 ♖a3 39 ♔f2 ♖a4 40 ♔e3 ♖a3+ 41 ♔d2 ♖e6 42 ♖f3 ♖a4 43 ♔c3 ♖h6 44 ♖g3 g6

Black could have tried to simplify with 44...♖xh2, but after 45 ♖xh2 ♖a3+ 46 ♔b4 ♖xg3 47 ♖h8 ♗g6 48 ♔b5! Black is either mated or loses his c-pawn.

45 c6 ♖h7 46 d5 ♖e7 47 ♖b7+ ♔a8 48 ♖g5 ♖a7 49 ♖xa7+ ♔xa7 50 ♔d4 ♖h7 51 ♖g2 ♖h4+ 52 ♔c5 ♖a4 53 ♖b2 ♖a5+ 54 ♔d4 ♖a4+ 55 ♘c4 g5 56 ♖b7+ 1-0

An efficient display that casts doubt on the viability of 4...d5. I recommend 4...g6, see the note to move four and game 43.

Game 46
Barczay-Sydor
Lublin 1969

---

1 e4 e5 2 ♘f3 ♘c6 3 ♗b5 ♘ge7 4 ♘c3

Here we examine White's alternatives where Black tries to play without ...g6.

After 4 d4 exd4 5 ♘xd4, the exchange 5...♘xd4?! is inferior (Black should really play 5...g6!), for instance; 6 ♕xd4 ♘c6 7 ♕e3 ♗e7 8 ♗d2 (also promising was 8 0-0 0-0 9

♘c3 d6 10 ♘d5 ♗e6 11 ♕c3 ♗xd5 12 exd5 ♗f6 13 ♕h3 ♘e5 14 f4, Stipunsky-Benjamin, New York 2000) 8...d6 9 ♘c3 0-0 10 ♘d5 ♖e8 11 ♗c3 a6 12 ♕g3 f6 13 ♗d3 and White has a nice initiative, Balabanov-Nasilov, correspondence 1978.

Following 4 0-0, I recommend 4...g6 as the most dynamic option, see Games 43-44. Black has three other ways of trying to develop:

a) 4...♘g6 5 d4 exd4 6 ♘xd4 ♗c5 7 ♘b3 ♗b6 8 ♘c3 (the position resembles something from the Scotch opening where Black has wasted time with ...♘ge7-g6) 8...0-0 9 ♘d5 d6 10 a4 ♗e6 11 ♗e2 f5 12 a5 ♗c5 13 exf5 ♗xf5 14 c3 occurred in Dzindzichashvili-Larsen, Tilburg 1978. White will capture on c5, when he is good and ready, obtaining the bishop pair and better pawns.

b) 4...d6 5 c3 ♘g6 6 d4 ♗d7, whereupon White has two tries:

b1) Keeping the tension in the centre is the less precise option; 7 ♖e1 ♗e7 8 ♘bd2 0-0 9 ♘f1 and now 9...♘h4!? proved to be adequate in Petersen-Nuoristo, Denmark 1999, but even clearer is the simplifying combination 9...♘xd4! 10 ♘xd4 exd4 11 ♗xd7 ♕xd7 12 cxd4 d5, which comfortably equalised in Buljovcic-Ivanovic, Zagreb 1974.

b2) 7 d5! is best. Then after 7...♘b8 8 ♕b3!? (8 ♗e2, intending c4 and ♘c3, gives White a nice space advantage) 8...♕c8 9 ♘a3 ♗e7 10 ♗xd7+ ♘xd7 11 ♘c4 ♘h4 12 ♘xh4 ♗xh4 13 f4, Westerinen-Larsen, Esbjerg 1978, White had the better game.

c) 4...a6 5 ♗c4 ♘g6 6 d4 exd4 7 ♘xd4, and now neither of Black's options are fully satisfactory:

c1) Objectively the best choice is 7...♗e7 8 ♗e3 ♘xd4 9 ♗xd4 0-0 10 ♘c3, but White's lead in development and his space advantage deny Black any route to equality; 10...b5?! (10...d6 11 f4 ♗e6 12 ♗xe6 fxe6 13 ♕g4 ♕d7 14 ♖ad1 yields White an edge, R.Byrne) 11 ♗d3 ♗f6 12 ♗xf6 ♕xf6 13 a4! b4 14 ♘d5, with excellent play for White,

R.Byrne-Böhm, Wijk aan Zee 1980. Black should have avoided the weakening ...b5, but in any case White's keeps a persistent edge.

c2) 7...♕f6?! 8 ♘f5 ♗c5 9 ♘c3 0-0 10 ♘d5 ♕d8 11 ♕h5 ♔h8 leads to the following diagram.

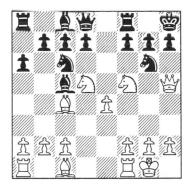

Black's opening looks dubious but there is perhaps no immediate refutation. In Van der Weide-Ernst, Dieren 2000 White in fact continued with the speculative 12 b4?! and won but only because of a blunder. The sharp 12 ♘xg7 is interesting but not that clear, so perhaps 12 ♗g5 f6 13 ♗d2 with a pleasant edge, but nothing concrete, is objectively best.

4...♘g6?!

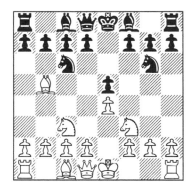

Playable but passive. A better try is 4...g6! (see Koch-Flear, game 47).

5 d4

The direct 5 h4!? was tried in Bologan-Arkhipov, Moscow 1995, when Black's best is probably 5...♘d4 (5...h5?! is a major concession) 6 h5 ♘f4 7 ♘xd4 exd4 8 ♘e2 ♘xe2 9 ♕xe2 ♗c5, with a type of Bird's Defence where the advanced h-pawn gives attacking possibilities for White.

5...exd4 6 ♘xd4 ♗c5 7 ♗e3

Again the 'Scotch' approach is another reasonable try; 7 ♘b3 ♗b6 8 ♘d5 0-0 9 0-0 d6 10 a4.

7...♗xd4 8 ♗xd4 0-0

Black can instead simplify further with 8...♘xd4 9 ♕xd4 0-0, but he has not completed his development. The e4-pawn helps maintain White's space edge into the middlegame.

9 ♗e3

Investing a tempo to avoid a later exchange of minor pieces.

A more recent game continued 9 0-0 d6 10 f4 f5 11 g3 fxe4 12 ♘xe4 ♗f5 13 ♘f2 ♘xd4 14 ♕xd4, Hracek-d'Amore, Manila Olympiad 1992, and White kept his edge, noting that 14...♗xc2??, would then lose a piece to 15 ♕c4+. The knight on g6 lacks squares but despite his space disadvantage, Black's position remains fairly solid.

9...d6 10 0-0 ♔h8 11 ♕d2 f5

The only chance to fight for space.

12 f4

Controlling the e5-square and forcing the knight on g6 to re-deploy at some point.

12...fxe4 13 ♘xe4 ♕e7

The manoeuvre 13...♘h4 14 ♖ae1 ♘f5 would be met by 15 ♗f2, followed by a timely g4.

14 ♘g3 ♘h4 15 ♖ae1 ♘f5!?

15...♕f7 is a possible improvement, taking the queen off such an exposed square, and following up with ...♘f5. In that case, White's superiority could have been kept to a minimum as 16 ♗xc6?! bxc6 17 f5?! would then fail to 17...♘xf5 18 ♘xf5?! ♗xf5 19 g4?! ♕g6.

16 ♗xc6

Not aiming to win a pawn (as Black can easily restore material equality), Barczay instead prepares a middlegame with opposite bishops where he has the attacking chances.

16...bxc6 17 ♘xf5 ♗xf5 18 ♗xa7 ♕d7 19 ♗d4 ♖xa2 20 ♖f3 ♖aa8 21 ♖g3 ♖g8?!

21...♗g6 (intending ...♖ae8) was the better alternative, trying to at least keep his rooks active.

22 ♕e2 c5 23 ♗c3 d5 24 ♗e5 c4 25 c3 ♗e4 26 h3 ♕e7 27 ♕f2 c5 28 ♖ge3 ♖a6

29 ♖xe4!

The exchange sacrifice is thematic; Black's most active piece is eliminated and he remains with no counterchances and weak pawns. Note how the bishop on e5 dominates the board.

29...dxe4 30 ♖xe4 ♕b7 31 ♖xc4 ♖a2 32 ♖xc5 ♖xb2 33 ♕g3 ♕a7 34 ♗d4

White can keep probing away with no risk

to himself.

34...♛f7 35 ♕h4 ♛b7 36 ♖g5 ♖b5?

36...♛f7 would have kept Black alive.

37 ♖xg7! ♕xg7 00 ♗xg7+ ♖xg7 39 ♕d8+ ♖g8 40 ♕d4+ ♖g7 1-0

White wins slowly but surely by advancing his pawns. However, Black couldn't be bothered to adjourn and resigned.

Game 47
Koch-Flear
French League 1996

1 e4 e5 2 ♘f3 ♘c6 3 ♗b5 ♘ge7 4 ♘c3 g6

A better option than 4...♘g6.

5 d4 exd4 6 ♘d5!?

With a threat!

White provokes a forcing sequence of moves where Black must play accurately to

survive.

For 6 ♘xd4, see Game 44.

6...♗g7

Taking off the knight seems dubious; 6...♘xd5?! 7 exd5 ♕e7+ 8 ♗f1 ♘d5 9 ♕xd4 f6 10 ♗f4 ♗g7 11 ♖e1, Johner-Tartakover, Karlsbad 1911, with big problems for Black.

7 ♗g5

Or 7 ♗f4!?, playing for the trick 7...d6? 8 ♗g5!, with pins galore. In fact now 7...♘xd5! is best, when 8 exd5 ♕e7+ 9 ♔f1 a6!? (better than 9...♕c5 10 ♕e2+ ♘e7 11 ♖e1 0-0 12 ♕c4 ♕xc4+ 13 ♗xc4 b5 14 ♗b3 ♘f5 15 ♗xc7 which gives White an edge; however 9...♘b4 looks possible, intending to meet 10 ♕d2 0-0 11 d6 with 11...♕f6.) 10 ♗a4 b5 11 ♗b3 ♘a5 12 ♗g5 f6 13 ♕d3 ♔f8 led to an unclear position in I.Zaitsev-Vul, Planernoe 1982.

7...h6 8 ♗f6

8 ♗h4? g5 9 ♗g3 d6, gives Black no problems.

8...♗xf6

8...♔f8 will probably transpose.

9 ♘xf6+ ♔f8

10 0-0

10 ♘xd4 should not be met by 10...♔g7?, because of 11 ♕d2! ♘g8 (11...♔xf6? 12 ♕c3 is catastrophic for Black) 12 ♘d5 ♘f6 13 ♘c3 ♘h5 14 g4, Murey-Dreev, Moscow 1989, where White had a big advantage. In fact Black should play 10...♘f5!, which seems satisfactory; 11 exf5 ♕xf6 12 ♗xc6, and now

he has two good ideas:

a) 12...dxc6 13 fxg6 ♔g7! was played in Nadanian-Vul, Moscow 1992, and Black has enough play according to Vul's analysis, for example 14 gxf7 ♖d8 15 f8♕+ ♖xf8 (15...♔xf8 is less good after 16 ♕f3) 16 ♘f3 ♖e8+ 17 ♔f1 ♗g4 18 ♕d4 ♗xf3 19 ♕xf6+ ♔xf6 20 gxf3 ♖ad8

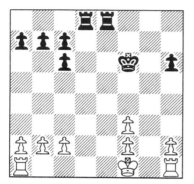

21 ♖e1 ♖g8 with an equal ending.

b) 12...♕e5+ 13 ♘e2 bxc6! and now 14 fxg6 ♗a6 looks too risky, so White should try 14 0-0, which Filipenko describes as unclear.

10...d6

In Lanka-Banas, Trnava 1989 White maintained a persistent edge after 10...♗g7 11 ♘d5 ♖e8 12 ♖e1 d6 13 ♕d2 a6 14 ♗xc6 ♘xc6 15 ♘xd4 f6 16 ♖e3 ♘xd4 17 ♕xd4 ♗e6 18 ♘f4 ♗f7 19 ♖ae1 and Black faces an arduous defensive task.

11 ♘d5

Filipenko suggests 11 ♘xd4 ♗g7 12 ♘xc6! ♘xc6 13 ♘d5 forcing 13...f6, as a better chance for White to keep an edge. He preferred this continuation to 12 ♘d5 ♘xd5 13 exd5 ♘xd4 14 ♕xd4+ ♕f6, which he assessed as equal. The 1997 game Baches Garcia-Lopez Martinez, confirmed this assessment; 15 ♕xf6+ ♔xf6 16 ♖fe1 ♗f5 17 ♗a4 a6 18 ♖e3 b5 19 ♗b3 ♖ae8 and the game was drawn a few moves later.

11...♗g4 12 ♘xe7 ♔xe7 13 ♗xc6 bxc6 14 h3!?

Sacrificing a pawn in order to keep the initiative. Instead 14 ♕xd4 ♗xf3 15 gxf3 ♔d7! looks fine for Black.

14...♗xf3 15 ♕xf3 ♖b8 16 c3 c5 17 ♖ad1

Black has a pawn, which compensates for his awkwardly placed king.

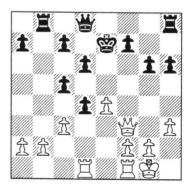

17...dxc3?!

17...♖xb2 was worth considering.

18 ♕xc3 f6 19 e5!

Open lines! Now Black has to tread warily.

19...♔f7

I rejected 19...fxe5?!, as this just invites the rook on f1 to join the attack after 20 f4.

20 exd6 cxd6 21 ♕c4+ ♔g7 22 ♕a6

White wins back his pawn but cannot avoid exchanges.

22...♕c7 23 ♕xd6 ♕xd6 24 ♖xd6 ♖hd8

24...♖xb2? is just bad after 25 ♖d7+.

25 ♖xd8 ♖xd8 26 ♖c1

White has the slightly better structure in the ending, but a draw is probable if Black doesn't play too passively.

26...g5!? 27 g4 ♖d5 28 ♖c4 ♖d2

see following diagram

Rather insisting on a pawn sacrifice to become active. The extra a-pawn is insufficient to win in these types of rook ending.

29 ♖xc5 ♖xb2 30 ♖c7+ ♔g6 31 ♖xa7 h5 32 gxh5+ ♔xh5 33 ♔g2 ♖c2 34 a4 ♖a2 35 a5 ♔g6 36 a6 ♔f5 37 ♖a8 ♔f4 38 a7 f5 39 ♖e8 ½-½

Summary

Although the Cozio has received much attention from strong grandmasters, I don't believe that Black can quite equalise. The three diagram positions below I judge as favourable to White, who should follow game 43 as his model. In game 44 Black should play 8...d6, instead of 8...d5, and in game 45 Black avoids the worst by avoiding 4...d5, and playing instead 4...g6. However it's in the main line, examined in game 43, that Black needs some new ideas to make the variation fully viable. The resulting positions are complex and offer counterchances, but with best play seem to be difficult for Black.

1 e4 e5 2 ♘f3 ♘c6 3 ♗b5 ♘ge7 4 0-0

> 4 ♘c3 *(D)*
>> 4...♘g6 – *Game 46*
>> 4...g6 – *Game 47*
> 4 c3 d5 5 ♘xe5 dxe4 6 ♕e2 ♕d5 7 ♘xc6 ♘xc6 8 d4 ♗f5 9 ♗f4 – *Game 45*

4...g6 *(D)* **5 c3**

> 5 d4 exd4 6 ♘xd4 ♗g7 7 ♗e3 0-0 8 ♘c3 d5 – *Game 44*

5...♗g7 6 d4 exd4 7 cxd4 d5 8 exd5 ♘xd5 *(D)* **9 ♗g5 ♕d6 10 ♖e1+ ♗e6 11 ♘bd2 0-0 12 ♘e4 ♕b4 13 ♗xc6 bxc6 14 ♕c1 ♖fe8 15 h3 ♖ab8 16 b3 ♗f5** – *Game 43*

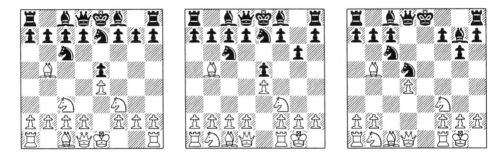

4 ♘c3 | *4...g6* | *8...♘xd5*

CHAPTER EIGHT

The Smyslov Variation

1 e4 e5 2 ♘f3 ♘c6 3 ♗b5 g6

I've called 3...g6 the Smyslov variation as it was primarily he who popularised the line over many years. There are many transpositions with the previous chapter on the Cozio variation, for instance; after 3...g6 then 4 0-0 ♗g7 5 c3 ♘ge7 6 d4 exd4 7 cxd4 d5, or 4 d4 exd4 5 ♘xd4 ♗g7 6 ♗e3 ♘ge7 7 ♘c3 are both examined in detail there. An opening such as 4 ♘c3 ♗g7 5 d3 ♘ge7 6 ♗g5 h6 7 ♗h4 g5 8 ♗g3 d6 9 h3 a6 10 ♗a4 b5, Rajna-Smyslov, Szolnok 1975, gives equal play from any move order! So these two chapters are best studied together.

White should play for d2-d4, either immediately or after the preliminary c2-c3. Only by a quick reaction in the centre can White hope to test Black's system of development. Recent developments suggest that Black's idea is fundamentally sound and this is one of Black's best alternatives to 3...a6. As to the choice between 3...g6 and 3...♘ge7, that's largely a matter of taste!

> ### Game 48
> ### Shirov-Azmaiparashvili
> *Montecatini Terme 2000*

1 e4 e5 2 ♘f3 ♘c6 3 ♗b5 g6 4 d4 exd4 5 ♗g5 ♗e7 6 ♗xe7 ♕xe7!

The soundest. Early deviations and 6...♘gxe7 are analysed in game 49.

7 ♗xc6

White can play 7 0-0, but this only delays the standard capture. Then Black has a couple of alternatives:

a) 7...♘f6 8 e5 (after 8 ♗xc6 dxc6 9 ♕xd4 c5 10 ♕e3 ♗g4 11 ♘c3 ♗xf3 12 ♕xf3 0-0-0 13 ♖ad1 ♖d4 Black was active enough to compensate for his slight pawn structure inferiority, Balashov-Smyslov, Moscow 1987; or 8 ♖e1 0-0 9 ♘xd4 ♕e5 10 ♗xc6 dxc6 11 c3, de Firmian-Berry, USA 1999, and yet again despite the White 4v3 majority being superior, Black kept his pieces lively and proved to have sufficient resources to hold the balance – note that in these type of positions Black should avoid too many exchanges, as simplified endings are likely to be better for White.) 8...♘h5 9 ♖e1 0-0 10 ♗xc6 dxc6 11 ♕xd4 ♗f5 12 ♘bd2!? (12 ♘c3 ♗xc2 13 ♕d2 ♗f5 14 h3 ♕d7 15 ♕e3 was messy in Galdunts-G.Giorgadze, Podolsk 1989), and the c-pawn cannot be taken, for example 12...♗xc2? (12...♖fd8 13 ♕c4 ♖d5! is best, with unclear play) 13 g4 ♖ad8 (after 13...♘g7 then 14 ♕c4 traps the bishop) 14 ♕c3 ♘f4 15 ♕xc2 ♕e6 16 ♔h1, Glek-Renner, Germany 1998, and Black had insufficient compensation for the piece.

b) 7...♕b4 (7...♕c5 8 ♗xc6 dxc6 9 ♕xd4 comes to the same thing) 8 ♗xc6 (8 c4!? is speculative and frankly ugly, but creates some practical problems; 8...♕xb2 9 ♘bd2 ♘ge7 10 e5 0-0 11 ♖b1 ♕a3 12 ♖b3 ♕a5 13 ♕c1 d6 14 ♘e4 with complications, Lengyel-M.Tseitlin, Budapest 1993) 8...dxc6 9 ♕xd4 ♕xd4 10 ♘xd4 ♗d7 11 ♘c3 0-0-0 12 ♖ad1 ♘h6 13 f3 ♖he8 14 ♔f2 f6, de Firmian-Azmaiparashvili, Moscow 1990.

The position is reminiscent of the exchange variation, where White retains a very small edge as his kingside majority is worth more than Black's queenside.

7...dxc6

The complications provoked by 7...♕b4+?, are lost for Black; 8 c3 ♕xb2 9 ♕xd4 ♕xa1 10 0-0 f6 (10...dxc6 11 ♕xh8 ♔f8 12 ♘g5 etc.) 11 e5! dxc6 12 exf6 (Dautov), for instance 12...♗f5 13 ♖e1+ ♔f8

14 ♕c5+ ♔f7 15 ♖e7+ and White mates.

8 ♕xd4 ♘f6 9 ♘c3

After 9 0-0 c5 10 ♕e5 ♕xe5 11 ♘xe5 ♗e6 12 ♘c3 0-0-0 13 ♖fd1 ♖d4 14 f3 ♖hd8 Black had no problems in Psakhis-G.Giorgadze, Debrecen 1992.

9...♗g4

This has replaced 9...0-0?! in current practice, because of games such as Sax-Smyslov, New York 1987, which continued 10 0-0-0 ♗e6 11 h3 ♖fd8 12 ♕e3 b5?! 13 ♘e5

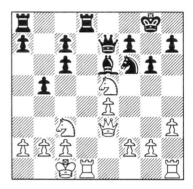

and White had an excellent position.

After 9...♗g4 White has a dichotomy.

10 ♘d2

ECO recommends 10 0-0-0, when 10...♗xf3 is forced (as White was threatening 11 e5), but now White's pawn structure is also compromised. The final assessment of this position will depend on whether or not White can obtain an attack by pushing his f-pawn. After the further 11 gxf3 0-0 12 ♕e3 Black has two moves:

a) 12...♘h5 13 f4 b6 (Dautov rejects 13...♕h4 because of 14 f5 gxf5 15 ♖d7) 14 f5 ♖ad8 15 ♖xd8 ♖xd8 16 fxg6 hxg6 17 f4, Luther-Dautov, Bad Lauterberg 1991, when White is much better according to Dautov. Again his kingside majority is more use than Black's queenside, but before taking this assessment for granted compare with Szmetan-Smyslov, below.

b) 12...♖fe8! looks a better try, to restrain the advance of the central pawns, and after

13 ♖de1 (13 ♖he1 has a downside in that the continuation 13...♘h5 14 f4 ♛h4 now has the added advantage of hitting the h-pawn) 13...♘h5 14 f4, then 14...♛h4 is now interesting, as here White doesn't invade on d7.

White can also push immediately with 12 f4 (instead of 12 ♛e3), when 12...♖fd8 (Dautov analyses 12...♘g4 13 f3 ♖fd8 14 ♛g1 ♖xd1+ 15 ♘xd1 ♘f6 16 f5 b6 17 ♘c3 ♖d8 18 fxg6 hxg6 19 ♛g5 as better for White) 13 ♛e3 b6 14 f5 ♖xd1+ 15 ♖xd1 ♖e8 16 fxg6 hxg6 17 ♛g5 ♛e5! (17...♘xe4? is rather embarrassing for Black after 18 ♛xe7 ♖xe7 19 ♖e1) 18 ♛xe5 ♖xe5 19 f3 ♔f8 20 ♘e2 ♖h5 21 ♘d4 c5 22 ♘c6 yields a double-edged ending where Black isn't worse, Szmetan-Smyslov, San Martin 1993. Here we note that the isolated h-pawn can be a liability.

It's possible that 10 0-0-0 could be White's best try, with reasonable chances of maintaining some sort of opening initiative, but I believe that ECO's view that 'White is clearly better' is too optimistic.

10...c5

By shielding the a-pawn and pushing the queen away with gain of time, Black prepares to castle long. Placing the king on the other wing is probably inferior as the following example suggests; 10...0-0 11 h3 ♗e6 12 0-0-0 ♖fd8 13 ♛e3 b5 14 f4 ♘d7 15 ♘f3 b4 16 ♘a4 ♘b6 17 ♖xd8+ ♖xd8 18 ♘e5! (if 18 ♘xb6?! axb6, Black is fine in view of White's weak a-pawn) 18...♘xa4 (after 18...♛e8 19 ♘c5 White's cavalry dominate) 19 ♘xc6 ♛e8 20 ♘xd8 ♛xd8 21 ♛xa7 and the rook and two pawns are far stronger here than the two pieces, Psakhis-Smyslov, Rostov 1993.

11 ♛e3 0-0-0 12 h3 ♗d7!

After 12...♗e6, White is able to achieve an ideal set-up; 13 0-0-0 ♘d7 14 f4 f6 15 ♘f3, and White is ready to use his majority actively. Illescas-Salov, Madrid 1997, then continued 15...♖he8 16 ♖he1 ♘b6 17 ♖xd8+ ♖xd8 18 f5! with a pleasant initiative for White.

13 0-0-0 ♗c6 14 g4 ♖he8 15 ♖he1 b6

With all his pieces on ideal restraining squares, Black is ready for anything. Here 16 g5 is White's critical option, pushing the knight away and taking some space, but after 16...♘h5 Black is eyeing the f4-square (if 17 f4 then 17...f6!?). In that case play would be fairly unclear, but after White's next he is just worse.

16 f4? ♘xe4!

A tactical shot that wins a pawn.

17 ♘cxe4 f5 18 gxf5 gxf5 19 ♘d6+ ♛xd6 20 ♘c4 ♛f6 21 ♖xd8+ ♖xd8 22 ♘e5 ♗e4 23 ♖g1

Shirov tries to retain active pieces, hoping to thus thwart Black's efforts to exploit his extra pawn, but f4 and h3 will be targets in an ending.

23...♛e6 24 b3 ♛d5 25 ♘c4 ♔b7 26 ♔b2 ♖g8 27 ♖xg8 ♛xg8 28 ♛f2 ♛d8 29 ♘e5 ♛d1 30 h4 a5 31 a4 ♔c8 32 ♘c4 ♛d4+

The exchange of queens and improvement in his pawn structure is exactly what Azmaiparashvili was looking for.

33 ♛xd4 cxd4 34 c3 dxc3+ 35 ♔xc3 ♔d7 36 ♘e3 ♔e6 37 ♔d4 ♗f3 38 ♔c3 ♗d5 39 ♘f1 ♔d6 40 ♘g3 ♗e6 41 ♘f1 ♔c5 42 ♘e3 c6 43 ♘c2 b5 44 axb5 cxb5 45 b4+ axb4+ 46 ♘xb4 ♗c4 0-1

Black's king will come to e4 and the f-pawn will fall.

Against 12...♗d7, coming quickly to the active c6-square, White has a difficult time proving any real advantage.

Game 49
Brynell-Martinovsky
Wrexham 1998

1 e4 e5 2 ♘f3 ♘c6 3 ♗b5 g6 4 d4 exd4

Alternatively 4...♘xd4 5 ♘xd4 exd4 6 ♕xd4 ♕f6 7 e5 ♕b6 8 ♕d3 c6 wins a pawn, but 9 ♗c4 ♕a5+ 10 ♘c3 ♕xe5+ 11 ♗e3 d5 12 0-0-0 then left White with a strong attack, I.Zaitsev-Suteev, USSR 1968.

5 ♗g5

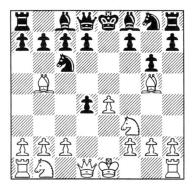

Instead 5 ♘xd4, is less critical; 5...♗g7 6 ♗e3 ♘f6!? (6...♘ge7 is also playable and will probably transpose to Chapter 7, game 44) 7 ♘c3 0-0 8 f3 ♘e7 9 ♘de2?! (better is 9 ♕d2) 9...d5 10 exd5 ♘fxd5 and Black is already a little better, Dückstein-Smyslov, Bad Wörishofen 1991.

5...♗e7

For those who like to grab hot pawns there is 5...♗b4+?!, but after 6 c3 dxc3 7 ♘xc3 ♗xc3+ 8 bxc3 f6 9 ♗h4 d6 10 ♘d4 ♗d7 11 ♘xc6 ♗xc6 12 ♗xc6+ bxc6 13 0-0 Black has problems to complete his development. White proved that he had excellent compensation and won easily in D.Gross-Murey, Clichy 1998.

More usual is 5...f6, which is essentially a positional concession, after which Black's development lacks harmony. There are then two logical retreats, 6 ♗f4 and 6 ♗h4:

a) 6 ♗f4 and then after 6...♗g7, White has a further choice:

a1) 7 c3?! (a dubious gambit) 7...dxc3 8 ♘xc3 ♘e5 9 ♘d4 c6 10 ♗a4 ♘e7 11 ♗b3 d5, Chernov-Breahna, Romanian Team Championship 1997, and for his pawn White didn't really have enough.

a2) 7 ♘xd4 is more sensible; 7...♘ge7 8 ♘c3 0-0 (or 8...a6 9 ♗c4 ♘a5 10 ♗e2 d6 11 0-0-0 12 ♕d2 ♘ac6 13 ♗c4+ ♔h8 14 ♘e6, Nikolin-Semenova, Rijeka 1997, when White is better due to the bishop pair and a territorial advantage) 9 0-0 ♔h8! (Black intends ...f5) 10 ♘xc6!? (now Black obtains counterplay on the b-file) 10...bxc6 11 ♗c4 d6 12 ♖e1 ♖b8 13 ♖b1 (perhaps 13 ♗b3 immediately) 13...♖b4 14 ♗b3 f5, with complications, Tan-Biyiasas, Manila 1976.

a3) 7 h4!? is aggressive and not so easy to meet:

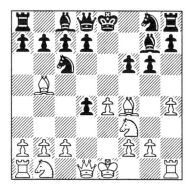

7...♕e7 (Kovalev gives 7...♘ge7 8 h5 0-0 9 hxg6 hxg6 10 ♘xd4 d5 11 ♘c3 ♘xd4 12 ♕xd4 c6 13 ♗e2 f5 14 e5 as a clear advantage to White, but perhaps 7...h5, which seems a practical reply is simplest, as in de Paula-Loureiro, Brazil 1999) 8 0-0 ♘e5?! (better are 8...♕b4, fishing in troubled waters, or 8...a6 playing for 9 ♗xc6 dxc6 10 ♕xd4 ♗g4, exploiting the weakened g4-square to obtain a playable Spanish Exchange variation; if instead 9 ♗c4 then simply 9...d6, when 10 ♘xd4? fails to 10...♘xd4 11 ♕xd4 f5) 9 ♘xd4 ♘h6 10 ♘c3 c6 11 ♗e2 0-0 12 ♕d2 and White had a pleasant initiative in Kovalev-Mariasin, USSR 1986.

ECO has a high opinion of 6 ♗f4, but 6 ♗h4 pinning and settling for a small edge is better in my opinion.

b) 6 ♗h4 ♗g7 7 0-0 (or 7 ♘xd4 ♘ge7 8 ♘c3 0-0 9 0-0 ♔h8, when Black's position looks a little suspicious, and practically awkward to handle, but with accurate play from a strong grandmaster Black equalises; 10 ♘de2 d6 11 a3 ♗e6 12 f4 ♗g8 13 f5 ♘e5 14 ♘d4 c6 15 ♗e2 d5 16 fxg6 hxg6 17 exd5 and now a draw was agreed in Glek-Hübner, Bundesliga 1993) 7...♘ge7 8 ♗c4 ♘a5 9 ♕xd4 ♘ec6 10 ♕d5 ♘xc4 11 ♕xc4 d6 12 ♘c3 ♗g4 13 ♘d5 ♗xf3 14 gxf3 ♘e5 15 ♕e2 0-0 16 f4 c6, Malaniuk-Ciruk, Linz 1997, and Black was only slightly worse.

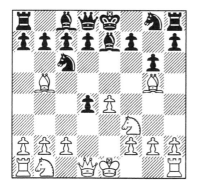

6 ♗xe7 ♘gxe7 7 ♘xd4 0-0
Black can also play for 7...d5 immediately,

when after 8 ♘c3 dxe4, White has two tries:

a) 9 ♘xe4 0-0 10 ♗xc6 ♘xc6 11 ♘xc6 bxc6 (11...♕xd1+?! enables White's king to come to an excellent post; 12 ♖xd1 bxc6 13 ♔d2! ♗e6 14 ♔c3 with a clearly better endgame for White, Godena-Ciolac, Marostica 1997) 12 0-0 ♗f5 13 ♘g3 ♗e6 14 ♕e2 isn't very much, but I prefer White slightly, Kikkola-Dobrowska, Poland 1997.

b) 9 ♗xc6+ ♘xc6 10 ♘xc6 ♕xd1+ 11 ♖xd1 bxc6 12 ♘xe4 ♗f5 13 0-0! was Nunn-Salov, Skeleftea 1989, when Nunn gives 13...♗xe4 (or 13...♖d8!?) 14 ♖fe1 f5 15 f3 ♔e7 16 fxe4 f4 17 ♖d3 as yielding a small edge for White.

8 ♘c3 d5

Black can't really play slowly as his dark squares will require constant attention, so nobody plays 8...d6?! here.

9 ♗xc6 bxc6 10 ♘b3!

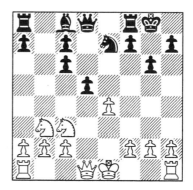

The recommended way to keep a pull. White wants to keep the better pawn structure and this stops counterplay based on ...c5.

10...dxe4 11 ♘xe4 ♗f5 12 ♘bc5 ♕xd1+

Otherwise, 12...♘d5 13 ♕d4? ♗xe4 14 ♘xe4 f5 15 ♘c5 ♖e8+ 16 ♔f1 ♕e7, was far from clear in Prié-Anic, French Championship 1996, but naturally after 13 0-0, White has an excellent game.

13 ♖xd1 ♖fd8

In the game Smirin-I.Sokolov, Wijk aan Zee 1994, Black kept as active as possible, but despite this, after 13...♘d5 14 0-0 ♔g7 15 c4 ♗xe4 16 ♘xe4 ♖ae8 17 ♘c5 ♘b6 18 b3 ♖e5 19 ♘d3 ♖e2 20 a4 ♘d7 21 ♖fe1 ♖xe1+ 22 ♖xe1, he was left with his static weaknesses and an unpleasant endgame.

14 ♔e2 ♔f8 15 ♖xd8+ ♖xd8 16 ♖d1 ♘d5 17 ♔f3 h5 18 h3

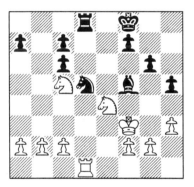

White consolidates his well-entrenched pieces and prepares to probe away at Black's shattered queenside.

18...♔e7 19 ♖e1 ♔f8 20 a3 ♘b6 21 b3 ♖d5 22 ♖e3 ♘d7 23 ♘xd7+ ♖xd7 24 ♖c3 ♗xe4+ 25 ♔xe4 ♖d6

It's not clear that the ending is objectively won, but with little hope of going active Black has to defend indefinitely. A disagreeable task.

26 ♖c4 ♔e7 27 ♔e3 ♔d7 28 ♖f4 f5?

Creating a fatal weakness on g5. Instead 28...f6, was the only chance.

29 ♖d4!

Stronger than 29 ♖a4 ♖e6+ 30 ♔f3 ♖d6 31 ♖xa7 ♖d2, when Black is active.

29...a6 30 ♖xd6+

30...♔xd6

White wins easily enough after 30...cxd6, but it's instructive to see how; 31 ♔f4 ♔e6 32 ♔g5 ♔f7 33 c4 d5 (or 33...♔g7 34 b4 ♔f7 35 a4 ♔g7 36 a5 ♔f7 37 b5 etc.) 34 cxd5 cxd5 (White wins because the queenside majority leads to the creation of an outside passed pawn) 35 ♔f4! ♔e6 36 ♔e3 ♔e5 (or 36...g5 37 ♔d4 ♔d6 38 b4 f4 39 f3 ♔c6 40 a4 ♔d6 41 b5 axb5 42 axb5 and so on) 37 f4+ ♔d6 38 ♔d4 a5 39 b4 etc.

31 ♔f4 ♔e6 32 ♔g5 ♔f7 33 b4 ♔g7 34 a4 ♔f7 35 a5 ♔g7 36 c4 ♔f7 37 b5 cxb5 38 cxb5 1-0

An excellent technical game exploiting Black's chronically weak queenside.

Game 50
Dolmatov-Kholmov
Sochi 1988

1 e4 e5 2 ♘f3 ♘c6 3 ♗b5 g6 4 c3 d6

Aiming to consolidate the centre before completing the development of his kingside.

The move 4...♗g7?!, however, fails to do so after 5 d4, when Black has no satisfactory continuation, for instance; 5...exd4 6 cxd4 d5 7 exd5 ♕xd5 8 ♘c3 ♕e6+ 9 ♗e3 ♘ge7 10 0-0, and Black's queen is badly placed. 'Putting the question to the bishop' with 4...a6, is the subject of game 51.

5 d4

5 ♗xc6+ bxc6 6 d4 f6, reminds one of a well-known 'Steinitz Deferred' line (3...a6 4 ♗a4 d6 5 ♗xc6+ bxc6 6 d4 f6 - C73), except that here Black has ...g6 instead of ...a6 and White an extra move c2-c3. These changes are not so radical, particularly as one of White's best plans is to continue with ♗e3, c4 and ♘c3. Stanciu-Suba, Romanian Championship 1973, continued 7 h4 h5 8 dxe5 dxe5 9 ♕a4 (trying to profit from the c-pawn being on c3) 9...♗d7 10 ♗e3 ♕b8, with a reasonable game for Black.

5...♗d7

6 ♕b3

Creating threats against b7 and f7 before Black has had time to get fully organised.

White's pieces are also more active after the exchange on e5, pre-empting any potential counterplay on the long diagonal. White can exchange immediately, or delay it one move:

a) 6 dxe5 dxe5 (6...♘xe5? leads to the loss of a pawn after 7 ♘xe5 dxe5 8 ♕d5 ♗g7 9 ♕xb7 ♘f6 10 ♗xd7+ ♘xd7 11 0-0 0-0 12 ♘a3, Strausz-Nilles, Il Ciocco 1978, while in this 7...♗xb5? is refuted by 8 ♘xf7! ♔xf7 9 ♕d5+) 7 ♕e2 (after 7 ♕b3 safest is 7...♕e7, covering weak points e5 and f7; 7 ♗g5 can be met with the solid 7...♗e7, as 8 ♗e3 ♘f6, intending ...0-0, ...♘g4 or ...♘xe4 depending on circumstances, is fine for Black) 7...♗g7 8

♗e3 ♘ge7 9 ♘bd2 a6 10 ♗c4 ♕c8 11 0-0 0-0 12 b4! (gaining space and influence on the queenside) 12...♘d8 13 a4 ♘e6 14 ♘g5 ♘c6 15 ♘xe6 ♗xe6 16 ♘b3 ♘d8 17 ♖ad1 b6 18 ♗d5, with a persistent edge to White, Tal-Smyslov, Biel Interzonal 1976.

b) After 6 0-0 ♗g7 7 dxe5 dxe5 (now 7...♘xe5 doesn't free the Black game, despite significant exchanges; 8 ♘xe5 ♗xe5 9 ♕b3 ♗c6 10 ♗xc6+ bxc6 11 ♘a3 ♗g7 12 ♖e1 ♘e7 13 ♘c4 0-0 14 ♗g5 ♔h8 15 ♖ad1 with pressure), the move 8 ♗g5, (provoking the concession 8...f6) is not bad, but following 9 ♗e3 ♗h6!? (it may seem odd in a ...g6 system to seek the exchange of this bishop; one can argue that this is Black's worst bishop, but after it's exchange then the dark squares may become weak; Geller and Keres propose instead 9...♘h6.) 10 ♕c1 ♗xe3 11 ♕xe3 ♔f7 (heading for g7 to cover the hole on h6) 12 ♖d1,

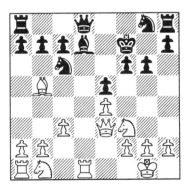

Tringov-Suba, Athens 1976, although White is clearly more active, the lack of pawn breaks may help Black to wriggle out.

6...♘a5

Alternatives are not so great either; the natural looking 6...♗g7? failing to 7 dxe5 dxe5 8 ♗c4 ♕e7 9 ♕xb7 ♖b8 10 ♕a6 ♘f6 11 ♘bd2 ♖b6 12 ♕a4, Razuvaev-Camara, Sao Paulo 1977, and 6...♗h6 leading to White obtaining a pleasant edge after the continuation 7 0-0 ♗xc1 8 ♖xc1 ♘ge7 9 ♘a3 0-0 10 dxe5 dxe5 11 ♘c4, as in Perenyi-Zsinka, Budapest 1977.

7 ♕a4 c6!?

Black could try 7...♘c6, cutting out some tactical tricks but at a cost in time. In that case Dolmatov intended to castle and then bring his rook to d1.

8 ♗e2 b5

Playing consistently, gaining some activity and space, but at the cost of potential weaknesses on this wing.

9 ♕c2 ♗g7 10 0-0 ♘e7 11 dxe5!

Effectively keeping the bishop on g7 quiet and opening the d-file to activate the rook.

11...dxe5 12 a4 a6 13 ♖d1

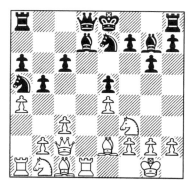

Black has to be careful, for example the routine 13...0-0? fails to 14 axb5 axb5 15 b4 ♘b7 16 ♖xa8 ♕xa8 17 ♖xd7, winning a piece.

13...♕c8 14 ♗e3 ♘b7 15 c4!

It's important to gain a concession from Black before he is properly organised.

15...b4

After 15...0-0 16 ♗b6, Black is rather tied up, and problems with the squares c5 and d6 will keep him on the backfoot.

16 c5

Declaring his intentions to use the d6-square and the a2-g8 diagonal.

16...♘a5 17 ♘bd2 0-0 18 ♘b3 ♘xb3 19 ♕xb3 a5 20 ♗c4 h6 21 h3

Cautious. Dolmatov later preferred the more forthright 21 ♖d6!? ♗e8 22 h4.

21...♗e8 22 ♖d6 ♔h7 23 ♖ad1

White dominates the board and it's clear that the opening and early middlegame have not been a great success for the second player. The bishop on g7 may help defend his king, but is still a poor piece, as it has no influence on the centre.

23...♕c7 24 ♕c2 ♘c8 25 ♖d8 ♗f6 26 ♖8d3 ♘e7 27 b3 ♘g8 28 ♕b2 ♕e7 29 ♖d6 ♗g7 30 ♕c2 ♘f6 31 ♗e2!

In view of Black's total passivity, White hasn't been in a great hurry, but now he intends to bring his knight to c4.

31...♗d7 32 ♘d2 ♘e8 33 ♖d3 ♗e6

Preparing to lop off the annoying knight when it arrives.

34 ♘c4 ♗xc4 35 ♕xc4 ♘f6 36 ♗g4!

Switching attention to the light squares. The immediate threat is 37 ♗d7 picking off the c6-pawn.

36...♘xg4 37 hxg4 ♖a7 38 g3!

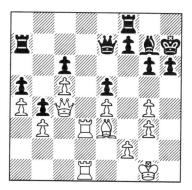

The bishop on g7 has been a spectator whilst White has strengthened his domination. The text move prepares to open another front on the h-file.

38...♗f6?

Dolmatov suggests 38...♖c8 39 ♔g2 ♗f8 40 ♖h1 f6 as a more stubborn defence.

39 ♖d6 ♖c8 40 ♔g2 ♗g7

I prefer 40...♗g5, meeting 41 ♗xg5 with 41...hxg5, and 41 ♕c1 by 41...♔g7.

41 g5! hxg5

41...h5 is brutally met by 42 g4! hxg4 43 ♖h1+ ♔g8 44 ♖xg6.

42 ♖h1+ ♗h6 43 ♕e2! ♖ac7

If 43...♔g7, then 44 ♕g4 ♖h8 45 ♖xc6 leaves Black's position in a shambles.

44 ♕g4 ♔g7

44...f6 is met by 45 ♖xf6! ♕xf6 46 ♗xg5.

45 ♖xh6! 1-0

Black had had enough. If instead he carried on, then 45...♔xh6 46 ♕h4+ ♔g7 47 ♗xg5 would force him to give up his queen in order to stop mate.

These variations look miserable for Black, which is why Smyslov and other leading 3...g6 exponents meet 4 c3 with 4...a6 (see the next game).

Game 51
S.Polgar-Smyslov
Munich, Women vs. Veterans 2000

1 e4 e5 2 ♘f3 ♘c6 3 ♗b5 g6 4 c3 a6!

Don't be put off by this move! Especially in a book dealing with the Spanish without 3...a6!? and, no, Black hasn't regretted not having played this on his previous move!

As we shall see, the exchange on c6 is not that worrisome, so Black picks a good moment for kicking the bishop.

5 ♗c4

After 5 ♗a4, then 5...d6 introduces a type of Steinitz Deferred (3...a6 4 ♗a4 d6 5 c3 g6) where Black's last move is not bad. The inclusion of 4...a6, 5 ♗a4 means that White can no longer play the plan based on ♕b3 seen in game 50. After the sequence 5...d6 6 d4 ♗d7 7 0-0 ♗g7, we reach a typical position:

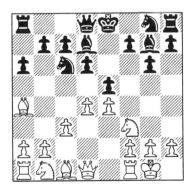

In three Xie Jun-Smyslov encounters White has failed to show any significant advantage; 8 dxe5 (or 8 d5 ♘ce7 9 ♗xd7+ ♕xd7 10 c4 ♘f6 11 ♘c3 0-0 12 ♗e3 b5!?,

Xie Jun-Smyslov, Women vs. Veterans 1996, with sufficient counterchances for Black) and now Smyslov has recaptured with both knight and pawn:

a) 8...♘xe5 9 ♘xe5 dxe5 10 f4 (otherwise White has nothing) 10...♗xa4 11 ♕xa4+ b5 12 ♕b3 exf4 13 ♗xf4 ♘f6 14 a4?! (better is 14 ♘d2 0-0 15 ♖ae1 ♘d7 16 ♕c2 with equality, Geller-Smyslov, Sochi 1986) 14...0-0 15 ♗g5 ♕d6 16 ♗xf6 ♗xf6 17 axb5 ♗e5 and Black had all the chances, Xie Jun-Smyslov, Women v Veterans 1999.

b) Trying for more tension with 8...dxe5!? in Xie Jun-Smyslov, Women vs. Veterans 1997, worked fine; 9 ♗e3 ♘ge7 10 ♘bd2 0-0 11 ♗c2 h6 12 a4 a5 13 ♕b1 b6 14 ♗b3 ♔h8 15 ♖d1 ♕e8 16 ♘e1 f5, and Black had the initiative. A good model of how Black can obtain his play in such lines. White's plan however looks laborious (the queen is not well-placed on b1 for instance).

Simplest for Black is to capture on e5 with the knight, with no problems to equalise, but capturing with the pawn may be worth a try if you want to set your opponent more complex problems.

5 ♗xc6 doesn't inspire; 5...dxc6 6 0-0 (6 ♘xe5 is met by 6...♕e7) 6...♗g7 is then much better for Black than the positions occurring after 3...a6 4 ♗xc6 dxc6 5 0-0. Here, Black's bishop is well-placed on g7 as White's weakened d3-square virtually obliges him to play for d4. After 7 d4 exd4 8 cxd4 ♘e7 (8...♗g4 9 ♘c3!? ♗xf3!? 10 ♕xf3 ♕xd4 11 ♗f4 gives White good play for the pawn) 9 ♘c3 ♗g4 10 ♗e3 0-0 11 h3 ♗xf3 12 ♕xf3, Chandler-Spassky, Vienna 1986, Black could try 12...♖xd4 (or 12...f5 13 ♗g5 ♕d7, as in the game wasn't bad either) 13 ♗xd4 ♕xd4 14 ♖ad1 ♕e5 15 ♖d7 ♖ad8 16 ♕d3 ♖xd7 17 ♕xd7 ♖c8 with an unclear position, according to Chandler.

5...d6 6 d4 ♗g7

The Lanka-Korchnoi game examined below (note to White's eighth move) actually transposed via 6...♕e7!? 7 0-0 ♗g7. The

advantage of Korchnoi's move-order is that 8 ♗g5 can be met by 8...♘f6 as well as ...f6.

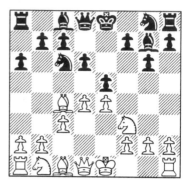

7 0-0

Or 7 ♗g5 f6 (I wonder if Black can actually envisage 7...♘f6!?, with the point that 8 dxe5 dxe5 9 ♕xd8+ ♘xd8 10 ♘xe5 is diffused by 10...♘xe4 11 ♗xd8 ♗xe5) 8 ♗e3 ♕e7 9 ♘bd2 ♘h6 10 h3 ♘f7 11 0-0 ♘cd8 12 b4 0-0 13 a4 ♔h8 14 ♖e1 ♘e6, Rozentalis-Balashov, Voronezh 1987, with equal chances and a rich position.

7...♕e7

Over-protecting the key e5 square and preparing ...♘f6.

Smyslov has also played 7...b5!? 8 ♗e2 ♘f6 9 dxe5 dxe5 10 ♕c2 0-0 11 a4 (the natural reaction, but it doesn't give White very much here) 11...b4 12 ♗e3 ♖e8 13 ♘bd2 bxc3 14 bxc3 ♘h5 15 g3 ♘a5 16 ♖fd1 ♕e7, Dolmatov-Smyslov, Moscow 1992, when White won a long game but not because of the opening.

The text is arguably more solid, avoiding any potential weaknesses associated with an early ...b5. Alternatively 7...♘ge7 is possible, and has scored well in practise, but it's not clear that this is the best choice of square:

a) 8 ♘g5 0-0 9 f4 exf4 10 ♘xf7?! (better is 10 ♗xf4 d5 11 exd5 ♘xd5 12 ♕f3 ♗e6, but this proved to be very solid for Black in Gufeld-Ignatiev, Kislodvsk 1968) 10...♖xf7 11 ♗xf7+ ♔xf7 12 ♕b3+ d5 13 ♗xf4 ♔g8 and Black won, Rogers-Zsu. Polgar, Wellington 1988.

b) 8 dxe5 dxe5 9 ♕e2 0-0 10 ♘a3 b6 11
♘c2 ♗b7 12 a3 h6 13 h4!? ♘c8! (heading
for d6) 14 ♖d1 ♘d6 15 ♘c3 ♘a5 and Black
was fine, Filipenko-Buturin, Lvov 1995.

8 dxe5

Not the only way to proceed. White can
also maintain the central tension with 8 h3.
Then after 8...h6 (cutting out the pin with
♗g5) 9 ♗e3 ♘f6 10 ♘bd2 0-0 11 ♖e1,
Lanka-Korchnoi, Debrecen 1992, White has
a shade of an edge but Black is very solid.
The game continued 11...♔h8 (11...♔h7,
protecting h6 was more precise) 12 a4 b6 13
♕c1 ♗d7 14 ♗f1 ♘g8 15 dxe5 dxe5 16
♘c4 and White made further progress by
manoeuvring his bishop from e3 to a3,
which may have given the idea to Zsofia
Polgar in our main game.

8...♘xe5 9 ♘xe5 dxe5 10 b3

White hopes that the bishop will be annoying on the a3-f8 diagonal.

10...♘f6 11 ♗a3 c5 12 ♗d5

The weak point on d5 cannot be occupied
by the knight so the bishop will have to do!

12...0-0

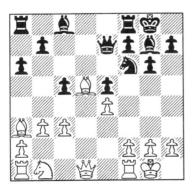

13 b4?

White should have tried the safer 13 c4
♖d8 14 ♘c3, but the text must have been
too tempting.

13...♖d8! 14 bxc5 ♘xe4

Positionally the exchange of the c-pawn
for the e-pawn is fine for Black, but the

struggle becomes sharp and the initiative is
paramount.

15 c4 ♕c7 16 ♖e1

16...♗f5!?

Smyslov makes an interesting choice. He
presumably rejected 16...♘xc5? 17 ♗xc5
♕xc5 18 ♗xf7+ ♔xf7 19 ♕xd8 e4 because it
fails to 20 ♘d2 ♗xa1 21 ♘xe4, with a decisive attack for White. Alternatively 16...♘f6
is met by 17 ♘c3, the fine outpost on d5
compensating for the slightly dodgy queenside pawns. However the immediate
16...♘xf2! 17 ♔xf2 e4 must have been
tempting! I can't see anything wrong with it.

17 g4

Consistent, but inviting the following
combination.

17...♘xf2! 18 ♔xf2 e4

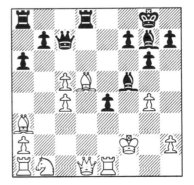

19 ♔g2

After 19 gxf5 ♕xh2+ 20 ♔f1 gxf5 White's

king is totally exposed and Black will be able to capture on a1 with a material advantage.
19...♗e6 20 ♘d2

20...♗xd5!

But not 20...♗xa1?, as 21 ♕xa1, followed by ♘xe4 allows White an attack.
21 cxd5 ♖xd5 22 ♕e2 ♗xa1 23 ♖xa1 ♖e8 24 ♘c4

24 ♘xe4 now fails to 24...♖de5! 25 ♘f6+ ♔h8, with ...♖e2+ to follow.
24...♖d3

With two pieces for rook and two pawns, White would have some holding chances but her king is too exposed.

25 ♖b1 ♕c6 26 ♔g1 ♖xa3! 27 ♘xa3 ♕xc5+ 28 ♕f2 e3 0-1

A possible finish could have been 29 ♕e2 ♕xa3 30 ♖xb7 ♕c1+ 31 ♔g2 ♕c6+ 32 ♕f3 ♕xf3+ 33 ♔xf3 e2, but resigning was less painful.

In conclusion, after 4...a6 the Smyslov Variation is perfectly playable for Black.

Summary

Black does best after 4 d4 exd4 5 ♗g5 ♗e7 6 ♗xe7, to play 6...♕xe7, and follow game 48, rather than the inferior 6...♘gxe7 of game 49.

After 4 c3, Black should probably play 4...a6 as in game 51.

Overall, it seems that the Smyslov is more solid than it's cousin the Cozio, but various exchange variations with ♗xc6 bxc6, can be a little dull and will not suit everybody.

1 e4 e5 2 ♘f3 ♘c6 3 ♗b5 g6 4 d4

    4 c3 *(D)*

        4...d6 – *Game 50*

        4...a6 5 ♗c4 d6 6 d4 ♗g7 7 0-0 ♕e7 – *Game 51*

4...exd4 5 ♗g5 ♗e7 6 ♗xe7 *(D)* **♕xe7**

    6...♘gxe7 7 ♘xd4 0-0 8 ♘c3 d5 9 ♗xc6 bxc6 10 ♘b3 – *Game 49*

7 ♗xc6 dxc6 8 ♕xd4 ♘f6 9 ♘c3 ♗g4 *(D)* **10 ♘d2 c5 11 ♕e3 0-0-0** – *Game 48*

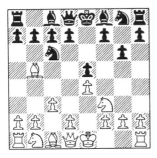
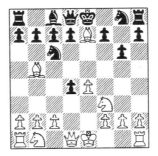
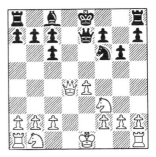

4 c3   *6 ♗xe7*   *9...♗g4*

CHAPTER NINE

Odds and Ends

1 e4 e5 2 ♘f3 ♘c6 3 ♗b5

When it comes to the weird and wonderful third move alternatives, a bit of common sense is a useful tool. Playing for a sharp risky refutation is often playing into your opponent's hands. He is more than likely well prepared for a 'book' refutation and in any case is hoping to provoke.

I suggest a safe positional approach bearing in mind the downside of your opponent's odd third move.

Game 52
M Chess 6-Efimov
Fiorenzuola d'Arda 1997

---

1 e4 e5 2 ♘f3 ♘c6 3 ♗b5 ♕e7

Others:

a) 3...♗d6 blocks in the queen's bishop and d-pawn so White should play 0-0, c2-c3 and d2-d4. How does Black then maintain a centre and complete his development?

b) After 3...f6, the weakness of the a2-g8 diagonal is an important factor. Tarrasch-Steinitz, Nuremberg 1896 continued 4 0-0 ♘ge7 5 d4 ♘g6 6 a3 (to maintain the bishop on the crucial diagonal) 6...♗e7 7 ♗c4 d6 8 h3 ♗d7 9 ♘c3 ♕c8 10 ♔h2, with a pleasant edge to White.

c) Following 3...♕f6, the queen may be exposed to a timely ♘d5 or ♗g5. After 4 ♘c3 ♘ge7 (4...♘d4 5 ♘xd4 exd4 6 ♘d5 ♕g5 is really provocative, but White can take the rook with 7 ♘xc7+ and get away with it; after 7...♔d8 8 ♘xa8 ♕xb5 9 d3 b6 10 ♗f4 d6 11 a4 ♕c6 12 ♕h5 g6 13 ♕b5 ♕xa8 14 a5 White maintains an advantage according to Alekhine) 5 d3 ♘d4 (5...h6!? is best met by 6 0-0 when 6...g5 7 ♘d5 ♘xd5 8 exd5 ♘e7 9 ♖e1 looks better for White, and 6...♘d4, will render the move 5...h6, a waste of time) 6 ♘xd4 exd4 7 ♘e2 c6 8 ♗a4 d5 9 0-0 g6 10 b4! (to probe the long diagonal) 10...♕d6 11 a3 ♗g4 12 ♗b2, Bogoljubov-Ed.Lasker, New York 1924, White has a type of Bird's Defence where Black has lost time.

For 3...♗b4 and 3...a5, see Game 53.

4 0-0

After 4 ♘c3 ♘d8

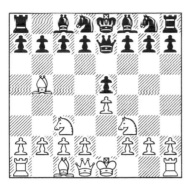

White can try to smash through (double-edged), or be happy with a positional edge (more practical), reminiscent of a slightly passive Philidor.

a) 5 ♘d5!? ♕d6 6 d4 c6 7 dxe5 ♕b8 8 ♗c4 cxd5 9 exd5, is given as an edge to White according to Vinogradov, but surely one doesn't have to play so riskily?

b) 5 d4!? c6 6 dxe5!? cxb5 7 ♘d5 ♕c5 8 ♗e3 ♕c4 9 b3 ♗b4+ 10 c3 ♗xc3+ 11 ♘d2 is another attempt at outright refutation. Kuindzhi continues 11...♕xe4?!, and prefers White, but 11...♕c6! (Flear), gives good defensive chances for Black.

c) 5 0-0 c6 6 ♗c4 d6 7 d4 g6 8 a4 ♘h6 9 h3 f6 10 ♗e3 ♗g7 11 ♖e1 ♘hf7, Rizzitano-Formanek, Philadelphia 1988, with a playable, but constrained position for Black.

4...♘d8 5 c3

After 5 d4 Black can continue with 5...c6 6 ♗c4 d6, in Philidor-style. Instead 5...f6?!, has been tried by the French IM Emmanuel Bricard. His idea is ugly but not as bad as the following game suggests; 6 ♘c3 ♘f7 7 ♗e3 g6 (I prefer 7...c6 8 ♗c4 d6) 8 dxe5 fxe5 9 ♘d5 ♕d8!? (or 9...♕d6) 10 ♘g5 ♘gh6?? (a terrible blunder, instead 10...c6 11 ♘xf7 ♔xf7 12 ♗c4 ♔g7, is better for White {development, insecure black king}, but Black is still on the board) 11 ♘e6 1-0 Vogt-Bricard, Bad Wildbad 1990.

5...c6 6 ♗a4 d6 7 h3

The computer intends to play d2-d4 and build-up sensibly behind his centre. Black can develop with ...g6, ♗g7 and ♘f6, but counterplay is not so easy to generate. Black's next anti-positional move tries to 'confuse' his electronic opponent but rebounds, and is refuted by energetic yet positionally correct play.

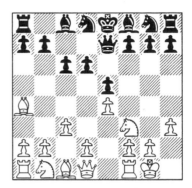

7...g5? 8 d4 f6 9 dxe5 dxe5 10 ♗e3 ♘e6 11 h4

Black's lagging development hardly allows him to launch a kingside assault, so this massaging of the black kingside pawn structure is justified.

11...h6

Perhaps 11...g4!?.

12 ♘bd2 ♕c7 13 ♗b3 ♘e7

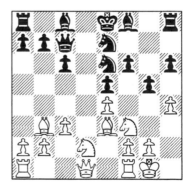

14 h5!

Stopping the knight using the g6-square.

14...♗d7 15 ♘c4 ♘c8

Necessary, but not really ideal.

16 ♘h2 ♗e7 17 ♘g4 ♔f7?

17...♘b6, intending ...0-0-0 is the lesser evil.

18 ♕f3 ♔g7 19 ♖fd1

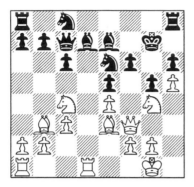

White has aggressively placed pieces and the Italian grandmaster now has to be very careful.

19...b5?

I prefer 19...♘f4, as after 20 g3 ♘xh5 21 ♘gxe5 fxe5, both 22 ♘b6 and 22 ♕xh5 are only slightly better for White.

20 ♘cxe5! fxe5 21 ♕f5

And the house of cards collapses.

21...♘d6 22 ♕g6+ ♔f8 23 ♘xe5 ♘f4 24 ♘xd7+ ♕xd7 25 ♗xf4 gxf4 26 ♖xd6! 1-0

Game 53
C.Hansen-Dreev
Kiljava 1984

---

1 e4 e5 2 ♘f3 ♘c6 3 ♗b5 ♗b4

The Alapin variation; a playable line where White has to play accurately to obtain a small edge.

After 3...a5 (Popov) 4 0-0 (4 d3? plays into Black's hands; 4...♘a7! 5 ♗c4 b5 6 ♗b3 a4 {whoops!}, Nikolov-Popov, Sofia 1990) 4...♘a7 5 ♗e2 (5 ♗c4!? b5 6 ♗xf7+ ♔xf7 7 ♘xe5+ is unclear, Kirillov-Popov, correspondence 1991-3, but why give a piece?)

5...d6 6 d4 ♗g4 (Backlund-Popov, correspondence 1992-4) and now I suggest 7 ♗e3! ♘f6 8 h3, leaving White with a safe edge. Basically, if White doesn't allow ...b5 with a gain of time and just consolidates his centre, then ...a5 and ...♘a7 look out of place.

4 0-0

White has two other serious moves:

a) 4 a3 ♗a5 5 b4 ♗b6 6 ♗b2 d6 7 d4 exd4 8 ♘bd2 ♗d7 9 ♗xc6 bxc6 10 ♗xd4 ♗xd4 11 ♘xd4 ♕f6 12 ♘2b3 ♘e7 13 0-0 0-0 14 ♖e1 ♖ae8 15 ♕f3 ♕g6, Kupreichik-Chetverik, Russia 2000, and White has an edge due to his firm control of the centre, but in the game Black held on.

b) 4 c3 ♗a5 and now:

b1) Pillsbury-Alapin, Vienna 1898 continued with 5 ♗xc6!? dxc6 6 ♘xe5 ♕g5, when White can continue with 7 d4 ♕xg2 8 ♕f3, when according to Keres and Geller White has an edge. A word of caution; White has his central pawns, but these may come under attack and proving anything concrete might be difficult in practise.

b2) 5 ♘a3 ♗b6 6 ♘c4 ♘f6! 7 d3 d6 8 a4 a6 9 ♘xb6 cxb6 10 ♗c4 h6 11 h3 0-0 12 0-0 ♖e8 13 ♗e3?! (I prefer 13 ♖e1!, intending to meet 13...d5, with 14 exd5 ♘xd5 15 d4 e4 16 ♘e5! keeping the better chances) 13...d5! 14 exd5 ♘xd5 15 d4 ♗e6 16 ♗xd5 ♗xd5 17 dxe5 ♘xe5 18 ♘xe5 ♖xe5 19 ♕d4 ♖e4 20 ♕xb6 ♕xb6 21 ♗xb6, Zso.Polgar-Berkovich, Amsterdam 1995, and despite the extra pawn the ending is very drawish.

4...♘ge7 5 c3 ♗a5

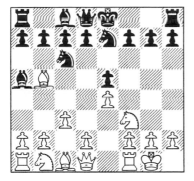

6 ♗xc6!

Obtaining the bishop-pair with the manoeuvre 6 ♘a3 0-0 7 ♘c4 is logical. Black can then react with 7...d5, when 8 ♘xa5 ♘xa5 9 ♕a4 (9 d4 ♗g4! is already equal according to Dreev) 9...♘ac6 is given by Suetin as equal. However, after 10 exd5 ♕xd5 11 ♖c1 ♗f5 White can try 12 d4!? exd4 13 ♗g5, with interesting play where I prefer White.

6...♘xc6 7 b4 ♗b6 8 b5 ♘a5

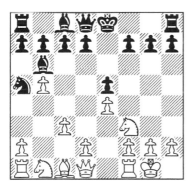

9 ♘xe5

White temporarily grabs a pawn, but at the cost of lagging development and loose pawns.

9...0-0 10 d4 ♕e8 11 ♘d2 d6 12 ♘d3 ♕xb5?!

Hansen points out that 12...f5 13 e5 ♕xb5 is more precise, with only a small edge to

White.

13 c4!

A shock for Black as the pawn cannot be taken.

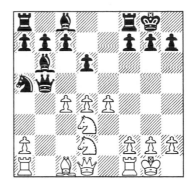

13...♕d7

13...♘xc4? just loses a piece after 14 ♖b1 ♕a6 15 ♘b4 ♕b5 16 a4.

14 ♗b2 c5 15 d5 ♗c7

White has a big advantage in view of his well-supported centre, whereas Black lacks space and effective development.

16 ♖b1

Immediately concentrating on the kingside with 16 f4! may be the most precise, as for instance 16...b5 17 f5 ♘xc4 18 ♘xc4 bxc4 19 ♕g4 f6 20 ♘f4 enables White to develop a strong attack.

16...♖b8 17 ♘f4 ♕g4 18 ♕xg4 ♗xg4 19 ♗c3 ♗d7 20 ♘h5 f6 21 f4

Hansen later suggested the prophylactic plan 21 a4 a6 22 ♖a1, when it's hard to see how Black can do much on the queenside.

21...b5?!

Better is 21...♗e8 22 ♘g3 b5, stopping the knight getting to e6.

22 f5! ♘xc4 23 ♘xc4 bxc4 24 ♘f4 ♖b6 25 ♘e6 ♗xe6 26 fxe6 ♖fb8 27 ♖xb6 axb6 28 a4 ♖a8 29 ♖a1 h5

The attempt to go active in a bishop ending with 29...b5, fails after 30 axb5 ♖xa1+ 31 ♗xa1 ♗a5 32 ♔f2 c3 33 ♔e2 c2 34 ♗b2 c4 35 b6 ♗xb6 36 ♔d2 and White will win in the long term as the e6-pawn is a decisive factor.

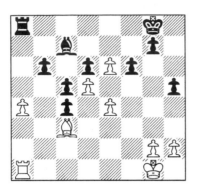

30 ♔f2 ♖f8 31 ♔e3 f5 32 ♖f1?

White should have tried to invade with his rook; 32 ♖b1! fxe4 33 a5! ♖b8 (after 33...bxa5, simply 34 ♖b7 is strong) 34 ♖b5 bxa5 35 ♖xb8+ ♗xb8 36 ♗xa5 and now Black can try 36...c3, to get some freedom, but after 37 ♗xc3 ♗c7 38 ♔xe4 g6 39 ♗f6 ♗a5 40 ♔d3, the king comes to c6 winning.

32...fxe4 33 ♖xf8+ ♔xf8 34 ♔xe4 ♗d8 35 ♔f5 h4 36 h3 ♗e7 37 ♗b2

37 ♔g6? fails to 37...♗f6.

37...♗d8 38 ♗a1 ♗e7 39 ♗c3 ♗d8 40 ♗b2 ♗e7 ½-½

Neither side can make progress.

Summary

The only half-reasonable move in this chapter is 3...♗b4, examined in game 53. The others are clearly inferior and not recommended.

1 e4 e5 2 ♘f3 ♘c6 3 ♗b5 ♗b4 *(D)*

3...♕e7 *(D)* 4 0-0 ♘d8 5 c3 c6 6 ♗a4 d6 7 h3 – *Game 52*

4 0-0 ♘ge7 5 c3 ♗a5 6 ♗xc6 ♘xc6 7 b4 ♗b6 8 b5 ♘a5 9 ♘xe5 0-0 *(D)* **10 d4** – *Game 53*

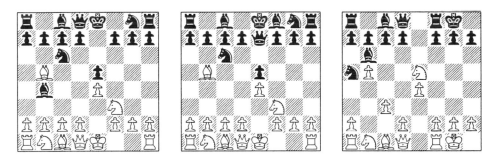

3...♗b4	*3...♕e7*	*9...0-0*

INDEX OF COMPLETE GAMES